Thanks for your interest in...

Fixing Congress

Mike Johnson

Praise for *Fixing Congress*

Mike Johnson and Jerry Climer combine decades of Congressional experience, knowledge, and years of day-to-day working on the important debates and policies that shaped American domestic and foreign policy. *Fixing Congress* is an encyclopedia of the rules of regular order that enabled America's representatives to debate and solve complicated fiscal issues. *Fixing Congress* is a must-read for every Member of Congress, Congressional staffers, scholars, and lecturers, but most importantly, for American citizens who want a more responsive Congress.

-Hon. Ray LaHood
Member of Congress, Illinois 18th District 1995–2009
US Secretary of Transportation 2009–2013

No two people could collaborate more ably on Congressional history and procedure than Jerry Climer and Mike Johnson. Staffers, writers, and educators have between them the wisdom and knowledge to convince a conservative Congress of the imperative of fiscal integrity through Regular Order. Our nation is in fiscal peril. Citizens can have a greater influence on the Members of Congress who can save us from economic disaster if they have the right tools to do it. *Fixing Congress* provides those tools and more.

-Hon. Robert L Livingston (R, LA-1)
Member of Congress (1977–1999),
Chairman of the Committee on Appropriations (1995–1999)

I have known Jerry Climer for many years and have observed him in his career as a dedicated professional in American politics and government. He has always been dedicated to improvement, with knowledge of the system and using that knowledge and experience to give us thoughtful, creative ideas. *Fixing Congress*, which he co-authored, is an excellent culmination of his career in public service. Climer & Johnsons's book is a good, thoughtful reading for the corporate world, where success depends on making decisions based on consistency. That factor has not been available for some time from the government regulatory and legislative process because of the "discombobulation" of the current system. *Fixing Congress* gives a detailed historical background of where we have been and where we are now and is an excellent pathway to reform in the future. The corporate world should promote the necessary reforms suggested in the book, making their decisions more confident and predictable in the future.

-Phil McClendon
Retired senior vice president and general counsel of Lafarge North America Inc., a New York Stock Exchange-listed company

Like many friends, I have lost confidence in our votes making a difference. *Fixing Congress* provides a thorough analysis, explaining reasonable and understandable causes of the disconnect. Explanations and solutions are based on the author's incredible Congressional experience, their grasp of history, population changes, and the effect on the representative-to-voter ratio. *Fixing Congress* provides credible, sensible analysis with substantial ideas for solutions to real problems we face. It gives me hope.

-Robert H. Quinn
former President/Owner: Fiberstock Inc., Philadelphia, PA; NC Order of the Long Leaf Pine.

MICHAEL S. JOHNSON
& JEROME F. CLIMER

FIXING CONGRESS

RESTORING
POWER TO
THE PEOPLE

Uncommon Solutions for
Unprecedented Problems

NEW YORK

LONDON • NASHVILLE • MELBOURNE • VANCOUVER

Fixing Congress

Restoring Power to the People

Published in New York, New York, by Morgan James Publishing. Morgan James is a trademark of Morgan James, LLC. www.MorganJamesPublishing.com

Proudly distributed by Publishers Group West®

ISBN 9781636983981 paperback
ISBN 9781636983998 ebook
Library of Congress Control Number:
2023951860

Cover & Interior Design by:
Christopher Kirk
www.GFSstudio.com

Morgan James is a proud partner of Habitat for Humanity Peninsula and Greater Williamsburg. Partners in building since 2006.

Get involved today! Visit: www.morgan-james-publishing.com/giving-back

To our spouses, Thalia Assuras and Mary Ann Climer, for their tolerance, their valuable advice, editing, research and fresh perspectives.

Also to . . .
our children, Jessie Vergano, Abby Hills, Erin Johnson, Garrett Johnson and Kate Domanski, and Greta Elizabeth Climer and Matthew Alexander Climer for their reactions and guidance on many subjects we cover, for research and overall support and to many family members and friends for their advice and suggestions.

And to . . .
the congressional staff with whom we were honored to work during our forty-years of connection to the US Congress, their help in educating us and willingness to follow us when we thought we knew what we were doing.

Table of Contents

Introduction

Are you fed up with Congress? It's a safe guess you probably are. Most people are. And based on survey research to street-corner conversations, that sentiment has been with us for many years.

This book aims to plumb the depths of the disenchantment, explore how and why Congress is failing the American people, and offer our readers insights into the institution that may give them greater influence over their future.

However, before introducing you to this work, we should introduce ourselves and our perspectives. Your authors are two experienced (some might say *old*) former professional congressional staff. They spent forty-two years for one and forty for the other, working for junior and leadership Members of Congress, Executive agencies, and organizations in the private sector well within the orbit of Congress. We are not academics, so this is not an academic exercise. We are not historians, so this is not a history book. We are also not the kiss-and-tell types, so this book does not dwell on the salacious or the scandalous, nor does it air the dirty laundry of those who have served there, although it is hard to avoid some of that.

We gained most of our experience plowing the fields of politics and government. That gave us a down-to-earth understanding of how Congress went off course and whether it works or does not work now. And most importantly, we'll dive into what can be done to help bring it back on course, representing your interests and giving you more access and control over what it does.

THE BIRTH OF THE BOOK

Mike was riding in a cab some years ago, returning to his office from meetings on the Hill (shorthand for Capitol Hill, in Washington, DC). Cab drivers are sometimes full of simple but sound wisdom. In a conversation about what was going on in politics, Mike mentioned a book about Congress written for incoming Members and staff. "Why don't you write a book like that for us," the driver asked, "so we'd know what the [explicative for heck] is going on too?" We thought it a pretty good idea.

So exactly how unhappy are people with Congress?

Most Americans—75 percent in a 2021 Gallop Gallup survey—disapprove of how Congress does its job. Only 14 percent approve. Another recent study put approval at 18 percent. Those survey numbers have not been any better for years. Few of us would last in a job with an evaluation like that.

The gripes against Congress are evident in countless social media posts, such as those contending Members of Congress:

1. Don't pay social security taxes and yet receive large pensions;
2. Put members of their family on staff and pay them with public money;
3. Retire after serving one full term with full pay for life;
4. Use campaign funds for personal expenses;
5. Receive healthcare benefits that are better than those of other federal employees and most private-sector employees, and for free to boot;
6. Pay more attention to lobbyists than their constituents; and,
7. Don't have to obey laws that affect the rest of us.

There are other complaints heard even more often that have more basis in reality. For example, people believe Congress is too partisan and controlled by the respective party leadership. People ask, "Do my views mean anything to anyone in government?"

A common criticism is that Members of Congress are more liberal or more conservative than the public and do not reflect the rest of the country. Another is that Members of Congress display visceral hate for each other, don't communicate, and, therefore, cannot reach a consensus on solutions to the nation's problems. The complaints are getting old and becoming harsher. The explosive atmosphere in Congress over the last four years especially has left many Americans disillusioned and, in some cases, frightened.

HOW THIS BOOK MAY HELP YOU GET THE GOVERNMENT YOU WANT

Our broader purpose is to address these criticisms and the rampant disillusionment with Congress and answer some questions about our representatives: Senators or Members of the US House.

We will try to set the record straight on some popular misperceptions of Congress and those who serve there. We will look at how the US House of Representatives and Senate operate now compared to past Congresses when, for better or worse, the national legislature was more productive and better able to meet public concerns. We'll also offer some context for the relationship of Congress to the two other branches of the federal government, the Executive (presidency) and the Judiciary (courts), and do it in both an informative and, hopefully, entertaining way. There's no shortage of humor in American politics, especially in the behavior of politicians. Early twentieth-century humorist Will Rogers once observed: "If I studied all my life, I couldn't think up half the number of funny things passed in one session of Congress."

(Oh, by the way, the seven allegations about Members of Congress listed earlier in this Introduction are all *false*, which shows the image of Congress is so poor that many folks are willing to believe and circulate almost any accusations.)

Finally, we'll evaluate the following:

- Proposed reforms about how Congress functions, how representatives are elected, how Members participate in the legislative process and communicate with their constituents, and how you can gain better access to that process to ensure that your views are heard, and your concerns met;
- The outside influences on Congress, especially constitutionally protected news media and lobbyists "petitioning the government." We'll look at our electoral process, the impact of money in political campaigns, and how congressional districts are redesigned every ten years; and,
- The internal operations of Congress—the great many rules and procedures that govern legislating—and how they impact your interests.

THE PAST IS PROLOGUE

We began this journey more than 230 years ago, on March 4, 1789, when the new experimental Republic started its life. Ratified on June 21, 1788, the Federal Constitution, considered revolutionary among world governments, provided the framework for the Congress, Executive, and Judiciary branches. Thus, it is essential to know what the fifty-five delegates to the Constitutional Convention had in mind and how their architectural design evolved as the national legislators brought it to life when the First Congress assembled in New York, then the US Capitol.

The history of our system of government provides context to how it performs today. Context is critical to understanding how government works, how to influence policy, and how to fix its broken parts.

We believe, too, and the record of Congress seems to bear it out, that government institutions in a Republic cannot function effectively or represent the interests of the public if the public doesn't trust the system or those who run it. It just doesn't work and can't be fixed unless the public knows how government works and how it is supposed to work and is actively engaged in ensuring the core problems match the right solutions.

Each year, more than twenty million tourists from across the country and worldwide visit Washington, DC, a beautiful city with hundreds of monuments, parks, and museums chronicling the Republic's proud and storied two centuries since the Constitution was ratified. At the end of Washington's National Mall is the Lincoln Memorial on the shores of the Potomac River. At the other end is the seat of our federal government, the US Capitol, under its majestic dome. Between three and five million people visit the Capitol each year, their eyes mostly tilted upward, taking in the historic Brumidi frescoes in the dome and the ceilings along the Capitol corridors.

On January 6, 2021, angry citizens marched on the US Capitol building. Illustrating a lack of understanding of the US Constitution and the Electoral College process they were attempting to disrupt, some of the "insurrectionists" threatened Members of Congress with death or kidnapping. The Capitol invasion left five people dead, dozens injured, and significant damage to the House and Senate. To date, 768 participants now face criminal charges. However, they did not change the outcome of the 2020 electoral vote for President.

With this debacle following the international COVID-19 pandemic and often violent racial protests, the public outcries for civility in our politics, a more responsive government, and much greater civic education in our schools have continued to grow. But, unfortunately for Congress, the damage wasn't limited to the building. Instead, Members of Congress were further polarized, personally angry, and seemingly unwilling to get things done.

We hope that reform of the institutions will lead to a time when visitors under the Capitol dome will look up and feel proud of more than the artwork in this historic edifice. We hope they will also be proud of what it stands for and the people who labor there.

When Benjamin Franklin left Constitution Hall that summer in 1787, after finishing the draft of the new US Constitution, the aging patriarch of

American independence was asked by a woman strolling by, "What kind of government did you give us, Dr. Franklin?"

He responded, "A Republic, madam, if you can keep it."

It was a good question in 1789 and a good one today. Can we keep it? Can it be fixed? Does it need radical reform? Does it need minor changes? Are there solutions to how Congress functions and how the Members of Congress solve the problems facing the federal government?

In *Fixing Congress*, we (1) identify the problems and the root causes and (2) strive for what the Prussian ruler and German Chancellor Otto Von Bismarck described as politics, which "is the art of the possible, the attainable—the art of the next best."

We believe we are at a critical juncture in the life of the Republic, particularly in the life of a system of government that depends on the involvement of an educated, informed, and engaged citizenry. But unfortunately, the country is in trouble. Our system of government is broken!

CAR REPAIRS AND REFORM

Fifty years ago, some teenagers, one of whom had just acquired his first car, were smart enough to change the oil and brake pads on the 1948 maroon Plymouth. Professional mechanics liked to call those amateurs "shade tree mechanics." Eventually, the shade-tree fixers would find their way to the local garage, where the professionals would repair what the amateurs messed up. Today, cars are computers on wheels, so complicated and intricate under the hood, they present a massive challenge to any amateur mechanic. Only well-trained and well-equipped technicians can keep the new vehicles on the road.

There's a similar analogy with today's government. It was once a collection of small offices operated by relatively few clerks and overseen by part-time legislators with no staff or office space. They were comparable to the shade-tree mechanics. Today, the government is a mammoth multi-trillion-dollar enterprise with millions of employees worldwide and thousands of agencies overseen by a full-time Congress. Moreover, Congress has 15,000 employees itself. It isn't your father's Oldsmobile, as the ads used to say.

Making sure a twenty-first-century government runs right requires citizens to have the right tools and sufficient knowledge of how the government works to keep it on the road.

We hope this book will be a toolbox *and* an owner's manual for responsible citizens.

It is time for a change.

"It takes three to make federal policy."

Chapter 1

How Did We Get Here? Laying the Foundation of a Democratic Republic

Assuming that most citizens are unhappy with Congress, doesn't it make sense to review what the Founders had in mind when it was created?

If the original design is not working, we should ask, "Can it be fixed? Can those original concepts, which are cemented into the structure of today's US Government, be reformed and brought into the twenty-first century, where the American people live?"

What do citizens expect in the behavior and actions of Members of Congress and their staff? What do they expect from the legislative and political processes that drive behavior and decision-making? What is expected in the degree of openness and efficiency and legislators' willingness to reach a compromise? Everyone calls for compromise, but do you support compromise if it means creating public policy that does not reflect your views?

What do citizens want in the role of political parties and other influencers on legislation?

What about your access to and influence over your representatives? How well do they reflect the interests and beliefs of those they serve? How do you decide if your representative is accountable? Who are they accountable to?

Does Congress today differ greatly from those of past decades? Today's broadly held belief is that Congress is much different from in times past. Is that so?

These are among the many questions about the state of our government that frustrate citizens and perplex politicians. Yet trying to answer those questions time after time, year after year, when nothing seems to change, makes you want to throw up your hands in disgust and disillusionment. The answers are not easy, but the answers are a gateway to the future and whether the great experiment in representative government will ultimately survive or fail.

We can all draw some general conclusions from the history of the First Congress that are important to understanding the current Congress. For example, the delegates to the Constitutional Convention in Philadelphia concluded a clear balance of power between the branches of government was necessary to ensure that actions had several filters and none of the branches could accumulate so much power as to become dictatorial. The separation of powers would protect representative government and power retained by the people. The Founders believed the Legislative Branch would be the one closest to the people and where the ideal of a democratic Republic would survive.

> The Founders believed the Legislative Branch would be the one closest to the people and where the ideal of a democratic Republic would survive.

The Founders also believed the Constitution had to be profound in its simplicity so that a rapidly growing nation would not be shackled by a document designed only for the nineteenth century. The Founders envisioned a nation that would ultimately grow, and the government would have to grow and mature with the country.

The Convention and the First Congress also taught us much about the concept of public service, human strengths and weaknesses, the motivations and proclivities of individuals who enter public service, and the strong but honest differences of opinions and beliefs that only a sturdy political system could bring together in consensus.

The First Congress was one of the most productive because enough of those in the House and Senate chambers believed they had no better alternative than to set aside their individual preferences for the higher cause of launching a new nation and a new system of governing it (that noble objective did not always prevail over behavior).

Could they imagine, at that time, the tremendous diversity of the United States in the twenty-first century and the expansion of representative government to practically all segments of the population? Probably not. But they did lay the foundation for it with the vision and foresight the electorate is searching for today.

The Members of the First Congress struggled with issues and dilemmas that Members of Congress struggle with today, from setting tariffs to regulating commerce among the states to the securing of individual freedoms to whether this nation should ignore the rest of the world or be a world leader—militarily, morally, and economically. Of course, some core issues appear in different specifics from one decade to the next. Still, they remain the fundamental questions that elected leaders are charged with deciding, blending, and amalgamating ideologies, political beliefs, and national and international dynamics.

How, then, did those historical times shape our governance today?

An excellent place to begin is New York in 1789, in a building called Federal Hall, at the lower tip of Manhattan, where the first session of the First Congress convened. It was months late in starting, waiting for Members to assemble a quorum. The new Members of Congress arrived alone. They had no personal staff, though they didn't need much help—they represented districts of a mere 30,000 or so people (a far cry from the 762,000-person congressional districts of today). The volume of correspondence Congressmen had to deal with was much less than the 50,000 pieces of mail, email, text, and more, which the average Member gets today.

No representative needed media advisers, poll takers, or strategic consultants, and the Members had no physical offices. Instead, they roomed in boarding houses and hotels across the city.

House Members were chosen by popular vote in their districts, while state legislatures selected senators in the states they represented. Senators, too, operated without staff or offices.

Although 48 percent of House Members and 56 percent of senators had college degrees, those without degrees were far more representative of the voting population at the time. Today 96 percent of Members of Congress have bachelor's or higher degrees, compared to 39 percent in the general adult population, according to the Census Bureau analysis of the 2020 census.

"There are few shining geniuses," wrote Congressman Fisher Ames of Massachusetts, describing his First Congress colleagues as sober, solid folks. "There are many who have experience, the virtues of the heart and the habits of business. It will be quite a republican assembly." According to a 1986 paper by the Congressional Research Service. (Note: the lowercase "republican" refers to the concept, not the party.)

All ninety-one Members of the First Congress were white, male, and landowners. The average age in the House was forty-three, and in the Senate, forty-six. They were paid $6 a day for their efforts (equal to about $163 today).

Like many who would follow in his footsteps, Ames soon discovered in the Second Congress, two years later, that familiarity could breed contempt when he complained about the "yawning listlessness" of many who served there.

> *"Their state prejudices, their over-refining spirit in relation to trifles, their attachment to some very distressing formalities in doing business," he said, tallying the reasons for his growing disenchantment. "The objects now before us require more information, though less of the heroic qualities than those of the first Congress."*[1]

Sound familiar? Maybe Congress hasn't changed after all.

Whether heroism was uppermost among the goals of the Constitutional Convention that met just two short years before the First Congress convened is debatable. Still, it was very much in evidence in the aftermath.

Delegates to the convention in Philadelphia in 1787 met to rewrite the Articles of Confederation, a document that had served unsuccessfully as the country's first governing charter. But instead of rewriting the Articles, the convention delegates decided on a more drastic and riskier course: they closed the doors, shuttered the windows on those sweltering, hot summer days, and, under the cloak of secrecy, wrote a new constitution, giving the central federal government more power but not total dominance.

And they didn't want politicians like Patrick Henry of Virginia to know what they were about to do. Henry abhorred the idea of a national government and eventually had a hissy fit. He opposed the ratification of the new Constitution. He wasn't alone.

No one was sure whether it would be ratified. New York and Virginia were in doubt up until the end. North Carolina failed to ratify the initial draft and only acted almost a year later, after the first amendments, called the Bill of Rights, had been proposed. But, in the final analysis, the new Constitution was ratified by all thirteen states, including Rhode Island, which repeatedly refused to send delegates to the Convention in Philadelphia.

The Convention delegates drew upon the experiences of the predecessors to the new Legislative branch, the Continental Congress, and the Congress of the Confederation, both of which had been unicameral bodies consisting of a single legislative chamber rather than two houses. They drew upon the political philosophers and parliaments of Britain and other European nations. They even drew upon the existing governing documents of Pennsylvania and Virginia. And in the process, they evolved a clear and definite role for the Congress to play: It would be the first branch of government, the one that was truly representative of the people.

"The grand depository of the democratic principles of government," is how George Mason of Virginia envisioned Congress. His remarks, as noted in the official History of the United States House of Representatives, continued: "The requisites in actual representation are that the Representatives should sympathize with their constituents, should think as they think and feel as they feel and that for these purposes should even be residents among them."[2]

Among the most important of the eighteen congressional powers enumerated in the Constitution is the "power of the purse," the authority to tax, and the authority to spend. The authors of the Constitution insisted this power resides in the House of Representatives, the only federal entity whose officials were, at the time, directly elected by the people. It also gave the House the power to impeach but not convict; that power belonged to the Senate, which was also empowered to confirm or deny presidential appointments and to ratify treaties.

The Legislative branch became the seat of the government and the font from which the nation's newly won independence would flow. Its importance is reflected in Article One of the Constitution, which creates the legislature. It is twice as long as Article Two, which establishes the Executive branch, and four times as long as Article Three, which defines the Judiciary.

Sometimes, it seems, the Founders thought of everything, including term limits, which had been among the provisions of the Articles of Confederation. The Constitutional Convention considered weaving term limits into the document. Instead, the delegates limited Members of the House of Representatives to two-year terms, naively assuming that would guarantee a constant flow of new blood into the Congress.

Throughout the history of what the Founders referred to as the Republic, the balance of power among the branches of government has shifted back and forth between the Executive, Legislative, and Judicial branches. Factors, such as the leadership abilities of those in charge, the political alliances they formed, and current national and international events, have contributed to changes in the power structure that drives the three branches.

Several Presidents have held considerable control over the Congress, usually in times of national emergency, but the Congress has also exercised substantial influence over chief executives. Sometimes both occur during a single administration, as with President Bill Clinton, a Democrat who sometimes dominated the Republican-controlled Congress, which also turned the tables on him. The same held for Ronald Reagan and the Democrat-controlled House. Similar circumstances affected the Obama Administration, which dealt with both Democratic and Republican-controlled houses of Congress.

The relationship between the Legislative and Executive branches was less tempestuous in the Republic's early days, particularly when the President's supporters dominated Congress. For example, historians contend that James Madison, who represented Virginia in Congress at that time, drastically edited a good deal of George Washington's first inaugural address. Later, Madison was appointed to head a committee of the House to prepare a response to the President's message he'd helped to write.[3,4]

Madison exemplified what influence a true leader can have, whether that individual is a legislator or the President. As a legislator, Madison was a driving force behind the Bill of Rights, which helped guarantee the success of the Constitution and remains a source of national pride today. But those who suspected the Constitutional Convention would create a strong central government were not all mollified by the addition of the First Amendment.

The Bill of Rights, a package of amendments that guaranteed the rights of the states and individual citizens, was Madison's way of compromising with those who felt, as Patrick Henry did, the people needed stronger protections against the government. It was, however, a hard sell. Individuals from the Federalist (those who favored a central government) and Anti-Federalist factions opposed Madison's amendments. Anti-Federalist Aedanus Burke of South Carolina, as noted by Gutenberg.org's transcription, captured the spirit of the debate when he called the amendments "little better than whip-syllabub, frothy and full of wind, formed only to please the palate."[5,6]

But Madison prevailed. The House of Representatives went right to work in the new capital—New York City—where Madison introduced his proposed amendments on June 8, 1789. The House adopted them on August 21, 1789, and in September of that year, both bodies sent the twelve amendments he originally proposed to the states for ratification on the last day of the First Congress. Ten were ratified. One of the two that were not adopted would have prohibited Congress from giving itself a pay raise while in session, which meant a raise could not take effect until after the next election. It was resurrected in 1992 and became the twenty-seventh and most recent amendment to the Constitution. The other non-ratified amendment related to the size of congressional districts.

Without Madison's commitment, the Constitution might never have been ratified. Those demanding the Bill of Rights's protections carried enough weight to table the entire document permanently. However, the assurance the amendments would be proposed cleared the way for the First Congress to convene, for President Washington to be sworn in, and for the process of selecting members of the Supreme Court to begin.

GETTING ORGANIZED

In other matters, before adjourning, the House flexed its oversight muscle early, instructing the Executive departments it had just created to report back to it on various issues. The House also appointed a committee on Ways and Means to advise it on fiscal matters. It dissolved it eight weeks later in favor of relying on advice from Secretary of the Treasury Alexander Hamilton—a reflection of the still-unresolved ambiguity in the roles played by the branches of our federal government. The Ways and Means Committee was reconstituted and made permanent on December 21, 1795. Until the mid-1800s, it had power over both taxation and spending.

The First Congress had more confidence in other actions it took. It created three federal departments: Treasury, War, and Foreign Affairs. It established the nation's court system, passed laws dealing with trade, patents, crime, mail, the military, and bankruptcies, and deliberated over slavery and relations with the native peoples they called Indians.

Congress also established rules governing its internal operations. And the House and Senate devised ways to communicate with each other and set salaries. The House also created the first permanent committee—the Committee on Elections—to judge the qualification of its elected Members, a prerogative the Framers invested in each chamber.

The first time President Washington visited Congress, he witnessed events that made it clear once and for all that, just as the Founders had intended, the Legislative, Executive, and Judicial branches of government are equals . . . but the Legislative was more equal than the others.

Washington and Secretary of War Henry Knox went to Federal Hall, where the Congress was meeting, to seek the Senate's advice—but more importantly, its consent. At issue was the creation of a commission to negotiate a treaty with the Creek Indians, who at the time laid claim to much of what eventually would become Florida, Georgia, and Alabama. If Washington expected a rubber stamp because he was the President, he was sadly mistaken. Several senators indicated they wanted to see documents related to the plan. Since no such documents were available, it was agreed the issue should be referred to a committee.

An uncomfortable period of silence and muttering followed, during which the cantankerous Senator William Maclay of Pennsylvania observed that Washington was visibly irritated. When Washington and Knox retreated from the chamber a short time later, the President vowed never to return. But he did two days later when the Senate approved the commission. The incident established the independence of the Senate in meeting its Constitutional responsibility to provide advice about and consent to treaties—and it also marked the last time a President has shown up in person to petition for that body's advice and consent.

Despite President Washington's disappointment, the First Congress exhibited harmony, civility, and willingness to compromise as hallmarks of decision-making. It considered 168 bills, of which 108, or 64 percent, were enacted. Its accomplishments happened in a little more than five hundred days, with almost no incidents of partisanship. There were no *organized* political parties at the time.

"There is less party spirit, less of the acrimony of pride when disappointed of success, less personality, less intrigue, cabal, management, or cunning than I ever saw in a public assembly," wrote Fisher Ames. The JSTOR digital library continues quoting Ames: "There was the most punctual attendance of the Members at the hour of meeting. Three or four have had leave of absence, but every other Member actually attends daily, till the hour of adjourning."[7]

"Small wonder they completed so much in such a short time," historian Robert V. Remini writes in *The House: The History of the House of Representatives*, "and all this without a staff of assistants to aid them."[8]

They got away with it because, despite the contentiousness surrounding various issues, life was relatively simpler then—if only because there weren't as many people looking over the shoulders of those in Congress and demanding their time and energy.

Today, elected officials and their staff represent almost every segment of society and US geography, virtually every religious belief, professional pursuit, education, and political persuasion. Critics point out, however, that the proportion of lawyers far exceeds the ratio of lawyers to the rest of the nation's population and that women and minority representation are still lagging in their proportions.

Yet Congress is more representative than it ever has been. The fact is that Congress was never intended to be a microcosm of its multitudinous constituencies. Today, that would be a practical impossibility, given the diversity of society and the subdivisions taking place among genders, races, ethnicities, ages, and socio-economic groups, among others. Subgroups of ethnicities, for example, have grown in population and have their own identities, their own issues, and their own concerns.

There are many more reasons why Congress is failing, and we will discuss them in the ensuing chapters. They range from problems of a technical and administrative nature to functions that strike at the heart of the first three articles of the Constitution, which form the Legislative, Executive, and Judicial branches of government, in that order.

They also include the negative influences from outside the government, especially the media and nontransparent activist organizations that exercise an undue influence on the legislative and political processes with excesses of wealth and stealth.

Are there needed changes in how constituents communicate with their representatives and senators? Unfortunately, the electronic communication revolutions and the lack of public education regarding the realities of public policy have weakened the communicative link between the citizen and the representative. In addition, there have been, for some time, debilitating problems with overlapping and inefficient jurisdiction of congressional committees and roadblocks in Senate rules, such as the filibuster, that delay or prevent legislation from acting.

But even more fundamental problems need to be addressed as well. For example, many people believe a flood, maybe a tsunami, of money flowing into political campaigns and the corollary evolution of full-time campaign operations are crippling the system, especially campaign donations from outside sources that can hide the origins of that revenue.

Other constitutional conflicts and contradictions arise because of the crippling dysfunction in relationships between the House and the Senate and between Congress and the President. In addition, there are other debatable issues, such as the gerrymandering of congressional districts, the relationships between the states and the federal government, and the media that also demand attention.

Identifying solutions, agreeing to them, and implementing them is a little more complicated than pointing fingers at the problems. Journalist H. L. Mencken is credited with a sage observation about solving problems when in 1920, he said, "There is always a well-known solution to every human problem—neat, plausible, and wrong."

Most Americans, especially the media, are drawn toward simple, one-sentence solutions that fit a newspaper headline, meet radio and television's twenty-second sound bite limit, or conform to word limits in an X (Twitter) post or a thirty-second campaign spot.

The curse of our politics is that those sound-bite solutions are no solutions. They are misleading. They misdirect efforts and public attention and end up delaying action. They distort the problems and encourage division that doesn't exist in any place else but the TV screen or the X (Twitter) feed. That, in turn, creates angst, incites anger, and eventually leads to gridlock. That is why taking some lessons from history may be the first element in regaining more citizen control over the government and making politics, especially the partisan influences, more responsive to and more reflective of the public.

The quotation on the National Archives building in Washington, DC, is appropriate and an excellent first lesson. "The past is prologue."

Businesses   *Congress*

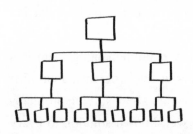

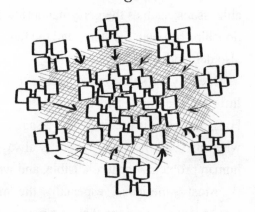

Congress is not hierarchical. Members only answer to their voters.

Chapter 2

Organization and Decision-Making

E very enterprise has a hierarchy, whether it is Microsoft or your local Parent Teacher Association (PTA). Every job site has its bosses. Every company has an organizational chart that tells you a little about who is supposed to do what and to whom they answer.

Congress does too. But most people can't penetrate its walls because the organizational chart is, well, not very organized and hard to navigate, so citizens have a difficult time influencing its actions or getting what they want from it.

Most people, again, according to survey research, believe Congress is more responsive to outside interests than them. So it stands to reason that if you know more about Congress and how the decisions are made, influence may be easier and results more worthy of your time.

The Congress is not a business; if you think it should be run like a business, think again.

Congress is a political institution like few others. Businesses are in business to make a profit. Congress is not. Congress has a bottom line that is much more difficult to define and processes and production lines you won't find in the private sector. Public policy that serves the public interest means something vastly different to a socialist from Vermont and a liberal from Minnesota, or a libertarian from Wyoming and a conservative from North Carolina.

Businesses usually have a strict and well-defined hierarchy that pinpoints who's in charge or who they want you to think is in charge. So, at a minimum, every employee knows by whom they can be fired or promoted.

Congress has a hierarchy, but by virtue of its political nature and constitutional duties, the House and Senate diffuse power among a wide array of its Members and staff.

For example, there are days when a Member of the House of Representatives has more power than the Speaker. One such day occurred on October 3, 2023, when a junior Member used such power and ousted Speaker McCarthy. There are also days when the Speaker can make or break the career of that same junior Member.

No Member of Congress is, in theory, answerable to any other Member. Each Member is answerable to the constituents back home, not fellow Members. When it looks like no one is in charge, that is sometimes the case. Leaders and some senior Members may have leverage over other Members, but it's both limited and conditioned upon a vast array of circumstances, and they can't fire them.

Decisions are not made the way they are in business. Constituents are not the same as customers. These distinctions can help a citizen take full advantage of the services and representation of their House Members and senators.

So, we need to open the House Chamber doors and look more closely at the dynamics behind them.

It would make sense for elected representatives to analyze a situation, examine the possible alternatives, weigh the advantages and disadvantages, and make decisions with the kind of efficiency and internal discipline often found in the workplace.

It's just not necessarily so.

Years ago, a retired businessman decided to devote his time to public service and won a seat in Congress as a Republican. Republican leaders, anxious to take advantage of his skills, appointed him to the Budget Committee, where he began pouring over the numbers.

Weeks later, the Republican leader asked the new Member what he had concluded about fixing the federal budget. Why it is clear, he responded, we are in terrible shape and have to raise taxes.

That might have been the correct business-model answer but the wrong one politically for Republicans, as President George H. W. Bush proved soon after that by breaking a campaign promise for "no new taxes" in his negotiation with Democrats over a new budget.

There are similarities with how business functions, to be sure, but governing is a system driven by constantly changing political currents, by voting blocks and interest groups, and by powerful media that can make or break a political figure easier and quicker than they can break a CEO. A business could not survive with three co-equal branches of decision-makers, with 535 independent policymakers elected every two years, an executive elected every four years, and courts that judge them.

Political campaigns may come a little closer to the look of a commercial marketplace than governance. In campaigns, simple, straightforward products (policies or candidates) are packaged and sold with attractive wrappings and catchy slogans. What defined Mitt Romney and Barack Obama, other major candidates in 2012, Donald Trump and Hillary Clinton in the 2016 elections, and Joe Biden in 2020 were slick, Madison Avenue television ads that defined the candidates before their opponents could define them. The same is true of many candidates for Congress. The simplicity of political ads, however, often distorts both issues and candidates so badly it makes governing more difficult once the campaigns are over (one reason governing is more difficult is that they are never over).

By some accounts, Donald Trump won the presidency because voters believed his experience as a businessman, a CEO, and a self-described negotiating whiz gave him the tools needed at the time to run the government. He was not a polished politician. Once again, however, that parallel between business and government proved elusive. Moreover, there were other driving forces behind Trump's election, not the least of which were millions of Americans who felt alienated from their government and ignored by their elected officials.

When and if politics ends and the governing begins, decision-making is not well served by slogans, simple solutions, easy answers, emotional appeals, and inflammatory behavior. Decision-making becomes a complex maze of conflicting interests, strong personalities, media, political power, massive amounts of federal dollars, and powerful government agencies competing for attention.

There are many examples of why and how rational decisions are not always the outcome Congress produces. The great healthcare debate that produced the Affordable Care Act, more commonly known as Obamacare, and the ensuing multi-year battle to repeal it, then repeal it, then replace it, and finally just repair it offers many examples of where business decisions to achieve a straightforward goal could not meet the challenges of a partisan and ideologically charged public debate. Shortly after taking office, President Trump, in one of his many moments of candor, conceded that health care was just too complicated.

Other examples are plentiful in education, immigration, cyber-security, emerging technologies, budgets and spending, the pandemic, international terrorism, conflict, energy, and environment, all among issues the Congress has failed to deal with in an effective and lasting way.

Congress resolved none of those issues with any finality in the 112th (2011–2012) Congress, nor the 113th (2013–2014), the 114th (2015–2016), the 115th (2017–2018), or the 116th Congress (2019–2020), leading to an entire decade of some success but mostly gridlock.

It may have been because there was no clear public mandate; interest groups were able to stall action or thwart compromise; Members were able to prevent votes because they couldn't get their amendments considered; Members were nervous about the negative political consequences of voting before the election, or there was too little or too much pressure from the media.

There may have been too many higher priorities or too little time to schedule bills on the Floor, or there was a full moon, or the dog ate their homework. The line between legitimate explanations and lame excuses is a thin one, indeed.

In succeeding chapters, we will explore why legislating does or doesn't happen. Still, our system of making laws and setting policies is complex and challenging to understand. It is organized to reflect the public's will, or lack thereof, and not to produce widgets efficiently. When voters are undecided and confused about what direction to take, politicians can be expected to be as well. Congress was designed as the seat of a democratic Republic guided by and responding to the will of the people rather than the other way around.

Many conflicting interests influence the legislative process in good and bad ways. They prevent bad legislation from becoming bad laws, but as we have seen in recent Congresses, they also can have an overbearing and paralyzing effect.

The bottom line is that Congress acts when it is motivated to act. Often, the most powerful motivator is not lobbyists, the media, or campaign contributions but job security or public pressure, which average citizens can apply if they know how.

| The bottom line is that Congress acts when it is motivated to act.

So when it comes to the congressional effectiveness or the lack of it, here are just some of the dominant influences on Members of Congress:

- The constituency, in the case of a Member of Congress, 762,000 constituents, and in the case of the senator, the entire state's population. The constituency is subdivided into a vast array of interest groups, including the local media, community organizations, business and labor leaders, religious leaders, local political leaders, key supporters and contributors, friends and family members, and others, all of whom may have a different perspective on what's good for the country and good for them.

- Congressional leaders, such as the Speaker of the House and the Majority Leader of the Senate and their partisan counterparts, the minority leaders of the House and Senate.
- Other congressional party leaders, such as the whips (those responsible for getting the votes, chairs of the *caucus* (Democrat's term to define their entire membership) and *conference* (Republican's word for their entire membership), and the numerous leaders of caucuses and coalitions involved in policy positions.
- Committee chairs and the senior minority members of the committees.
- Subcommittee chairs and the senior minority members of the subcommittees.
- Senior staff of the committees and subcommittees.
- The national media, internet blogs, and social media.
- Washington-centered organizations, trade associations, unions, and other interest groups that may reflect the interests of or represent the interests of the Member's constituency back home.
- The White House and the Cabinet Departments of the Executive branch.
- The politician's personal and professional ambitions, aspirations, objectives, and philosophical disposition.

THE BALANCING ACT

Members of Congress, when they are first elected, must learn to balance political awareness, sensitivity to voter attitudes, the realities of the legislative process, constituent service, and the impact of the influences just listed.

They must accept, for example, that:

- Their power is situational and temporary. Members of the House and Senate arrive in Congress from various backgrounds and for a variety of reasons. The positions they hold are not based on skill, experience, or knowledge. Their tenure is subject to the whim of the electorate.

- Decisions made in Congress are based on consensus. Because power there is transient, there are no accepted rules for how a Member should decide whether to support or oppose a measure. It should come as no surprise, then, that when a Member is forced to take a position, it is shaped as much by outside pressures and the imperative to compromise as by principle or logic. Group or party influence is powerful.

- There is a never-ending tension between following the people and leading them—and often balancing conflicting obligations. Members of Congress are forever challenged to weigh their beliefs against public opinion or what's good for the country versus what's good for the voters. Fortunately, the answer is usually good or bad for both, but not always. Some Members vote their perception of how constituents view the issue at hand, believing it is the safest course and why they were elected to Congress. Others act on their beliefs, even when they think most constituents might disagree with them. They are then obligated to go home and explain why their chosen course is the right one. A number of them venture further into their Constitutional responsibilities and engage in activities and issues with a national or international impact that may not interest constituents. Many Members blend all three patterns of behavior. Among the reasons it's hard to decide whether a Member should vote their conscience, or their constituency is the leeway provided by the Founding Fathers when they took what they considered the best qualities of a republic and best qualities of a democracy and created our Democratic Republic. A *Democracy* is governed by majority rule—in our case, the ballot box. The majority can be wrong and is not required to be rational. A *Republic* is governed indirectly, by men and women chosen from among the citizens to make decisions on behalf of all.

- Melding both forms of representation is not easy, particularly when a representative knows more about an issue than the constituents.

The fate of many elected officials has been doomed when a strongly held belief or principle conflicted with the strongly held opinions of voters back home. Former Senate Majority Leader Lyndon Johnson experienced that conflict when as President, he tried to convince his fellow Southern Democrats to support the Civil Rights Act of 1964. Even though Johnson previously had resisted such change when he served in the Senate and despite the assurances of Democrats that they would support the measure when it came to a vote, many of those Democrats voted nay. They voted for their constituency. Had it not been for former Senate adversaries, such as Republican Senator Everett Dirksen of Illinois and Republican Congressman William McCulloch of Ohio, Johnson might never have mustered the votes he needed to turn civil rights into the law of the land.

Here are some other congressional service basics to remember when thinking about how Members do their jobs:

- The entire House of Representatives must be elected every two years, forming an entirely new Congress that must elect (or re-elect) party leaders, adopt its own rules, and appoint its officers; Members of the Senate serve six-year terms, but the terms are staggered so that only one-third of the Senate changes every election, making the Senate an evolving body.
- Senators represent entire states; House Members represent districts within each state, districts that are a fraction (around 762,000 constituents) of the size of most states and whose inhabitants tend to be more cohesive in their attitudes. A few states—Alaska, Delaware, Montana, North Dakota, South Dakota, Vermont, and Wyoming— lack the population needed to justify more than one House member.
- Senators serve on a larger number of committees and have larger staffs; House Members typically don't even have committee spe-

cialists on their staffs until they achieve seniority or serve on a key committee, such as Appropriations, nor are they required to develop expertise in as broad a range of committee topics.

- The efficiency and effectiveness of Members of Congress are challenged every day by their schedule of debates and votes on the House and Senate Floor, committee hearings, meetings with constituents, meetings with congressional leaders, meetings with interest groups, media demands, briefings, and caucus meetings, time with staff, time for research and reading, and time to answer correspondence, emails, and phone calls. That leaves little time to think.

- Another unspoken influence on a politician's behavior is their career path and what opportunities may lie ahead. Of course, self-preservation is a constant in all our lives, and for politicians, the instincts are even more acute, because nothing in politics is certain, and little is even predictable. But like most other people, politicians have ambitions. An old curmudgeon with decades of Capitol Hill experience once reminded Jerry, "All House Members want to be Senators, and all Senators want to be President."

Thus, it is not true that Congress is organized in a hierarchical fashion like most other institutions. Yet, it does have an organizational structure that we will explore in depth in the coming chapters. Every Member of the House or Senate knows well by whom they can be fired. That would be you and your fellow citizens.

The respective majorities name the House Speaker or Senate Majority Leader.

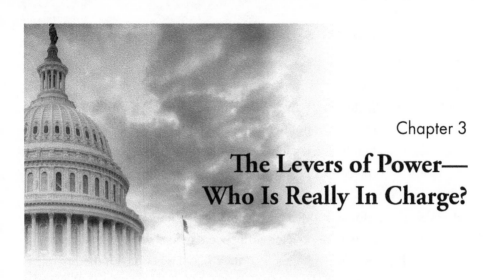

Chapter 3

The Levers of Power—
Who Is Really In Charge?

Nearly all men can stand adversity,
but if you want to test a man's character, give him power.
—Popularly attributed to Abraham Lincoln
but probably said by Robert G. Ingersoll about Lincoln

Power corrupts. Absolute power is kind of neat.
—John Lehman, former Secretary of the Navy 2003–2004

Voters tend to think of their congressmen and congresswomen, senators, and a select few others who are the focus of press attention—and the President, of course—as the powers that be in national government. That view is valid, but there are far more powerful figures who make things happen with little notice or attention.

A recent study by George Mason University found evidence that Congress's most partisan and vocal Members get far more attention than the less partisan ones. For example, the study, conducted by the Center for Media and Public Affairs, found that during the 2022 election cycle, Congresswoman Marjorie Taylor Greene, an obstreperous Georgia Republican, received ten times the media coverage of Nebraska Republican Don Bacon, considered one of the most bipartisan Members and one of the most hotly contested candidates in 2022 ". . . name-calling, partisan bickering and provocation dominate the political news cycle, to the exclusion of substantive coverage about the actual work of Congress," the report concluded.

Every workplace has power players, people, and places that are centers of authority, where the decisions get made. For example, each elected Member of the House and Senate has the final authority to cast a vote, but behind them are many un-elected influencers who shape those decisions.

We call them power players, and they may be people on the organizational chart who exercise authority or influence; they know how to pull the levers of power. They may be effective coalition builders, individuals with expertise or insight into issues, effective fundraisers, political operatives, or just politicians who have sway with the press because they often leak valuable information to them.

THE POWER PLAYER!

It doesn't take long in a new job to identify who they are, but it may take longer to understand whose power is relevant to the decisions that affect you.

There's a humorous story about former New Jersey Senator Bill Bradley that former MSNBC host Chris Matthews used to tell that brings home the point: The senator was the guest of honor at a dinner one evening and seated at the head table, waiting for the food to be served. A waiter placed a single pad of butter on Bradley's bread plate.

> *"I'll have two pads of butter, please," the Senator instructed.*
> *Replied the waiter, "Sorry, there is just one per guest."*
> *"Well, I think you can give me two," Bradley insisted.*
> *"One to a guest," came the reply.*
> *"Do you know who I am?" Bradley asked.*
> *"No, sir."*
> *"I am Bill Bradley, a United States Senator, former Hall of Fame professional basketball player and college All-American at Prince-*

ton. I am a Rhodes Scholar and author. And I am the guest of honor at this dinner. Now, I would like another pad of butter!"

There was a pause, and finally, the waiter replied, "Senator, do you know who I am?"

"No," Bradley admitted.

"I am the person in charge of the butter."

It's always good to know who's in charge of the butter.

Congressional power players impact the ebb and flow of legislative and political life. They affect you, your family, and your community, some-times—often—without you ever knowing anything about them. That is why it is important to determine who the power players are in your congressional offices and who the power players are in deciding the fate of your representatives' efforts on your behalf.

The first point of contact with the Legislative branch will probably not be your Congressional representative or one of your two senators, but more likely any of their staff to whom you will be introduced in more detail in the next chapter. Staff members can be power centers in their own right, but eventually, the Member of Congress will be the responsible/accountable player. However, they must be able to influence many others at various levels throughout the policy-making process, ultimately including the President, before an idea becomes law.

Let's look at the mechanics of where these players must act and with whom they must interact.

THE CRAPSHOOT:
COMMITTEES AND SUBCOMMITTEES

Committees have been called the "workshops of Congress." In 1885, the professorial, future President Woodrow Wilson (his first name was Thomas) put it this way: "Congress in session is Congress on public exhibition, whilst Congress in its committee rooms is Congress at work." That was said in the day when media was not allowed inside committee rooms and was perfectly illustrated to Jerry shortly after he arrived on Capitol Hill.

He was staffing a committee markup (the drafting of the legal words of a proposed law) when the top minority (Republican) Member offered an amendment. The Chairman asked for an explanation and liked what he heard. He then turned to the committee staff and said, "Take his name off that amendment; put mine on there." Then, looking up and without missing a beat, he said to the full committee membership, "Everyone in agreement?" Hearing no objection, he declared the amendment accepted. To this day, that amendment carries his name and is the law, with history ignoring or unaware of the major role the minority member played. But that Republican went to his grave knowing he'd improved law and improved Congress's work.

The committees and their subcommittees are mini-legislatures. Committees have four main functions:

1. Conduct oversight (the process of reviewing how well laws are being executed) and investigations of governmental agencies, organizations, and individuals whose activities fall under the jurisdiction of the committee;
2. Conduct hearings and briefings to collect information and insights that can be turned into the knowledge and expertise needed to legislate;
3. Authorize and monitor the mission and operations of federal programs and agencies; and
4. Craft and either pass or defeat bills and resolutions that originate in the committee or are assigned to it out of the thousands introduced in both houses in each Congress.

Serving on the ideal committees is one of the most coveted elements of congressional service. Membership in committees and subcommittees can make the career of a legislator. It also serves as a pathway to power within Congress, affords the Member access to the media, and serves as a venue for benefits to the home state or district. It was widely assumed that former Speaker Kevin McCarthy made deals with recalcitrant Members to get their votes for Speaker—chief among them key committee assignments. And time—less than 300 days—proved that deals with the Devil come back to haunt Speakers and other mere mortals. Eight of the same Republicans who demanded concessions from McCarthy in January voted on October 3, 2023, with all Democrats, on a resolution introduced by renegade Florida Rep. Matt Gaetz to vacate the Speaker's chair. McCarthy's short-lived tenure was over.

Usually, a newly elected Member will not get the top committee or committees of choice. That may have to wait a couple of terms (each *term* consists of the two-year life cycle of each Congress, broken into two *sessions*), but a skillful politician and committed legislator can turn any committee assignment into a policy and political benefit.

Because there are so many more members in the House than in the Senate, House Members specialize in a particular set of issues and may build a reputation as the "go-to" person in that field of expertise.

There are twenty permanent or standing committees in the House and sixteen in the Senate. Most of those committees are called authorizing committees because they create federal programs and policies and oversee them. The exception is the Appropriations Committee, which allocates the money needed to fund those programs and policies. As stated in the US Constitution, "No money shall be drawn from the treasury, but in consequence of appropriations made by law; and a regular statement and account of receipts and expenditures of all public money shall be published from time to time."

On the House Energy and Commerce Committee, for example, at the outset of the 118th Congress (2023–2024), six subcommittees dealt with specific areas of the full committee's jurisdiction. They included communications and technology; energy, climate, and grid security; environment, manufacturing, and critical materials; health; innovation, data, and commerce; and oversight and investigations. In the House and the Senate, there are, as of this writing, committees on rules, and in the House a separate

committee on House Administration that oversees internal House administrative operations. The average citizen will rarely have any reason to interact with these committees.

The Senate and House both have these committees, and each of these
entities constitutes a power center occupied by power players who have a
major impact on their area of federal policy. They include:

- The Armed Services;
- Agriculture (Agriculture, Nutrition, and Forestry in the Senate);
- Appropriations;
- Budget;
- Foreign Affairs (Foreign Relations in the Senate);
- Judiciary (covers crime, the courts, and the Department of Justice);
- Intelligence (we've heard the jokes); in the Senate, this is a select
  committee;
- Small Business (Small Business and Entrepreneurship in the
  Senate); and
- Veterans Affairs.

The precise titles differ from one chamber to the other. Each also has a
committee that deals with its Members' ethics. In the House, it is a standing committee (permanently established in the rules), and in the Senate, a
select committee (*select* committees are usually temporary).

The rest of the committees in the House and Senate have different names
and jurisdictions but essentially cover the waterfront of federal interests.

The Senate has committees on:

- Banking, Housing and Urban Affairs;
- Commerce, Science, and Transportation;
- Energy and Natural Resources;
- Environment and Public Works;
- Finance (mostly taxes, trade, and health care);

- Health, Education, Labor, and Pensions;
- Homeland Security and Governmental Affairs; and
- Indian Affairs.

The other House Committees are:

- Education and Labor;
- Energy and Commerce;
- Financial Services;
- Homeland Security;
- Natural Resources;
- Oversight and Accountability;
- Science and Technology;
- Transportation and Infrastructure; and
- Ways and Means (mostly taxes, trade, and health care).

Wow! If that's not enough to confuse the average citizen, consider that under the auspices of those committees, there are seventy-one subcommittees in the Senate and about one hundred in the House, not counting select committees (the House abandoned the Select Committee on Modernization and created a new Select Committee on the Strategic Competition Between the United States and the Chinese Communist Party in the 118th Congress), special committees, and joint committees that address specific issues or operations. For example, there is a Joint Committee on Printing. Imagine that?

The majority party in each Chamber controls the committees, deciding how many Democrats and Republicans will sit on each. In the House, the majority party dictates the ratios and usually does *not* reflect the ratio of the entire House. In the Senate, the ratios are subject to negotiation between the parties but usually reflect the ratio of Republicans to Democrats.

The majority party decides who the committee Chair will be, often by seniority but not always. The minority leadership usually decides who will be the Ranking Member (The *ranking member* is the minority party's person in charge of that committee or subcommittee). The majority also controls staff funding allocations. There are approximately 1,300 committee staff in the House and 900 in the Senate. The Chair has extensive authority over the committee's activities, and they are a major power in Congress. The Ranking Member, directs the minority's committee activities, such as hiring staff, deciding which witnesses to ask to testify or requesting research reports, etc.

One of the greatest powers of a Chair is the power to say no. There are approximately 10,000 bills introduced each Congress, yet only a few hundred will become law. The committee chairs perform a gatekeeping role over what bills are considered out of all those sent (the institutional phrase for sending a bill or resolution to the committee is "referral" or "referred") to the committee. Still, it's more like managing a legislative mortuary. For reasons we will discuss later, the power to say *no,* held by House chairs, is greater than that of their Senate counterparts because the House rules make it more difficult for individual Members to go around a committee directly to the House Floor.

Chairs hold sway over the consideration of bills and influence whether amendments are made in order (*made in order,* a term of art used in Congress that means "allowed"), both in committee and on the Floor. For example, Republican Senator Charles Curtis of Kansas first introduced the Equal Rights Amendment in 1921, but it failed to get out of committee in either House until 1946.

Committees establish their own rules, normally consistent with their respective House of Congress rules.

The power exercised by individual Members of the committees and subcommittees who are not chairs or ranking Members depends on any or all of the following conditions:

1. How long the Member has been on the committee (called seniority);
2. Whether the Member belongs to the majority or minority party;
3. Whether the Member is also in the party leadership in the House or Senate;

4. Whether the Member has particular expertise in a given issue area;
5. Represents a state or district with particular interest or influence in a given issue area;
6. Whether the Member is on another committee that also has jurisdiction over the same issue area; or
7. Whether the Member has access to the media, an association with an interest group, or is connected to someone of considerable power in the Executive branch with muscle to flex—all different power levers and players in their own rights.

Chairmen and Ranking Members are also selected because of their political clout among other Members, such as their class (class defines Members initially elected in the same year, sort of like high school). Historically, those leadership roles went to the Member who'd served the longest. However, seniority is no longer an absolute process because Republicans established six-year term limits for such chairmanships in 1994.

In those days, when seniority was the only criterion, Jerry once witnessed a baffling scene when a roll call vote was being taken on the House Floor. The Chairman of a very powerful Committee approached the Floor being literally lifted, under his shoulders, by two staff members who took him onto the Floor, where it was evident his age and incapacity kept him from knowing where he was, much less what he was doing. Staff put his voting card in his hand and guided his hand to insert the card into the reader, guided his hand to press the button, and then removed him from the House chamber. Scenes like that led to the end of the formerly consistent practice of seniority as the only criterion for chairmanship.

Committee chairmen throughout history have exercised ordinate and excessive influence over public policy and public spending.

THE CLOUT OF COMMITTEE STAFF

Prepare yourself; we are now digging deeper into legislative policymaking and discussing additional power players, most of whom are never heard of or from by the public. For example, when talking about staff in many committees and Member offices, there are unwritten rules that say a staff member quoted in public will soon be a former staff member. The Members are individual power players, but, realistically, so are some staff members, and sometimes, the committee staff can be more influential than some Members.

The committee *chief of staff*, called the staff director, is loyal to the chairman, the person by whom they were hired, and can be fired without the concurrence of anyone else. The staff director hires and fires staff, runs the committee operations, and coordinates with the chairman's congressional (often called "personal") staff. One of the surest ways for a chairman to get into political hot water back home is to allow the committee's agenda to get out of sync with the expectations of the constituents who elected them.

The committee *chief counsel* (lawyer) plays a key role on the committee. Can any center of power get along without a lawyer? The work of the counsel can vary. On some committees, the counsel is like the legislative director in a Member's personal office but is more likely to be called the committee's policy director or deputy staff director. In addition to experience, the chief counsel has a thorough knowledge of the rules, history, and traditions of the committee, a legal background, of course, and policy expertise relating to the issues before it. The chief counsel is usually the one you see whispering in the ear of the congressman, congresswoman, or senator at a televised hearing, reminding them to pick up the dry cleaning. Seriously, the counsel usually knows more about the law's background, objectives, evolution, and weaknesses than anyone else in the hearing room and is generally a welcomed advisor while the proceedings take place. An example one might hear is, "Mr. Chairman, you may want to call on Congresswoman McGillicuddy next, because of her work prior to coming to Congress," or, more to the point, "You may want to press the witness on who was present in the May 11th meeting when we were told the decision was actually made."

Most committees have abundant *legislative staff* with expertise in various specialties, from communications to technology to food packaging. A committee's legislative staffer may serve as a resource for Members' personal staff, so if you inquire in a congressional office about the status of a piece of legislation or want an issue explained, the answer may originate with a committee staff aide.

Modern technology has made committees much more accessible to the public. The committees have websites where you can get the names of and links to their members, committee reports, committee rules of procedure, transcripts of committee hearings, press releases, copies of testimony, staff briefing papers on issues, and links to live webcasts of hearings. Unfortunately, some committees do not keep those sites up-to-date. The same often applies to the subcommittees too.

PINNACLE OF POWER: CONGRESSIONAL LEADERSHIP AND THEIR STAFF

Like all major organizations, someone must make the trains run on time, and in Congress, those folks are a step above the committees on the hierarchy ladder. They are the leaders.

In the House and Senate, within the minority and majority, Members seek out and are elected or appointed to leadership positions. Why? Because those positions are powerful roles and have more influence in establishing policy and political imagery.

The top leadership office in Congress is the Speaker of the House, the only House leadership position designated by the Constitution, which also puts the Speaker third in line to the Presidency behind the Vice President, who is also President of the Senate, as prescribed by the Constitution. The Constitution also does not specifically require the Speaker to be an elected member of the House, but so far, all have been. The Constitution also provides for the selection of a Senate President Pro Tempore.

> The Constitution also does not require the Speaker to be an elected member of the House, but so far, all have been.

The Speakership is truly an exceptional phenomenon in the hierarchy of the American Republic. The Speaker is a unique figure with power and opportunities to shape the nation's public policy. There have been some exceptional ones. Thomas Reed of New York, who wielded considerable power over the institution, for example, was once asked by a constituent for a copy of the rules of the House. He sent the inquirer an autographed picture of himself.

Then there was Joseph Cannon of Illinois, who accumulated so much power in the office that angry Members on both sides of the aisle nearly toppled him. He was followed by Champ Clark of Missouri, who served during the entry into World War I, and Nicholas Longworth of Ohio, whose savvy leadership guided Congress through the first years of the Depression. A decade later came the great Sam Rayburn of Texas. His Speakership included the longest period of one-party control over the House. Next, Thomas P. "Tip" O'Neill, the classic Boston liberal, led the House during the ascendency and Presidency of Ronald Reagan, the godfather of traditional conservatism.

Successors after Tip left a mixed legacy as the nation slowly sunk deeper into the mud and mire of partisan rigidity and extremist politics. He was followed by the controversial and autocratic James "Jim" Wright of Texas, who was deposed after relentless criticism from future Speaker "Newt" Gingrich. Following Wright was "Tom" Foley of Washington State, one of the more congenial leaders who served with Minority Leader Bob Michel of Illinois, also one of the last in an era of relative civility and bipartisanship.

After losing his congressional seat, civility was not dead when Speaker Foley presided over the House for the last time in the waning days of the 103rd Congress (1994). As Republicans were about to assume control of the next Congress (for the first time in forty years), Foley invited Mike's boss and friend, Bob Michel, who had served his entire forty-year career in the minority, to preside over the House, as he, too, was leaving Congress. It was the first time in our recollection that a member of the minority party had been given that honor beyond the ceremonial exchange between an outgoing and incoming Speaker. Mike watched the moment with much of the rest of C-SPAN's audience. The look on Michel's face spoke volumes as he stared up at Speaker Foley, wondering if he had heard him correctly. Foley repeated himself, and Michel joined him on the dais. It was one of rapidly dwindling grand gestures of dying civility and camaraderie among Democrats and Republicans in the House. A widely respected ABC news analyst, the late Cokie Roberts, said of Michel's retirement, "What you really see is the end of civility in the House of Representatives in a very important way."

Gingrich was elected Speaker in 1995 (the first Republican Speaker in forty years) with an ambitious agenda to which was added the impeachment of President Bill Clinton, a watershed event in the relations between the parties and the Legislative and Executive branches. Gingrich declined to seek reelection following the GOP's 1998 election losses and pressure from his Republican colleagues. He was succeeded by Dennis Hastert of Illinois (who later, as a former Speaker, was sentenced to jail for pre-congressional activities). Hastert was followed by the tough partisan and progressive Nancy Pelosi of California, who stands in the pantheon of legislators as the first woman to ever ascend to the Speakership. Next came John Boehner of Ohio and Paul D. Ryan of Wisconsin; both had short-lived (four years each) Speakerships, which preceded the return of Pelosi in 2019 and the election of Kevin McCarthy in 2023.

There was probably no Speaker greater, however, than Speaker Henry Clay of Kentucky, who in 1811, at age thirty-four and a freshman member of the House, was chosen to lead the House as Speaker. He served on and off until 1825.

By 1820, Washington, DC, was a literal swamp, perpetually under construction. Above it all, on a place called Jenkins Hill, stood the half-completed US Capitol building, overlooking much of the growing Capitol City.

Inside the Capitol, the House and Senate were in heated debates at the epicenter of the slavery debate and the admission of Maine and Missouri to the Union, as reflected in the excellent Clay biography by David S. Heidler and Jeanne T. Heidler. Initially crafted by Illinois Senator Jesse Thomas, the historical Missouri Compromise was maneuvering through Congress to preserve the Union. Speaker Clay, struggling with his views on slavery, employed every ounce of power and persuasion to win final passage. He believed the carefully crafted measure, for which he received more credit than deserved, was the only guardrail standing between the country and civil war.

After much negotiation, the compromise was given final approval by the House. However, the crusty and crotchety Rep. John Randolph of Virginia would not relent in his opposition. He moved that the bill be reconsidered. Clay refused Randolph's request because reconsideration could not occur until the House finished several petitions and committee reports. Here is how Clay used his gavel and preeminence in procedure to make the Missouri Compromise one of the hallmark pieces of legislation of all time:

> *Occasionally Randolph piped up to repeat his motion, but he was each time ruled out of order. Finally, with all old business completed, Randolph offered his motion, but Clay announced that because the clerk of the House had already taken the Missouri bill to the Senate, it could not be reconsidered. Randolph was dumbfounded. He blurted that the clerk had violated a Member's prerogative to ask for reconsideration, but his motion of protest was defeated too. Randolph sat fuming. Clay had done it to him again.[9]*

Clay, who eventually had a duel with Randolph that resulted in only their clothing being damaged, became known as the Great Compromiser because of his incredible talent, legislative skill, political instincts, and flexibility. He also clearly illustrated the power of Speakership.

Arguably, few other Members of Congress exercised political power and persuasion more effectively than Clay. He served many years in the US Senate but could never capture his Holy Grail, the Presidency.

Clay was a cunning strategist and a mesmerizing public speaker. He made formidable enemies, even of former friends, and Clay instinctively knew how to overcome challenges. He used his friendships developed during evening fireside chats with fellow freshmen Members of Congress at Mrs. Dawson's boarding house to promote his candidacy for Speaker and his agenda. Uppermost on his agenda was satisfying Americans' mood for vengeance against the British in 1811 and moving the country toward war.

From *Kings of the Hill* by Lynne and Richard Cheney, writing about Clay and the new Members of Congress:

> *They hadn't gone to the trouble of getting themselves elected and then traveling all the way to Washington by saddle horse and coach and flatboat over muddy roads and swollen rivers simply to continue the national humiliation. The House of Representatives could lead the country, lead it right to war, if it had "some controlling or at least some concentrating influence," as William Lowndes put it in a letter to his wife. And no one was better suited for that than Henry Clay, the man who had stood on the floor of the Senate and so eloquently proclaimed, "No man in the nation desires peace more than I. But I prefer the troubled ocean of war ... with all its calamities and desolations to the tranquil, putrescent pool of ignominious peace."[10]*

Clay would soon radically transform the Speakership, "which had previously been largely ceremonial into a power center," which Clay "would use it to propel the country into war," the Cheneys wrote.

As we return to the other leadership positions, it is important to remember the majority and minority leaders come next in line in authority, followed by the whips, all of whom are elected by their respective caucuses or conferences and who exercise considerable power in their own right but are much less publicly known.

The whips are called *whips* because of their political ancestry in the British Parliament. There and here, the whips are assigned the responsibility of whipping the Members into shape and motivating them to vote how their leadership wants them to. The term shows up as far back as the sixteenth century but, in the current usage, evolved in the eighteenth century from the term *whipper-in*, which describes the huntsmen's assistant—the person who had to herd stray hunting dogs back to the pack using, what else? A whip. That is not to suggest that current Members of Congress or Parliament are to be compared to hunting hounds. They are not dogs.

Former Senator Trent Lott of Mississippi, a former whip himself, entitled his memoir *Herding Cats.*

Next in line in the power structure in the House are caucus or conference chairs, who are primarily responsible for internal and external communications.

Leadership also includes a policy committee chairman responsible for coordinating policy positions and researching and analyzing issues coming before the legislative body. The House Democratic caucus also has the office of assistant leader.

Most leaders are permitted to hire additional staff above their congressional office staff limit, currently eighteen employees. A Member who holds one of the leadership positions regularly sits at the strategy table meetings.

The leaders perform five basic functions:

1. Overall management of their respective bodies;
2. Management of Floor procedures and the flow of legislation;
3. Media relations;
4. Political operations, and
5. The development and coordination of policy positions, including the appointment of Members to committees and task forces.

First and foremost, leaders represent a home district constituency just like every other Member of Congress. Troubled waters lie ahead when they or their staff lose touch with that reality. The most striking modern example is Speaker Foley, who was defeated for reelection to the House in 1994, partly because his constituents became convinced he was paying too much attention to Washington, DC, and too little attention to them.

Another example is that of former House Majority Leader Eric Cantor of Richmond, Virginia, who was defeated in a primary in 2014—again in part because his opponent was able to capitalize on constituent unrest over his leadership role.

The primary elected leadership offices in the Senate are:

- President of the Senate (the Vice President).
- The President Pro Tempore (usually filled by the longest, continuously serving member of the majority party).
- Majority and Minority Leaders (the real power).
- Majority and Minority Whips.
- Chairman, Vice Chairmen, and Secretary of the Democratic Caucus.
- Chairman, Vice Chairmen, and Secretary of the Republican Conference.
- Chairman of the Democratic Policy Committee.
- Chairman of the Republican Policy Committee.
- Chairman of the Democratic Senatorial Campaign Committee (political arm not funded by tax money).
- Chairman of the National Republican Senatorial Committee (political arm not funded by tax money).

Remember that when party control changes in the House, the incoming majority gains a new leadership office—the Speakership—while the outgoing majority must shrink. Being in the minority means fewer leadership offices, smaller budgets, and a draconian reduction in staff. When control of a Chamber shifts from one party to another, it also sets off a major round of office shuffling and furniture moving. The majority party has its pick of the best office space in the Capitol buildings. In Congress, the spoils belong to the victors.

The partisan political arms of the caucuses and conferences are not provided appropriated federal funds for their operations, nor are they provided taxpayer-funded staff or office space. Their respective leader is, however, considered part of the extended family of elected leaders in both the House and the Senate.

Leadership staff must perform a delicate balancing act. Since both Chambers give leadership a great deal of power in decisions about the development and flow of legislation and policy issues, proponents, and opponents of key issues, those both inside and outside Congress want to have the ear of the leaders. And there are never enough ears to go around.

That dynamic put increasing demands on leadership staff, many of whom are known to have the ear of the leaders and are in a prime position to influence the political and policy decision-making process.

Some of the most capable senior leadership staff working for the top leaders are looked upon by many as unelected members of their respective bodies. Some staff keep that exalted position in the proper perspective (one of those staff is former House Speaker Kevin McCarthy's Chief of Staff, Dan Meyer, whose career spans several leaders and senior White House service); others do not. Some can handle the adulation and power and keep their arrogance in check; others do not. That is why it is critically important that those elected to public office hire staff who understand and respect the great constitutional distinction between them and the elected Member. The Constitution made no provision for staff. Those who are given power and fail to understand its limitations and responsibilities can seriously damage the legislative process, jeopardizing the respect they may have from their leader and the public.

One example: Mike once sat in a meeting in secluded offices in what used to be the attic of the Capitol with visitors from former Speaker Paul Ryan's State of Wisconsin. It was 2017, and the meeting was chaired by the tax counsel on the leadership staff to discuss tax reform proposed by Speaker Ryan. The visitors got a tongue lashing from the tax counsel, who criticized them for not being as familiar as he with the long-range global implications of the bill and didn't fully appreciate the important work the Speaker was doing for the country. "You don't live in the real world," the counsel yelled at the Wisconsinites. "I live in the real world."

Staff is critical to the work of Congress in an age when no Member can understand the depth and breadth of 2,000-page pieces of legislation. Unfortunately, however, staff, isolated within the confines of Washington, sometimes fall victim to their exaggerated presumptions about their role in the institution, especially their ultimate subservience to the citizenry. A competent staffer knows when to exercise power, but a great staffer knows when not to.

POLITICIANS WHO MASTERED
THE EXERCISE OF POWER

We can learn more about the current environment for controlling the levers of power from the chronicles of American history, filled with fascinating stories of individuals who exercised enormous power in politics and government, particularly in Congress, and had the good judgment to know when to exercise it and how. But unfortunately, history is also ripe with stories of those who languished in mediocrity because they could never figure out who was in charge of the butter.

When you think of historic governmental leaders, who do you think about?

Most of history was written about Presidents and founding fathers who became Presidents but very few exceptional Members of Congress and senators. So we offer the following profiles of just seven of the more than 12,506 Americans elected to the House or Senate who made history. We do so not only for the fun of reading congressional history but to illustrate various ways the levers of power are wielded in your Congress. Some solely by their election and a quick trip to ignominy. Others by the boundless stories of heroism or cowardice, profiles of courage or timidity, individuals with great character alongside political charlatans. They are men and women who rose from poverty to power and from wealth and privilege to the humbling nature of public service and, sometimes, gruesome politics.

In 1957, a commission created by the Senate and chaired by a young senator from Massachusetts named John Kennedy, who had just written a book called *Profiles in Courage,* was charged with naming the Senate's most outstanding Members. The commission initially settled on five and directed that their portraits hang in a special place in the Capitol.

Among them were three who served in the same tumultuous period between the War of 1812 and the Civil War. They were:

- Daniel Webster of New Hampshire and Massachusetts, known as the "Great Communicator" for his oratory excellence and constitutional authority;

- John C. Calhoun of South Carolina, an avowed racist who was known as the "cast-iron man" for his defense of slavery and the right of states to nullify federal law; and
- Clay of Kentucky, the "Great Compromiser," engineered some of the most far-reaching legislative milestones of the period.

They became known as the Great Triumvirate, drawing their power and influence from their knowledge of the process and their ability to build coalitions and craft solutions, including the Missouri Compromise. They shaped much of the nation's public policy in foreign affairs, national banking, national transportation, international trade, and settling the western frontiers.

They were all effective Members of the House of Representatives, candidates for President, and Cabinet members. Calhoun was Vice President under President Andrew Jackson but resigned over disagreements with the President on the issue of state sovereignty and slavery.

Webster served as Secretary of State under President William Henry Harrison and his successor, John Tyler, with whom he had disagreements and resigned. Harrison, by the way, paved his path to the Presidency with the slogan "Tippecanoe and Tyler Too," a reference to Harrison's military assault on an Indian village in the Indiana territory founded by none other than Chief Tecumseh and his brother, Tenskwatawa, an Indian high priest. Tecumseh was not in the village at the time.

Clay served as Secretary of State under President John Quincy Adams, whose election to office was decided by the House of Representatives, where Clay was Speaker. Clay was accused of engineering Adams's election in exchange for the Cabinet post.

The Kennedy Commission also cited Robert La Follette of Wisconsin and Senator Robert Taft of Ohio, whose portraits joined those of the Great Triumvirate.

"Fighting Bob" La Follette, the son of a Wisconsin farmer, got his nickname as a leader of the progressive movement in America that flourished in the late nineteenth and early twentieth centuries. He was a rebellious and engrossing reformer who spent his life in politics and public service, fighting what he saw as entrenched power and corruption in politics and business.

He advocated for a direct primary system for nominating people to public office and supported the 17th Amendment establishing the direct election of senators (we'll have much more to say about that change's impact on our democracy later). In addition, he was among a coalition of pacifists in the Senate who opposed US entry into World War I. La Follette served in the House from 1884 to 1890 and was Governor of Wisconsin before entering the US Senate, where he served from 1906 to 1925, the year he died.

When La Follette was sworn in as Governor, his progressive soul mate, Theodore Roosevelt, was inaugurated as Vice President of the United States. Their paths crossed many times while La Follette championed progressivism in the Senate, and Roosevelt did so in two terms in the White House. After his second term, Roosevelt traveled the globe for much of the next four years while his designated successor and close friend, William Howard Taft, served his first term as President.

Both Roosevelt and La Follette became disillusioned by what they saw as Taft's abandonment of the progressive movement and sought the Presidency as independents in 1912, in what became a brutal campaign. They both lost, as did Taft. Democrat Woodrow Wilson won the election with the eventual support of La Follette.

Robert Taft, the son of President William Howard Taft, mastered the rules and precedents of the Senate and used his considerable political skills to increase his influence and leverage. After Taft led the successful fight to overturn President Harry Truman's veto of his Taft-Hartley Act, the *New Republic* described his victory this way: "The Congress now consists of the House, the Senate and Bob Taft," according to the Senate Historian.[11]

Taft exercised considerable influence, even when in the minority. He leveraged his position as Chairman of the Republican Policy Committee and Chairman of the Committee on Labor to establish himself as the point of the spear of conservative politics in America. Taft was an effective coalition builder among Democratic conservatives and the foremost adversary of the New Deal programs of Presidents Roosevelt and Harry Truman. In addition, he successfully moved his agenda, restricting the power of labor unions that had been infused into the National Labor Relations Act, otherwise known as the Wagner Act.

Taft declined the job of Senate Majority Leader in 1946, understanding that he could be more productive without the mantle of leadership weighing him down. Still, he did become Leader in 1953, working effectively with President Dwight Eisenhower, against whom he ran for the Presidency in 1952. Unfortunately, Taft did not serve long. He died of cancer that year.

In 2004, the Senate added two more colleagues to the august list of the Senate's greatest, moving their official portraits to the Senate reception center to join the other five. Guess who joined Taft?

Taft's nemesis, Senator Robert Wagner of New York, came to the US from Prussia with his family at age eight, settling in a New York tenement house. He started his career in Democratic politics as a ward heeler for the notorious Tammany Hall political machine. He rose through the ranks and was elected to the US Senate, where he served from 1926 to his death in 1949, as Senate leader and chairman of several committees, including Banking and Commerce. But his power also emanated from his close relationship with a former New York General Assembly colleague, Franklin Delano Roosevelt.

Maybe more than any other member of the Senate, Wagner shepherded through Congress the significant laws that framed the President's New Deal: the National Industrial Recovery Act, the Federal Emergency Relief Administration, the Civilian Conservation Corps, and the Wagner-Steagall Act, which created the public housing authority. However, his crowning achievements were the Social Security Act, the cornerstone of our nation's retirement system, and the National Labor Relations Act, called the Wagner Act, considered the most important labor legislation of the twentieth century and the target of Senator Taft's fury.

Rounding out the wall of portraits is that of Arthur Vandenberg of Michigan, who had a difficult childhood growing up in rural Wisconsin. He had to quit school and get a job early to compensate for his father's bankruptcy in 1893. Vandenberg eventually returned to school, left again, and became a successful journalist at the *Grand Rapids Herald* and, eventually, a media entrepreneur. He was a millionaire before age thirty. In 1928, he was appointed to the US Senate to fill an unexpired term, becoming the fifth former journalist to join that body, according to the Senate Historian.

The Chicago Tribune's Walter Trohan, according to Spartacus Education.com wrote of Vandenberg: "I knew Vandenberg quite well . . . I confess I was not fond of him . . . Politicians as a class are vain, but he was vain beyond most of the tribe. His chief conversation was on his last speech or the one he had in preparation."[12] Early in his career, Vandenberg was a "New Deal Republican" but later opposed the President on constitutional grounds. He also helped defeat Roosevelt's attempt to pack the Supreme Court.

The Michigander was an early isolationist, opposing our entry into the war in Europe against Germany. "He supported the isolationist Neutrality Acts of the 1930s but wanted and sponsored more severe bills designed to renounce all traditional neutral 'rights' and restrict and prevent any action by the President that might cause the United States to be drawn into war. He was one of the most effective of the diehard isolationists in the Senate."[13]

Vandenberg, however, later converted to internationalism with his support of Roosevelt's Lend-Lease program to sell arms to Great Britain. Sixteen other Republicans joined Vandenberg in pushing Lend-Lease over the top in the Senate. In 1945, he gave the "speech heard round the world," publicly announcing his conversion from isolationism to internationalism. Vandenberg was rumored to have had an affair beginning in 1938 with a woman who resided with her husband on the floor above Arthur and Hazel Vandenberg in a Washington apartment building. It was that woman, Mitzi Sims, who was said by Trohan of the *Tribune* to be a British agent in the US, one that helped convince Vandenberg to change his position on Lend-Lease and isolationism.

Vandenberg became Chairman of the Foreign Relations Committee in 1947, at the start of his fourth and last term in the Senate, and in that capacity, again, according to the Senate historian, advanced the Truman Doctrine, launching the Marshall Plan for the recovery of Europe and creating the North Atlantic Treaty Organization, insisting that "politics stop at the water's edge," a principle of foreign policy that survived the remainder of the twentieth century. It was eventually abandoned in the heated partisanship of the Bush, Obama, and Trump Administrations. Vandenberg died of cancer in 1951.

The same profiles in the exercise of power can be found among the more than 12,506 individuals who have served in the House since 1789, many of them Speakers of the House, such as Clay, and committee chairs. One of the most effective and colorful of those chairmen was Wilbur Mills, an Arkansas Democrat who ruled the powerful Ways and Means (W&M) Committee from 1957–1974.

Mills' position as Chairman had even more power back then than it wields today. As Chairman of W&Ms, he was de facto Chairman of the Democratic Committee on Committees, the small insider group that decided on which committee a Member would serve. So if Mills liked you, you got a plumb assignment; if not, a not-so-good assignment.

To illustrate real power: Even before taking the Oath of Office in 1967, the newly elected and first African American Congresswoman, Shirley Anita Chisholm, after being critical of her own Democratic leadership, asked for assignment to a major committee. This offended Mills, who believed new Members were like children, best seen but not heard. Although Chisholm's district consisted of a new Brooklyn congressional district, Mills assigned her to the Agriculture Committee, knowing she did not have a single farm in her district. He ultimately relented and moved her to the Veterans Committee, slightly more relevant but irrelevant in the national policy-making scheme.

Jerry joined Mr. Mills and other Members from Arkansas for dinner, at which he learned more about the levers of power and how that power is attained. In response to a question, Mills explained how he maneuvered major legislation through Congress. It boiled down to spending the first year making the country aware of the problem and the urgency to solve it; his example was the creation of Medicare. Next, he'd hold field hearings in major media markets (such as St. Louis, Chicago, Los Angeles, Dallas, etc.), where the selected witnesses would testify to the dire straits created either by the cost of health care or the fact that spending on surgery had bankrupted their family. The following year was a protracted series of congressional hearings in DC, where all sorts of solutions were publicly presented. However, Mills said he had already decided on the legislative track he would follow. Then, late that year, he presented his bill and held markups in the Ways & Means Committee that ultimately adopted the plan Mills had in mind from the beginning.

The process was mostly out of public view, with Mills, or others so empowered, leaking information that shaped public opinion. When the legislative process was finished, the country had a new federally funded program. Even though Mills had enormous internal power, he also knew how to use that power to sway the nation's public opinion.

Power, like most else in politics, is a relative element. Issues come and go. Conditions change. People change. Power seldom lasts very long.

Power often convinces politicians they are invincible. This may have been the case with Mills when his car and companion, a reasonably well-known exotic dancer, veered off the road and ended up in the Tidal Basin by the Jefferson Monument in DC.

His long and illustrious career ended in disgrace. After undergoing alcoholism treatment and forfeiting his chairmanship, he survived the immediate election but declined to run for reelection in 1976.

Members must be careful not to become captive to the many influences around them..

Chapter 4

Congressional Staff: The Influence of the Unelected

There are two things that are most important to your success
[in Congress]: the people you choose to help you in your office
and selecting the committees you want to serve on.
—Sam Rayburn, the longest-serving Speaker of the House,
advice to new Members

O n a hot July 1998, a gunman entered the US Capitol's first floor, fatally shooting Capital Police Officer JJ Chestnut. He wounded a staff member before entering a corridor and shot Officer John Gibson. Mortally wounded, Gibson returned fire, wounding the assailant. He was captured but declared incompetent to stand trial.

We will never know how many Members or congressional staff would have been wounded or killed had Gibson not returned fire.

Three years later, a group of heroic Americans died downing a passenger plane whose terrorist hijackers intended to fly into the Capitol, killing those who worked there and destroying one of America's most significant landmarks and its seat of government.

In the ensuing years, staff working in Washington's US House and Senate offices or congressional offices around the country are regularly reminded they are at risk.

On January 8, 2011, Congresswoman Gabby Giffords was conducting a constituent gathering in a supermarket parking lot in Casas Adobes, Arizona, when an assassin opened fire. Rep. Giffords was severely wounded; a staff member, Gabe Zimmerman, lay dead with five others, including a nine-year-old girl.

Six years later, on June 14, 2017, Rep. Steve Scalise of LA was badly wounded along with four others, including congressional aide Zack Barth, when an angry man opened fire on a baseball field in Virginia.

Five years later, protestors stormed the Capitol on January 6, 2021, threatening Members and staff.

Congressional staffers work in a risk-prone environment today more than ever. They work in a bullseye that ranges from harassment from angry constituents and frequent harangues of press and political foes to the harsh reality of domestic and international terrorists. Staffers work behind street barriers, magnetometers, security cameras, and armed officers. Unfortunately, this has had the unintended consequence of placing physical and mental barriers between them and the public they serve.

Following the January 6th assault on the Capitol, Speaker Pelosi further clouded the visual image of the People's House by having barbed-wire and physical barricades erected around the entire Capitol complex, which have since been removed.

Thankfully, most Members express their gratitude for staff efforts.

The staff does much of the work behind the scenes on legislation, finding and neutralizing the political landmines, crafting amendments, polishing images, and making sure that mountains of paperwork, communications, and problems get driven from the inbox to the outbox.

Imagine being associated with legislation intended to prevent forest fires, provide worker training for veterans, improve educational opportunities for young children, or reduce the flow of illegal drugs into the country. Helping a senior citizen with a Social Security problem can keep a smile on a staffer's face for the rest of the day. In fact, being successful in the name of the Member for whom they work is potentially more rewarding than their paycheck.

On most days, 15,000 staff perform their jobs like many people everywhere in America. Some perform well, some not so well, some with ulterior motives, some with a deep dedication to public service, some enamored with the exercise of power and influence, and others with the humility that politics often demands. Some work with one eye focused on the task at hand and have the other searching for a career in the private sector where salaries can be twice to four times that of pay on the Hill. They all toil under varying degrees of excitement, boredom, overwhelm, incredibly long hours, and burn-out by an overbearing boss.

Knowing how and why staff function is understanding the circuitous routes through the politics and process of Congress to influence your Congressman or Congresswoman. They are the gatekeepers, the palace guards, and the workhorses.

Senators and House Members may, within the limits of the law, congressional rules, and smart politics, hire who they please and make independent decisions about salary levels, working hours (with some limitations), office space, equipment purchases, and a whole range of other functions. Congress is not one workplace but 435 independent offices in the House, six nonvoting delegate offices from the District of Columbia and US territories, and one hundred offices in the Senate.

Each House Member may hire up to eighteen full-time permanent staff and four part-time staff, including interns. In the Senate, there are no fixed limits on the number of staff. But each senator receives an allowance to hire personnel based on the population of their state. Accordingly, a California senator will have significantly more staff than a senator from North Dakota.

Some House Members and senators are entitled to hire more staff assigned to assist them on their committees, such as when they chair committees or subcommittees or serve in leadership positions.

The Speaker of the House has the largest staff. They have eighteen full-time staff to handle affairs involving the congressional office and home district. Additionally, the Speaker also has a staff of approximately fifty, called leadership staff, who help manage the functions and activities of the House of Representatives. (More on leaders later.)

STAFF ROSTER

Here is the general breakdown of staff the average House Member may hire. Staff are very influential with the Member and an essential avenue for communications with constituents (titles are common to the role but not dictated by law or the rules of Congress; legally, all are classed as clerks):

Chief of Staff

Legislative:
- Legislative director (LD)
- Legislative assistants (LA)
- Legislative correspondents (LC)

Communications:
- Communications director or press secretary
- Deputy director or deputy press secretary

Outreach and Constituent Services:
- District director (for representatives, resident commissioner, and delegates)
- State Director (for senators)
- Director of Constituent Services
- Caseworkers

Support and Administrative Staff:
- Office manager(s)
- Technology specialist or systems manager
- Scheduler (who may also be Executive Assistant to the Congressman/Senator)

- Assistants to senior staff
- Staff assistants/receptionists
- Interns

The Chief of Staff has responsibility for all Washington and home district office operations, oversees the staff, serves as a liaison to outside organizations, and usually serves as the top advisor to the Member. The Chief must also understand the ethics rules better than anyone on the staff (in many cases, Members will hire a counsel to deal with legal matters, such as ethics rules and laws.

The legislative team deals with policy and most aspects of lawmaking. They also monitor rules and regulations promulgated by the Executive. They meet with constituents, interest groups, government agencies, and staff from other offices. They handle truckloads of constituent mail and electronic correspondence.

The Legislative director (LD) is responsible for developing legislative strategy and coordinating with other Members' staff, the leadership, and the committees on specific legislative issues. They also oversee their Member's legislative staff—four or five people in the House or more than ten in the Senate. They include:

- Legislative assistants (LAs) assigned specific issues (e.g., agriculture, Veterans Affairs, international relations, or defense matters). If you contact a Member's office about an issue, you may want to talk directly with the LA who handles your subject of interest for faster communications.
- Legislative correspondents (LCs) respond to what has been estimated to be an average of 50,000 communications per year, which the Member receives from constituents.

It used to be that the most valued communication from a constituent was a hand-written letter, indicating that the constituent was interested enough to put pen to paper and concerned enough to spend time composing their thoughts. But since a fatal mail-based anthrax attack on Congress in 2011, "snail mail" has been curtailed by the roughly fourteen days it now takes to inspect it before it even reaches the Member's office.

Another source of communication is constituent telephone calls, usually answered by staff assistants who work in the reception area. In 1879, the first telephone was installed in the Capitol and answered by just one man, the doorkeeper (stationed outside the Floor of the House). The phones have not stopped ringing since, and today are answered by tens of thousands of employees who frequently have two phones to oversee, a desk phone and a cell phone.

Emails are now the largest communication volume, easily amounting to 75 percent or more of the messages most offices receive. Members are also overwhelmed by emails from professional interest groups with access to massive amounts of data about congressional districts, with which they can target both the mail, email, and their messages. There are thousands of organizations in Washington with that capability, including groups like the AARP, the National Rifle Association, teachers, doctors, and bricklayers.

All of this suggests that to maximize your communication with a congressional office—House or Senate—it is helpful to contact the right staff person in the Washington, state, or home district office.

How offices respond to mail varies from office to office, and the degree to which the Member participates in that process varies too. Some Members take a personal interest and have a sample of mail brought to them for a response. Other Members get summaries.

The communications director, once known as the press secretary, helps manage the Member's public visibility: drafts news releases and commentaries for newspapers and social media, posts information to the Member's website, and designs printed mail sent to constituents. More importantly, the communications director manages and engages in relations with local, regional, and national media—plus the avalanche of information and propaganda circulated through social media.

Back in the home district or state, the staff provides constituent services—solving problems with the federal government that constituents face. The district or state director and their staff also serve as the eyes and ears for the Member so changing public attitudes or growing problems are made known to the Member. They attend meetings and visit senior centers, churches, schools, and workplaces. In addition, the local staff answers mail and helps with a wide range of problems called *casework*. Bridging the gap between residents and federal agencies ranges from cases involving immigration, military, Social Security, Medicare and Medicaid, veteran's service, and federal grants and contracts.

Another important staff Member is the scheduler or executive assistant (usually one staffer in House offices and two in most Senate offices), who is principally responsible for coordinating the Member's meetings and appearances. Members of Congress have incredibly tight schedules. They receive hundreds of invitations for events in Washington, the home district, and the state. They juggle committee hearings, the votes, and debates on the Floor schedule, time in the office with staff, media interviews, and countless other commitments, including travel schedules, just getting back and forth to the nation's capital. Congressional offices usually establish disciplined processes for arranging meetings. It is best to follow them but be prepared to circumvent them.

Some communications with congressional offices are subconsciously intended to blow off steam. It isn't very polite and doesn't accomplish much. Moreover, it is highly disrespectful of the staff who get the brunt of such bluntness. Jerry experienced this firsthand when a telegram arrived shortly after a new federal policy had been announced. It read: "Go to [H]ell, tough letter to follow." Some correspondence today is much worse, from vulgar to threatening.

Letting your representatives and senators know how you feel about important issues is important. In that process, constituents should seek information and learn from them how legislation is written and how it can be influenced. Your communications will compete with thousands of others for the attention of your legislators and their staff. Citizens who understand how Congress works and who pull the levers of influence are more effective at affecting the process and ensuring their message comes across, gaining more attention than others.

Here are some tips:

- Make sure you are communicating with the right individual. For example, suppose your VA pension check is in error, you have an immigration problem, or you have a question about Social Security procedures. In that case, the best approach is communicating with the staff who handles VA, immigration, or Social Security. Most areas of citizen concern are assigned to a specific staff person in a congressional office. They can probably solve the problem far faster than it will take you to get a meeting with the Member or insist on communicating with a more senior staff person.

- If you want to express your opinion on a general issue, making that position known to the staff assistant may be sufficient. However, if you have a concern that may seriously impact you, your family, or your community, ask which staff member handles the issue.

- If you advocate for or against specific legislation, meet with the district or state director or talk with the legislative aide or director. Depending upon what you learn, consider requesting a meeting or call with the Member. Many issues introduced in Congress or hyped in the media are unlikely to ever see the light of day in the House or the Senate. Making your opinions known at the highest levels may not be necessary. But a staff person can give you the odds of more action happening.

- If your interest is more political/partisan than legislative, you may want to talk with the chief of staff or state or district director or be directed to campaign staff. By the way, it is unwise to discuss campaign business in a congressional office. Never deliver a campaign contribution to a legislator or staff on federal property. It's against the law.

- When communicating with the congressman, congresswoman, or their office, ensure your interaction is action-forcing. That is, make sure it requires a response or some form of follow-up that moves your request forward. It may be just insight into where the Member stands on an issue. Ask to be apprised of status changes or guidance on whom else you should talk to. Ask for additional information or any relevant reports, speeches, or statements. You may want to get the Member to cosponsor a piece of legislation, speak out on an issue, attend a meeting, or contact a federal agency on your behalf if that contact is not restricted by law, regulation, or congressional rules, and talking with staff first may help you understand such limitations.

- Before making contact, know what you want to get out of it and be sure that what you want is *reasonable and doable*. Sometimes the better part of wisdom is to ask the congressional aide or the Member what they and you can do to produce the best result. You may not get the response you hoped for, but you will know where you stand and better understand what to do next.

- Be clear, concise, well thought out, reasonable, and complete in your communications. If you provide information, *ensure it's correct* and contains both sides of the story. They should hear the pros and cons of a situation from you rather than someone else who may have a bias.

- Take good notes on your contact with whom you talked, including when and what was said or done.

Your congressman and their staff work for you, but they also work for around 762,000 other congressional district residents and, in the case of a senator, the state's entire population. Legislators are individuals. Each of them treats the job differently and will undoubtedly treat you differently depending upon the time of day, what you want, and whether they can help. Sometimes the outcome depends on you and the relationship you establish with them.

Legislation only becomes law if both Houses and the President agree.

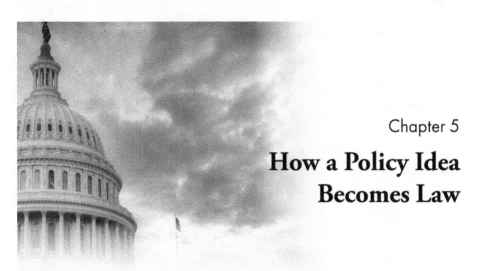

Chapter 5

How a Policy Idea Becomes Law

Congress is where an idea becomes a proposal and a proposal becomes a bill, and a bill becomes a law, which sometimes becomes public policy.

Question: How does an idea become a law?

Answer: Anyway, it can.

The Founding Fathers created the Congress in the general likeness of the European parliaments and the legislatures already functioning in the states, particularly Virginia and Pennsylvania. They also borrowed from political philosophers ranging from seventeenth-century British philosopher John Locke, French historian Voltaire, eighteenth-century English teacher, and scholar William Wollaston to British Member of Parliament sympathetic to the grievances of the American colonies, Edmund Burke.

For example, Edmund Burke's prescription is clearly reflected in our Constitution. He wrote:

> *To make a government requires no great prudence. Settle the seat of power, teach obedience, and the work is done. To give freedom is still more easy. It is not necessary to guide; it only requires to let go the rein. But to form a free government—that is, to temper together these opposite elements of liberty and restraint in one consistent*

*work—requires much thought, deep reflection, a sagacious, power-
ful, and combining mind.*[14,15]

But the Founders also experimented with new ideas of their own. Intentionally, they weren't very specific about how the process would work. But
they wanted power diffused.

The Founders gave the two chambers of Congress, the House and
Senate, a free hand in writing their rules for turning ideas (bills and resolutions) into the laws of the land.

But the writing of our laws isn't always done the way we were taught
in high school—or college, for that matter. In fact, it seldom is. But there is
a textbook version of how a bill becomes a law. Here it is:

Only senators and representatives can introduce legislation in Congress. A lot of people think the President can, but he can't. He must get a
Member of Congress to do it for him. (Note: Getting an idea turned into a
bill that is introduced—officially submitted—means almost nothing. The
legal counsel drafts the bill, but the overwhelming number of bills never
see the light of day or receive any action in either House.)

A senator introduces a bill or resolution by placing the written language
at the desk of the Clerk of the Senate.

A House Member drops the language for the bill or resolution in the
hopper, a box on the Floor of the House.

The legislative language is assigned to a committee or committees in
the chamber in which it was introduced, based on which committee(s) has
jurisdiction over the subject matter by the legislation. A bill introduced in
one chamber or House of Congress *does not* automatically get introduced
in the other. The Speaker assigns jurisdiction in the House, and the Senate
Parliamentarian (acting on behalf of the Senate President, the Vice President of the US) determines jurisdiction in the Senate.

New legislation can ignite turf wars between committees fighting for
areas of control, but most bills are assigned according to well-established
precedents in both chambers.

For example, suppose a bill is introduced in the House that deals with the internet. In that case, it will be assigned to the Energy and Commerce Committee, which has jurisdiction over most telecommunications issues. But if that bill also has a provision that creates a new tax on the internet, it will also be assigned to the Ways and Means Committee, which has jurisdiction over taxes. Additionally, if it has a provision dealing with intellectual property, it may also be assigned to the Judiciary Committee.

The respective committee chairs in each of the committees of jurisdiction may then decide to assign the bill to a subcommittee.

The workhorses of the legislative process are the committees and subcommittees in the House and Senate. Most legislation proposals are referred to subcommittees, so subcommittees shoulder the lion's share of the work. Generally, the legislation is thoroughly evaluated at the subcommittee level, where hearings are conducted to obtain expert testimony for or against it.

Of course, that assumes the committee leadership considers the idea worth studying or action. Most bills get buried at the committee or subcommittee level. It is not uncommon, however, for a piece of legislation to be kept in the full committee for hearings and consideration.

When hearings are completed, the legislation is usually amended and, in some cases, completely rewritten.

That process is called a "mark-up," where the subcommittee or committee Members mark up (change) the text of the legislation, adding or extracting words or phrases, changing whole sections, or adjusting effective dates or instructions to the Executive branch on how Congress wants the legislation enforced and administered (expressing what is called "congressional intent").

The same process could even occur at the full committee level with or without action by the subcommittee. And this mark-up process could be repeated in other committees that may have jurisdiction.

If the full committee approves it, the House bill then goes to the Rules Committee, where it is debated again. The Rules Committee is the traffic cop of the House, deciding which bills get sent to the House Floor and under what conditions—how many hours of debate and how many amendments will be considered by the full House.

In the Senate, the majority leadership decides when the full Senate considers a bill. While senators have more freedom to amend legislation on the Senate Floor, the Majority Leader can exercise powers to inhibit amendments.

When the House passes a bill, the Clerk sends it to the Senate or vice versa. However, suppose versions passed by the House and Senate are different. In that case, the bills are sent to a specifically created conference committee of representatives and senators, who must resolve the differences between the two body's wording and send the legislation back to each chamber for final approval.

When both houses pass *identical* versions, the bill goes to the President for signing or veto. If the President signs the bill, it becomes law. If he vetoes it, both houses of Congress must re-approve it by a two-thirds margin before it can become law.

And that, in theory, is how a bill becomes a law.

Or is it?

It should be understood from the outset that the odds of a single bill (or idea) becoming law are slim, very slim. For openers, if a Member of the House or Senate introduced a bill in the 112th Congress, in session from January 2011 to January 2013, the chance of that bill becoming law was less than one in fifty. In that Congress, 9,987 pieces of legislation were introduced, and only 230 became law.

The 115th Congress (January 2017 to January 2019) was a little more productive. Legislators enacted 442 bills out of 13,556 introduced, the most adopted since the 101st Congress from 1989–1991, the first two years of President George H. W. Bush's Presidency, whose full term was one of the most productive on record. The 116th Congress produced 344 new laws out of more than 14,000 introduced, while the 117th produced just twenty more out of about 16,000 introduced.

But don't be misled by these statistics, which are representative of most congresses and differ depending on how legislation is labeled and counted.

About one-third of the bills and resolutions passed are not life-changing. For example, the 116th Congress (2019–2021) passed legislation renaming 109 post offices across the country—most were in separate bills.

Furthermore, most legislative language took different routes into the law books. Some parts of those thousands of introduced bills may have been attached or incorporated into one of the few bills that did pass. Because so few pieces of legislation get through Congress, those that do are often broad, bloated, amalgamated, transformer-like versions of their former selves, with sometimes hundreds of individual provisions that weren't there at the birth of the bill. In the 116th Congress, for example, the GovTrack website calculated that Congress passed 1,229 bills if you count those incorporated in other legislation. And during the 117th Congress, according to the website, it passed 1,231.

At the close of the 112th Congress (January 2013), the Senate passed and sent the House an emergency supplemental (appropriations) bill with $60 billion in authorized spending for the victims of Hurricane Sandy that swept through the Northeast in late October 2012.

However, in the House of Representatives, the bill was delayed because some House Members were upset that the Senate had slipped into the legislation $400 million in extraneous spending that had nothing to do with Hurricane Sandy. The same situation occurred in 2019 with a bill to provide emergency funding for areas in several states and Puerto Rico hit by hurricanes and wildfires. The dispute then was over how much money Puerto Rico should receive. Unfortunately, that exercise is not unusual.

Appropriation bills rushed through the House or the Senate at the end of a Congress are often laden with additional spending for extraneous purposes. Therefore, they call those bills a freight train or a Christmas tree bill (with lots of ornaments).

The House and Senate have not passed and sent to the President all twelve of the called-for appropriation bills funding the federal government since 1996. Instead, Congress has thrown the bills not passed individually into a huge supplemental appropriation bill containing thousands of pages of legislative language and provisions most Members never read. While the chambers are putting together the supplemental package, they pass temporary Continuing Appropriation Resolutions to fund the Government for short periods, which can be anywhere from a week to several months, to get Congress passed funding deadlines.

When Congress can't get the individual bills done, or a supplemental or even a temporary Continuing Resolution, much of the Government shuts down, as it did for a record thirty-five days from December 22, 2018, until January 25, 2019. However, all governmental activities are not stopped. Some functions, such as defense, are considered too essential to be interrupted.

Finally, getting away from appropriation-type legislation, not all bills and resolutions are intended to become law. Members of Congress have different motivations for introducing a piece of legislation. Some try to imitate the Kansas City Chiefs' colorful quarterback Patrick Mahomes, who fakes out his opponents on the field by looking at one receiver to his right while throwing to another receiver to his left.

Members introduce bills to:

- Satisfy constituent interest in a subject;
- Establish a benchmark for or ownership of an idea or issue;
- Draw attention to an issue, sometimes in the hope that a bill will result in media attention or a committee hearing on the subject;
- Establish a position on an issue that they may eventually incorporate into another piece of legislation;
- Introduce an issue or an idea to attract opposition and demonstrate its invalidity, as is the case when the opposition party introduces the President's budget as an amendment and forces a vote on it to show that the President's party does not support it.

A good example is House Resolution 109, introduced on February 7, 2019, by freshman Congresswoman Alexandria Ocasio-Cortez of New York and sixty-seven original (those who sign on the day it is introduced) cosponsors, all Democrats.

The same day, Senator Edward Markey of Massachusetts introduced an identical measure, Senate Resolution 59, with eleven cosponsors, ten Democrats, and an Independent, six of whom were announced candidates for President.

The legislation had no chance of passage from the minute it was introduced. The resolutions were entirely partisan and symbolic. Moreover, the House version was so broad, it was referred to eleven different committees, two elements that can and usually do spell doom from the beginning.

The legislation, dubbed the *Green New Deal*, purported to advance the cause of environmental protection. But it was an amalgamated social democratic (the objectives of socialism under a democratic system of Government) agenda, deliberately ill-defined and so glittering in its generalities, it defied serious discussion or specific criticism.

The legislation claimed it would create millions of new jobs, zero greenhouse gas emissions, increase investments in infrastructure, and more investment in industrial production, plus set clean air and water goals. It called for climate and community resilience, renovation of buildings, cleaning up hazardous waste, fair competition in business, healthy food, economic security, and justice and equality. But unfortunately, they left out the kitchen sink and a chicken in every pot.

The Green New Deal did, however, draw more glowing press attention to the congresswoman, and it had considerable appeal to the progressive and socialist base of voters in the Democratic party. It laid claim politically to that agenda. But as a legislative instrument, it had no value.

REAL WORLD LEGISLATING

Back in the real world of serious legislating, Members usually test the integrity of an idea before they get too far into the process. That usually means testing the waters with five or six key individuals and organizations:

1. The constituents back home: If the idea falls like a rotten apple in the orchard of constituent opinion, particularly those with a

special interest in the subject, then the Member has three choices: (a) try to convince the constituency of the merits; (b) modify the idea to minimize resistance from back home; or (c) drop the idea and go fishing.

2. The influencers: For a bill to become a law, those in power will have to support the process, such as the subcommittee and committee chairmen, senior Members of the committees, members of the party leadership, and in some cases, the leaders of influential caucuses. The Member will have to win support from enough individuals with critical influence to feel confident they can move the bill forward. If too much resistance exists, three options identical to *a, b,* and *c* above exist.

3. The Executive branch: At some point in the process, the Executive branch will have to weigh in on the bill's merits, so supporters must do some selling with one or several relative Cabinet departments that have jurisdiction or influence over the bill's provisions. Other agencies, particularly the White House's Office of Management and Budget (OMB), arguably the most powerful agency in Government (because it controls the Administration's purse strings and regulatory actions), or the quasi-independent agencies would be likely touchstones. (This is the real-world explanation of what happens. Occasionally, one party will pass legislation without coordinating and count on it being vetoed so the issue can become campaign fodder.)

4. Outside interest groups: Thousands of outside interest groups exercise influence over public policy. Several probably represent your interest. It doesn't matter what the subject is; an organization in America is dedicated to influencing that subject. Those organizations' support can go a long way toward getting a bill enacted or defeated.

5. Colleagues in Congress: Probably the most valuable support and guidance a Member can solicit is from colleagues in Congress. The

more cosponsors a Member can recruit for their legislation, the better chance it has of being considered in committee, sent to the Floor, and introduced in the other body.

6. The media: It is common for legislators to test ideas with the media. It is helpful to know whether an idea is considered newsworthy, whether it can be explained in a manner attractive to media coverage, or whether it generates such a harsh reaction, it may need substantial change.

Clearly, the legislative process is so complex that we could write a chapter on each one of these steps. Even though we know you want us to, we won't.

Suffice it to say, your Member of Congress, or any Member of Congress, must jump through a lot of hoops, turn a lot of somersaults, twist a lot of arms, and bend a lot of ears to move even a simple piece of legislation. Simply promising to introduce an idea on the campaign trail may sound good, but it can be a promise with many unintended consequences and interpretations. An idea is only the seed from which the policy position sprouts, the legislative language blooms, and the fruit of the law appears. The fruit, of course, then must be picked, cleaned, sorted, packaged, transported, priced, and sold. And through all of that, it could turn out to be rotten or contaminated with pesticide residue and subject to a recall.

As we have said before, based on what we have learned from history, the Founding Fathers intended the process to be slow, cumbersome, and sometimes difficult. While they recognized the need for a national government to replace the loose confederation of states, they were also leery of a strong federal government, particularly a strong presidency.

MISS DEMOCRACY "LAN' SAKES, WHAT'LL I DO WITH 'EM?
NOVEMBER 1912

Most ideas do not become law.

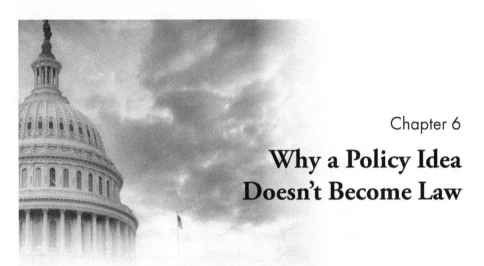

Chapter 6

Why a Policy Idea
Doesn't Become Law

The Founding Fathers likely never envisioned a legislative process serving 320 million people in a Congress of 535 Members from fifty states, almost as diverse as the then-existing countries of Europe.

They did envision a legislative body where it would be difficult to enact new ideas into laws. But on the other hand, they did not want to make it easy for the government to impose itself on the citizenry. So they created checks and balances among the three branches of government—the Legislative, Executive, and Judicial—and the two houses within the legislature—the House and Senate—for that purpose.

One of the questions that deserves the attention of the American people in this twenty-first century is whether it has become too difficult for Congress to act, to take up an idea and turn it into the law of the land. Whether you want a smaller or bigger government or the government to do more or less doesn't matter. But, in most cases, either objective requires Congress to act, to do something to bring about change.

Congressional critics, and there are a lot of them, argue there are compelling reasons to answer yes, that it has grown too complicated for Congress to solve problems. As a result, most Americans look upon the institution unfavorably. But different folks can hold that common view, viewing Congress unfavorably, but for conflicting and opposite reasons. Some want Congress to impose rules on every aspect of personal life and to increase spending for every conceivable reason while reducing defense spending and allowing almost anyone to enter the country. Others hold Congress in an unfavorable light because it has not gotten the government out of regulating details of everyday life: it hasn't cut federal spending and deficit, protected our borders, and reduced taxes on everyone while saving Social Security and Medicare.

Congress, in recent years, has consistently violated its own rules and even toothless laws that it imposed on itself. For example, Congress failed to adopt a budget for the nation, as required by law, in eight of the last ten years. Even worse, modern Congresses have failed for the past twenty-two years to individually adopt the congressionally required twelve appropriation bills that fund governmental services. And before that, it only passed all twelve individual appropriations in fiscal years 1977, 1989, 1995, and 1997.

If the orderly adoption of budgets is your criteria for good government, things have looked sad for over forty years. Before the Congressional Budget Act of 1974 was adopted, Congress did not even try to create a unified budget.

The government is now routinely funded by huge "continuing" or omnibus appropriation bills that few Members of Congress even read. In 2013, the failure of Congress to pass either form of appropriation forced a government shutdown for fifteen days. The 115th and 116th Congresses raised that bar, keeping part of the government closed for thirty-five days in a battle with President Trump over border security.

Recent Congresses have also failed to pass the authorization bills (*authorization bills* do what they sound like—give specific statutory authority and rules to conduct activities but do not provide funding). The Department of Homeland Security has never been reauthorized. The Department of Justice hasn't undergone reauthorization in more than fifteen years. But Congress does back-door implied reauthorizations that, so far, have withstood court challenges.

In 2011, Congress created a *minor crisis* by its failure to extend the legal existence of the Federal Aviation Administration. That forced people out of work and cost the Treasury more than $30 million a day in uncollected tax revenues, a number the *Christian Science Monitor* questioned (if you can call $30 million a "minor" crisis). In addition, Congress has failed to resolve numerous additional individual laws that were about to expire but covered its tracks by passing stopgap reauthorizations that allowed most of these operations to continue to function temporarily under the old laws.

Congress, through its neglect, has allowed the Executive branch to exercise considerable power through regulation and Executive Orders. The Obama Administration took full advantage of congressional gridlock with a wide variety of energy and environmental actions, many of which were then undone by the Trump Administration. Trump's Administration made broad use of Executive powers too. One of the most controversial was to declare a national emergency at our southern border to go around Congress to fund new and expanded immigration barriers (a.k.a. the wall). The Biden Administration followed suit by "forgiving" millions owed to the public through unpaid student loans. The program faced legal challenges and was eventually deemed an overstep of Executive authority. Normally, that would be the end of the matter, but Presidents in recent decades have made a hobby of finding other ways to bypass their constitutional limitations.

> Congress, through its neglect, has allowed the Executive branch to exercise considerable power through regulation and Executive Orders.

This volatility created by both parties does not serve the nation well: it confuses individuals, other governments, and businesses trying to make plans. It ultimately reduces efficiency and effectiveness in government and private activities. More importantly, this shifting of power undermines the structural objectives of three equal branches of the federal government by shifting excessive power to the Executive, simply because legislators don't have the leadership ability and political courage to pass legislation with clear and specific congressional intent.

The point in policy terms: Immigration is just one of many far-reaching issues and national concerns on which Congress and the Executive branch have failed to come to terms. Others range from cyber-security and terrorism to the national deficit, the looming bankruptcy of Social Security and Medicare, and ongoing crises in education and educational opportunities undermining the US's global competitiveness. In a rare display of bipartisanship, the Biden Administration and more centrist congressional Republicans agreed on a massive infrastructure bill in 2021. But even that legislation has not met expectations because, predictably, getting the funds where they are needed is easier said than done.

Again, the criticism of Congress has nothing to do with whether you believe the federal government ought to be active or passive, bigger, or smaller, limited or unrestrained. Congress would have to act to accommodate any point of view.

The extent of legislative and political gridlock within Congress and between Congress and the Administration suggests our system is not functioning anywhere near the level the nation's problems demand.

There are several reasons why Congress and the Executive branch are unpopular and unproductive. Much can be learned from history and the constant waves of change that overtake the country at any given time, from good times to bad, from war to peace, from one generation of leaders to another, from one technological age to another, and from bull markets to bear markets.

History tells us that Congress and the Presidency are almost always in popular disfavor when the economy is bad. Moreover, they face more unrest when the country has been in extended periods of military conflict in which the lines between victory and defeat are blurred. Unrest has been especially true in the international struggle against non-state-sponsored terrorism.

Dissatisfaction is high when a tectonic conflict exists between influential but rigid ideological extremes. Likewise, there is disillusionment without strong visionary leadership or well-defined common challenges.

The most recent period of intense public disaffection is virulent for other reasons. We have let our institutions of government and politics sink into serious disrepair, along with those institutions that have been the pillars of our society since our founding. Gallup regularly conducts polls on the approval or disapproval of sixteen institutions. As of 2020, thirteen had less than 50 percent of public confidence. Seth McLaughlin reported in the *Washington Times* in January 2022: "Small businesses and the military remain well-respected, and police squeaked back above 50 percent after slipping in 2020—the only institution that saw an increase in confidence last year." Kevin Kosar, a friend now at the American Enterprise Institute, told McLaughlin, "I think the more the public sees anything in government and the longer it sees it, the gloomier it gets."

The problem has come down to a matter of respect, Mo Elleithee wrote in the Foreword to Ed Goeas and Celinda Lake's new book *A Question of Respect*. "Americans have stopped respecting our institutions, our political opponents, and even one another. The lack of respect has fueled a toxic polarization that has made this one of the most divided eras in modern history."[16]

Recent Pew Research Center data on the public's religious composition "finds the religiously unaffiliated share of the public is six percentage points higher than it was five years ago and 10 points higher than a decade ago." At the end of 2021, Pew reported the largest religious population in the country is still Christians, who make up 63 percent of the adult population, but that is down ten points from a decade ago.

Is there any wonder that chronic problems with the Legislative and the Executive branches inhibit good governance and reduce public confidence in the institution, which has been stuck at one of its lowest approval levels since polling data was first collected?

Gallup reported that those who have a "great deal" or "fair amount" of confidence in the government's ability to solve domestic problems declined from a high of 70 percent in 1972 to a low of 19 percent in 2014, with improvement in 2020 at 41 percent. Gallup also reported in 2021 that only 12 percent had a "great deal/quite a lot" of trust and confidence in Congress.

MANY REASONS BILLS DON'T BECOME LAW

The absence of public trust is a serious impediment to public policy development. But while admittedly conjecture on our part, we believe there are many other reasons why bills don't become law and why governmental and political processes seem like they are decomposing. So here are our top eleven:

I. When people are divided, there is no clear mandate for governing, so the path to reaching a consensus on any issue is more complicated. Neither Democrats nor Republicans feel obligated to compromise when enough of their constituents aren't interested in compromise.

American people have a history of rallying around the flag when the country is challenged or when an overwhelming majority believe the common good is threatened. Unfortunately, this has not happened since the US was attacked in 2001. Gradually, the unity, patriotism, and sense of common purpose those attacks spawned faded. The justification for the war on terror became less clear and more difficult to understand as more lives were lost or permanently damaged, and more tax dollars were drained.

American voters are divided politically and ideologically, separated by allegiance to their core values, political parties, political movements, and core beliefs.

They are further pulled apart by the magnetic forces of the emotional extremes at both ends of the political spectrum.

Americans are divided culturally, as well. We have aspired to be a cultural melting pot, but our differences are not melting away or melding together. Instead, the cultural divisions make communicating more difficult and governing much more complex.

II. Too much power, especially in the House of Representatives, is concentrated in too few hands, those of the congressional leaders and powerful committee chairs. There are times when the concentration of power serves a good purpose, but too much power in the hands of a few can frustrate Members of Congress and leave them and their constituents without a voice in the process. The House has at times revolted against the mighty few, once in a historical rebellion against House Speaker Joe Cannon in 1921 and again in 1974 in a revolt of rank-and-file liberal Democrats against Southern committee chairs, shielded by their seniority. In both cases, Members were frustrated by their inability to participate in the legislative process, offer amendments, change language, or even get legislation considered on the Floor. While significant reforms have often resulted from revolts, expediency, and political imperatives usually drive the power back to the leaders. Part of the reality is that legislative leaders are also partisan leaders whose interests are served by retaining or gaining back partisan majorities, turning their leadership into a partisan juggernaut that leaves little room for bipartisanship, compromise, or civility.

III. There's no difference and no break between campaigning and governing. Related to the partisan nature of congressional leadership is the constant influence of the twenty-four-hour, seven-day-a-week, fifty-two-weeks-a-year campaigns, that consume so much of a legislator's time and make it more difficult to discuss and debate issues in an atmosphere conducive to creating public policy. The nature of campaigns has also led to massive increases in the cost of campaigns, and the influence of outside sources of contributions detracts from the local focus of campaigns.

IV. The rules and procedures that govern the flow of legislation, communication with the citizenry, and the daily lives of politicians are in some areas archaic. In other areas, they are stifling, oblivious to the new age of technology, or simply not helpful to lawmakers who want to make laws. Congress constantly needs reform and modernization, better management, and greater responsiveness to the people it serves, but that change does not come easily. Members of the Leadership are reluctant to open the process they control to changes that may diminish their control. Three times in the twentieth century, Congress created special committees of both the House and the Senate to take a hard look at itself and reform the process. It is long overdue for the first such effort in the twenty-first century. The House of Representatives took a step forward in the 115th and 116th Congresses and created special committees to conduct a comprehensive review. That committee was extended in the 117th Congress and folded into the House Administration Committee in the 118th. It was a model for bipartisan productivity, generating more than one hundred solid recommendations for improving how Congress functions.

V. Members of Congress don't work together well, and one of the reasons is they don't know each other. In previous decades, they lived in Washington, DC, and got to know one another in social settings, which made it harder to throw verbal brickbats in public debates.

VI. The federal government is gargantuan. It is a nearly $4 trillion enterprise run by a President and 535 Members of Congress who often come to their jobs without anywhere near the skills and experience they need to run the government. Moreover, as they come to work, they often face problems and national concerns that have festered for years, some growing into full-blown crises and others so badly ignored they may no longer be solvable. Roughly, federal spending has equaled about 25 percent of the gross national product in recent years, and revenues nearly 20 percent. No organization in the US begins to reflect that size and complexity or imbalance in revenues/expenditures; thus, no one can honestly claim experience in guiding such an enterprise.

VII. The combination of news and entertainment media (we call it infotainment) in an undisciplined wild, Wild West of internet gossip, quasi-information, and blatant propaganda has become a formidable influence on our governmental and political processes that is more damaging than beneficial. The media view the destruction of the established order, public or private, as a sign of accomplishment because salacious gossip and public flogging always attract readers and viewers and generate revenue. It didn't go unnoticed among the media that the bombastic, sarcastic, and divisive Donald Trump was good for business.

VIII. The professionalism of politics. Our political system has gone from one of the citizens' leading governments and volunteerism in public service and community involvement to a highly politicized system in which so-called career politicians and full-time professional staff perform many of the government's critical functions. Highly professional advisers and full-time campaign staff greatly influence candidates' selection and public servants' election. They are often professional public hangers-on who have spent their entire lives on government or campaign payrolls, to both the disadvantage and expense of good government.

IX. The economy, society, and the institutions that reinforce them are undergoing a degree of change more remarkable than during the Industrial Revolution, which dominated our way of life and dictated our future as a nation more than a century ago. Factors, such as the rapidity of technological advancement and the accelerated rate of the social and economic integration of diverse races, ethnicities, religions, genders, generations, income levels, and educations, combined with global and moral change, have annihilated respect for authority or shared beliefs and threatens our security. They all make reaching a consensus on public policy, political values, and a visionary approach to the nation's future nearly impossible. What it means to be an American is no longer a settled question, and shared values are nigh on to non-existent. Is it any wonder politicians throw insults at one another rather than address these volatile changes?

X. The link between the people and the elected (Members of Congress) has stretched beyond breaking. What began as reasonably cohesive and small constituencies of 30,000 people in each congressional district have grown into gigantic 762,000-population congressional districts where commonality of perspective, goals, and values is impossible to discern. Ours is one of the worst ratios of elected official-to-voter in the democratic world. The elected official no longer has an intuitive feel for the folks back home and relies instead on polling and artful orchestration of evolving majorities to stay in power.

XI. The distinctions between the House of Representatives and the Senate have been marginalized. Now both reflect the passions of the public as defined by nightly polling data, news media, etc. The Senate's old role of reflecting cooler thought and the perspective of citizens of the individual states is lost. The distinction between the states is not expressed, and volatile majorities attempt to dictate one-size-fits-all solutions to moral and fiscal questions.

All these influences, taken together, create an environment in which governing cannot meet public expectations or public needs. It is time to rethink how and why our representative government is not functioning better and how the public believes it should work. It is time, too, that the people contribute to this process, not by criticizing what is, but by focusing on how it should be and then on what is possible.

Let's count the ways to thwart governing.

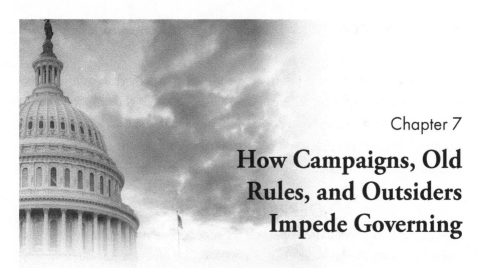

Chapter 7

How Campaigns, Old Rules, and Outsiders Impede Governing

*A national political campaign is better than
the best circus ever heard of . . .*
—Journalist H. L. Mencken

When we look at what's wrong with Congress, we can look first at the eleven items listed in the last chapter. But there are just three that we want to give special attention to.

The first is the grueling political process of getting to Congress and staying there. The second is the maze of rules, procedures, traditions, politics, leadership, precedents, laws, and constitutional mandates that make legislating difficult. And the third is the kaleidoscope of ever-evolving influences on our system of government; Americans engage the government through the media, special interests, partisan organizations, civic institutions, other governments, and so many more.

Let's begin with the first bucket, the process by which people become politicians, how they get to public office in the first place, and what they must do to stay there.

The American political campaign has been a curse and a blessing of our system of representative government since campaigners uttered the first slogan. Members of Congress must run the campaign gauntlet, sometimes repeatedly, before they can cast a single vote or introduce a simple amendment.

Campaigns have been comical, mean, mesmerizing, informative, persuasive, and boring—sometimes all at the same time. They are the guts of the political system and have profoundly impacted it at every level of government. Yet voters keep voting for people they think will get the job done and months later wonder "why nothing is getting done."

GERRYMANDERING

One of the more harmful influences on the process is gerrymandering, the practice of drawing the boundaries of congressional districts to the advantage of partisan interests rather than the interest of the people who live in those districts. It is one of the most perplexing political issues because it has defied solutions.

Experts have been devising ways to reduce gerrymandering for decades, maybe centuries, but politicians always find a way to protect their self-interests. Gerrymandering has implications that cross many partisan, demographic, economic, and racial lines. Some say it is a legitimate exercise in democracy.

Gerrymandering is one of three legislative inhibitors that evoke some of the most blatant hypocrisy from both parties. The other two are raising money for campaigns and the Senate filibuster, discussed later in this chapter.

Gerrymander was coined in 1812 as a jab at Congressman Elbridge Gerry of Massachusetts. He was instrumental in drawing a partisan district that looked just like a salamander. But the practice goes back to the very first elections for Congress, and James Madison was one of the first targets of gerrymandering. His nemesis, Patrick Henry, sought to use the practice to prevent Madison from being elected to the First Congress.

In the nation's infancy, congressional constituencies contained smaller populations much more likely to have common interests. Most people lived in rural areas and were employed in agriculture, but there were also smaller cities and towns where trading occurred. Even then, trading was tied to agriculture. As populations grew and manufacturing and service industries developed, more significant economic, social, and educational disparities appeared. Map makers could still draw most congressional districts to reflect a community of interests. It was standard practice many years ago to see one congressional district dominated by urban, merchant, and manufacturing interests, while a neighboring congressional district reflected agricultural interests.

As the country's population tripled over the past one hundred years, census data became more detailed and research about voter behavior more precise. As a result, politicians and political parties became more adept at drawing congressional district boundaries to favor one political party and point of view. The practice has become so sophisticated that cities, towns, even neighborhoods and city blocks are carved up and separated into different districts, making it easier for a representative to represent a compatible constituency without having to navigate contrary points of view among the general population.

As of the 2018 congressional elections, there were an estimated eighty-five competitive congressional districts in the country, out of 435 districts, or just 19 percent. Of course, not all the lack of competition is attributable to gerrymandered boundaries. Still, it has pronounced influence over who runs for office, who wins, and, most importantly, how they behave once sworn in and handed their congressional voting card. Other researchers see people preferring to live close to like-minded fellow citizens and thus self-segregating, not by race or religion, but by ideological or cultural lines.

The redistricting process following the 2020 census continued several well-established gerrymandering trademarks that have scarred redistricting for a long time. Before the process concluded, it was clear that gerrymandering was playing a key role in drawing congressional districts to suit partisan desires at the expense of districts that would best serve those who live within them. It was also clear that the political hypocrisy was as outrageous as ever, both parties accusing each other of gerrymandering atrocities, even though the abuses were evenly divided between them. Democrats smothered Republican prospects in New York, Illinois, and Maryland. Republicans did the same to Democrats in states such as Texas and Alabama. Highly touted commissions created to diminish the partisanship in legislatures doing the redistricting proved once again: There is no such thing as nonpartisanship in politics. Commissions failed to meet expectations in states such as California, Washington, Utah, Iowa, Michigan, and Virginia.

In Colorado and Arizona, the commission maps got high marks. But in others, the ultimate outcomes were decided by the courts. And the process of turning to the courts is now being challenged in the Supreme Court.

THE CHANGING NATURE OF POLITICAL CAMPAIGNS

After the districts are defined geographically, campaigns get into full swing in those districts that are more competitive.

Campaigns in the US have been shaped by cycle creep, the insidious movement by the parties and states to extend the campaign season by staging earlier and earlier primaries or caucuses, at which nominees are chosen.

Campaigns have also been extended by wall-to-wall media coverage that is no longer put on pause between elections. Hyperventilating over political theatrics and engaging in constant speculation about political outcomes doesn't cost much, requires less expertise, and avoids the more complicated and less attractive work of understanding and reporting complex policy questions that voters should know more about before casting ballots.

Just days after President Barack Obama won re-election in 2012, media speculation began about who would run in 2016. Even before the next off-year elections in 2014, most candidates for the Presidency in 2016 were on the trail, trying to become known or better known.

No candidate took more advantage of the media attraction to the circus than Donald Trump. His coverage far exceeded that of any other candidate for months on end. It certainly can be argued that the media won him the Republican nomination in August 2016.

> *The (Shorenstein) report shows that during the year 2015, major news outlets covered Donald Trump in a way that was unusual given his low initial polling numbers—a high volume of media coverage preceded Trump's rise in the polls. Trump's coverage was positive in tone—he received far more "good press" than "bad press." The volume and tone of the coverage helped propel Trump to the top of Republican polls.*

> *The Democratic race in 2015 received less than half the coverage of the Republican race. Bernie Sanders' campaign was largely ignored in the early months but, as it began to get coverage, it was overwhelmingly positive in tone.[17]*

Members of Congress begin campaigning for re-election the day after they are elected. Fundraising cycles never end. Campaign offices never close. As early as six months after a new Congress convenes, the campaign arms of the congressional leadership, the political consultant industry, pollsters, and the media have shifted into high campaigning gear. The time for governing is just about over before it ever starts.

There was no relief for the public from campaigns in the first months of the 116th Congress in January 2019. Partisanship began driving legislative activity from the first day, dictating what Congress took up, what it investigated, and how the majority party treated the minority party. *The Hill newspaper* reported in early April 2019: "Roughly 100 days into the new Congress the business of legislating is slowing to a crawl on Capitol Hill. Of the 10 bills that have been signed into law so far this year only two were substantial enough to require roll call votes. . . ."[18]

Congressional leaders had already abandoned the passage of a federal budget by March and were moving on to appropriations. Senator John Thune said, "Things that are sort of incremental" are likely the "only things that are actually going to get done this year." Senator Roy Blunt of Missouri: "We need to now move forward just the fundamental things that need to be done to fund the government. If we did that, and two or three other things . . . that would be really good legislative year."[19]

FUNDRAISING OR GOVERNING

The full-time campaign cycle contributes, too, to the rising cost of campaigns and what it takes to raise larger and larger amounts of money—another negative influence on the development of public policy, according to some critics.

According to the Campaign Finance Institute, in 1986, when adjusted to reflect the buying power of 2010 dollars, the average winning House Member spent over $700,000, and a senator spent over $6,000,000. In 2010, winning representatives spent an average of $1,400,000, and their colleagues in the Senate spent almost $9,000,000. The spending in 2016, according to Open Secrets, was staggering, with a total of $6.5 billion spent on campaigns, of which $4 billion went into congressional races. By 2018, the organization said total spending for all congressional races was $5.7 billion.[20,21]

Clearly, something needs to be done. But some campaign experts don't see the costs as exorbitant. To create some context, total US advertising in 2021 amounted to about $304 billion, according to Statista.[22] Compared to a Big Mac or a house, $6.5 billion spent on campaigns sounds large. However, compared to advertising for consumer goods, very little is spent on political advertising. Media gladly accepts that $304 billion but loves to criticize spending on the more important priority, the selection of those who will protect our freedoms and govern the spending of more than one-third of all income in the nation. The real issue should not be how much is spent but how it is raised. The costs of a campaign and the inability to raise it inhibit many good people from running for public office.

The incredible amounts of money needed also greatly increase the role of outside interests, diminishing the influence of local citizenry and local campaign contributors in some cases. One incumbent candidate in Virginia in 2022 raised 61 percent of her campaign contributions from outside Virginia. Another raised 55 percent.[23] Money buys the strong edge media advertising delivers; that can be the deciding factor in some races. Saturation negativity works tragically, and it costs a lot of money.

It is said there are no voids in politics. They are filled as fast as they are created. That is true with attempts to reform campaign finance. When Congress restricts contributions, often making the public believe funding is being reformed, it usually proves to be a mirage. Those bent on getting around the reforms will find a way to create new funding mechanisms or streams of money that skirt the new rules. Contributors and fundraisers funnel money and services through more creative channels. As is the case with gerrymandering, hypocrisy abounds in partisan fundraising. There is no better example than the phenomenal growth of "dark money."

Dark money is contributions to a web of interest groups mostly set up through the tax code as nonprofit organizations. There are big distinctions between these organizations and other campaign funding organizations. The dark money contributions are unlimited in size and can come from almost any source, from labor unions to corporations. Moreover, hence the moniker, contributors do not have to be disclosed to the Federal Election Commission. That enables mega-donors to pour millions of dollars into political activities without detection. While the money doesn't go directly to the candidates, it is spent by the donor advocating for or against positions taken by candidates or for turn-out-the-vote efforts focused on certain demographic groups known to support or oppose certain candidates. As a result, dark money has a profound and sometimes decisive influence over the outcomes, especially concerning total advertising dollars spent on campaigns.

The Supreme Court's 2010 *Citizens United* decision, which, in simple terms, said corporations were individuals with respect to campaign contributions, unleashed the flood of dark money.

Kenneth Vogel and Shane Goldmacher wrote in The *New York Times* on January 29, 2022, after an in-depth study of dark money politics:

> *"Dark money" became a dirty word, as the left warned of the threat of corruption posed by corporations and billionaires that were spending unlimited sums through loosely regulated nonprofits which did not disclose their donors' identities.*

They went on to say,

> *Then came the 2020 election. Spurred by opposition to then President Donald Trump, donors and operatives allied with the Democratic Party embraced dark money with fresh zeal, pull-*

ing even with and, by some measures, surpassing Republicans in 2020 spending.

These new mega-money machines create additional secrecy and deception by setting up elaborate webs of nonprofits among which money is contributed, so tracing becomes even more difficult, all in the name of charitable giving.

> *"The findings (of the* New York Times *analysis)" Vogel and Goldmacher said, "reveal the growth and ascendancy of a shadow political infrastructure that is reshaping American politics, as mega-donors to these nonprofits take advantage of loose disclosure laws to make multimillion-dollar outlays in total secrecy. Some good-government activists worry that the exploding role of undisclosed cash threatens to accelerate the erosion of trust in the country's political system."[24]*

The secrecy is only one detriment.

Another is that money from outside the state or the district where the candidates are running frequently dwarfs that locally raised, diminishing the influence and impact of local citizens in electing their representative.

In Jerry's adopted state, North Carolina, his analysis of the 2022 US Senate race, for example, concluded that outside interests spent over $100 million supporting or opposing North Carolina candidates. The FEC reported that the party nominees raised around $40 million dollars, and voters within North Carolina did not contribute all of that. The bottom line is that outside interests are dominating highly contested congressional races.

One example, CNN reported that the Washington, DC-based Club for Growth independently spent over $12 million attacking former Governor McCrory and promoting Congressman Budd in the Republican primary.[25]

The bottom line: outside organizations that do not disclose the names of donors spent more than the two top contenders raised and spent from individuals . . . or even all reportable sources.

The other major campaign funding sources include the national political parties themselves, official party campaign organs that focus exclusively on House and Senate races, Political Action Committees (PACs), leadership PACs, and Super PACs.

So who is influencing elections, local donors and voters, or out-of-state big money using facilitating organizations? When districts had smaller populations and, therefore, common interests, it was not necessary to pay for research telling a candidate how people viewed taxation, trade, energy policy, immigration, or health care; candidates relied more on a natural and intuitive feel for what voters believed, and they were able to gather their information by talking to people in local churches and restaurants, walking the neighborhoods, and visiting factories and feed mills.

Some of what campaigns are supposed to deliver to voters gets lost in the delivery. Both the voters and the candidates lose out. Campaigns are supposed to serve as the vehicle by which voters get a general feel for or view of a candidate's character, basic philosophies, managerial strengths, experience and expertise, and general political skills. Some of those characteristics do come through, but often, what the voters get is a camera-ready Madison Avenue portrait of the candidate, reinforced by a nasty assassination of the character of the opposition. That dominating advertising may not speak to the substantive concerns of voters but instead appeal to emotional reactions.

Advertising is paid media, and news stories are called *earned media*. The earned (not paid) "news" coverage is sometimes not much more enlightening than negative or positive advertising. For example, it is much easier for the media to report on mud wrestling contests than forums about transportation infrastructure. Likewise, it is more profitable to point cameras on scandals and candidate behavior twenty years ago than the complex mathematics of Social Security solvency or the consequences of the national debt.

No candidate is immune from a negative campaign. George Washington, Thomas Jefferson, Andrew Jackson, Henry Clay, Abraham Lincoln, Grover Cleveland, and Missouri Senator Thomas Hart Benton (one subject of John F. Kennedy's book, *Profiles in Courage*) were among countless victims of ruthless campaign tactics. The allegations that Russia somehow manipulated the US election were tame compared to previous allegations about the influence of various Popes and those horrible foreign powers, England and France. Nevertheless, they allegedly had a harmful influence on American campaigns.

Campaigns can inhibit good governance by forcing candidates into a straitjacket of pledges, petitions, and promises. But, once a representative gets to Washington, they discover an environment far from conducive to keeping sweeping campaign promises, making policy by enacting new laws or amending or repealing old ones.

> Campaigns can inhibit good governance by forcing candidates into a straitjacket of pledges, petitions, and promises.

In some respects, governing has become no more than an extension of campaigning. There is so much time spent creating a perception that problems are being identified and solutions advocated that it disguises the reality that they are not.

The 116th Congress (2019) outset offered some good examples of how campaign mentality may impede governing. One was House passage on March 3, 2019, of HR 1, a catch-all piece of legislation called the For the People Act, to improve ethics, restore integrity to campaign financing, prevent the purging of election rolls, strengthen voting rights, make it easier to register and vote, expand early voting, several other so-called "anti-corruption reforms," and make a partridge in a pear tree the national bird. (OK, everything but that last bird bit.)

Introduced by Maryland Congressman John Sarbanes and reintroduced in subsequent congresses, the legislation was largely the work of the Democratic House Leadership in fulfillment of campaign promises to "clean the swamp" in Washington. The legislation carried the highly marketable anti-corruption mantra, a theme that registered very favorably with media and voters.

But the legislation contained some fatal flaws (called *poison pills*), known to its authors. As a result, the left-wing American Civil Liberties Union praised its good points but declined to endorse it.

The ACLU wrote:

> . . . *even with all the good HR 1 (2019) would do, if enacted in its current form, it would unconstitutionally infringe on the speech and associational rights of many public interest organizations and American citizens. It is incumbent upon the drafters of HR 1 to correct these issues.*[26]

Senate Majority Leader Mitch McConnell said the bill would weaponize the Federal Election Commission, then an evenly bipartisan campaign finance watchdog. The new bill would give it a partisan majority, wiping out even the pretense of bipartisanship. The bill also provided for injecting millions of the public's tax dollars into campaigns.

So the intent of HR 1 was not passage but campaign-like messaging, leaving the perception of delivering on a major campaign promise and putting Republicans in the uncomfortable position of voting against allegations of corruption. McConnell, meanwhile, was preparing a similar Republican PR stunt in the Senate.

The Democrats Green New Deal resolution was not a piece of legislation in the normal sense. Instead, it was a non-binding wish list of goals and ideals, each one of which should require separate bills to implement. In other words, it was political gamesmanship that the media continued talking about for months, right into the 2020 campaigns, where it became a centerpiece of the so-called "democratic socialism" agenda of candidates for President and Congress.

The goals promised zero net greenhouse gas emissions but through a fair transition for communities and workers, millions of new high-wage jobs ensuring prosperity and economic security for all people, jobs for everyone—even if they are unwilling to work—clean air, clean water, climate and community resiliency, healthy food, access to nature, and a sustainable environment. It also called for justice and equity by stopping the oppression of Indigenous Peoples, communities of color, migrant communities, pre-industrialized communities, depopulated rural communities, the poor,

low-income workers, women, the elderly, the "unhoused" people with dis-
abilities, and youth. See how our politics has matured? Decades ago, that
kind of vacuous hyperbole and political glitter would have been called "pie
in the sky" posturing and dismissed. Yet, surprisingly, even liberal Michael
Bloomberg used those exact words in early 2019 as the ruse was presented.
Or said another way: even legislating has become campaigning.

It was brought to the Senate Floor for a vote in March 2019 by Majority
Leader McConnell for no other purpose than to embarrass its supporters,
to the consternation of its sponsors and cosponsors, including six senators
running for President. The vote was an odd 0–57, with all the Democrats
voting present and Republicans voting no.

The lingering campaign atmospherics give rise to other factors that
make governing life difficult. One is the dramatic transformation of news
media over the last several decades. The industry has reinvented itself, and
the impact on public governance has not been good. We will explore the
media more thoroughly in the next couple of chapters. In the meantime,
other factors impede governing.

BUT I DON'T KNOW YOU

Another factor inhibiting lawmaking is the erosion of or lack of personal
relationships among policymakers and a broader erosion of social and
political civility across the country.

Members of Congress, when not around reporters or TV cameras, still
maintain some social comity in Washington. Still, the closer personal relationships, the professional interactions, and many natural political incen-
tives to get along and work together are difficult to find.

The once protected and nurtured atmosphere of civil discourse that
enabled Members of Congress to disagree but not be disagreeable has been
blown away by the partisan, political, and now personal invective that infects
and afflicts the governmental process and, regrettably, much of society.

Some of the erosion can be blamed on the pandemic that shuttered
many Americans in their homes, including House Members of Congress

where absences were excused, and they allowed proxy voting (*proxy*, a vote cast by another Member), an unprecedented move. The House voted on December 23, 2022, to stop using proxy voting in the House. (Ironically, by casting proxy votes.) But as has been the case for decades, committees can allow proxy voting under certain circumstances.

Some erosion can be blamed on less apparent changes in how Washington and Congress function. For example, personal relationships do not flower among Members because more Members leave their families behind to live in the home district while they are in Washington. As a result, one of the strongest magnets for bonding, friendships, and fellowship at a personal level—the family—is no longer present.

When Congress radically increased the number of airplane trips home a Member may make as an official expense, it facilitated leaving the family back in the home district where children could remain in their familiar schools. Spouses could continue their work and social lives. In the mid-1960s, Members were reimbursed for only two trips home per two-year Congress. Today there is no limit, but the expense is attributable to the overall Member's office allowance.

The cost of living in Washington, DC, also encourages families to remain in their home districts. A member, only in town for a few nights each week, can spend those few hours in a small, relatively inexpensive apartment close to the Capitol or even in his office. Contrast that to buying or renting a house big enough to accommodate an entire family whose moving, educational, and living expenses are not reimbursed by the government.

The bottom line is that it is logical and politically important for Members to commute to their home districts and for workweeks in DC to be short, resulting in an isolated environment that inhibits Members from getting to know one another very well. Another opportunity for Members to get to know one another is official government travel, particularly to foreign countries. The media began labeling such trips as *junkets* many decades ago, highlighting abuses of official travel. Subsequent restrictions on foreign travel threw out the baby with the bathwater. Travel often fostered lasting friendships that made the workplace more civil. The travel also made their world bigger and helped instill a sense of commonality that brought them closer together. While it is said that a long trip will either make you fast friends or permanent enemies, modern Members have limited opportunities to find out. The irony is that no nation on the globe is more integrated and interdependent with the world, yet our legislators are as poorly exposed to that world as legislators anywhere.

The media justifiably focused intense light on the abuses. Those few Members with the power to authorize trips would sometimes organize a doozy, travel to the Caribbean or the South of France, punctuated with golf games on championship courses or extended shopping trips for Persian rugs. Some quasi-governmental or private trips were further compromised by lobbyists—evil creatures living in the Washington swamp. The media's focus on these exceptional situations, as opposed to any of the value of the trips, resulted in a political liability that caused most Members to avoid trips like the plague.

Another valuable asset of a bygone era was bipartisan congressional retreats and conferences at out-of-the-way venues. The retreats were an opportunity for practical discussions of issues before the House, some of it more political, some more policy-driven. Participants focused on the subject with less interruption, especially from the media. More importantly, they provided Members of Congress and often their families a unique environment to get to know one another personally, expand their political horizons and give new perspectives to the two sides of important issues. In addition, they often engaged in long-range planning and strategic thinking that seldom gets much attention in Washington. The retreats eventually collapsed under the weight of nasty partisanship and a growing distrust between the two sides that only exacerbated the personal invective.

RULES OF THE ROAD CREATE ROADBLOCKS

While Congress, like most other institutions, has rules—and a lot of them: temporary, permanent, arcane, and outdated—all these rules occasionally impede legislating. It is an institution governed by the Constitution, public laws, historical precedents, tradition, and the whims of leadership. All these influences, melded with the unique political culture of the institution, affect behavior and the outcome of deliberations, making passing laws more difficult.

We will explore other influences in upcoming chapters, particularly the media, interest groups, and public judgments. Still, before we get there, we need to take a new look at old rules, especially those being abused or over-used and grinding down the legislative process to a nub of its former self. One of the pearls of wisdom we once found in a fortune cookie was this: "Constant grinding can turn an iron rod into a needle."

Some rules and procedures in the House and Senate date back to the Founding Fathers as a means of discouraging or limiting government, not propagating it. Whatever their intent, however, the cumbersome process hasn't kept the government small and unobtrusive. When the government is seen as the solution, and it comes time to act to get something done, the rules don't make that any easier.

THE FILIBUSTER

One of those rules, and maybe the one most talked about, is the Senate filibuster.

The filibuster, made famous by Jimmy Stewart in the 1939 Frank Capra movie *Mr. Smith Goes to Washington*, permitted a US senator or group of senators to debate on the Senate Floor for an unlimited amount of time to prevent a vote on a piece of legislation. The Capra film was based on a real filibuster in 1934 by Louisiana Senator Huey Long against one of President Franklin Roosevelt's New Deal programs, the National Recovery Act.

The filibuster is a practice or precedent designed to protect the rights of the political minority in the Senate by allowing unlimited debate on most measures—talking a bill to death—unless its proponents can garner sixty votes, a practice known as *cloture*, to shut off debate. Some contend the threat of filibusters also encourages bipartisanship, which is good.

The debate over the filibuster has consistently generated more heat than light. It can spark strong and strident partisan differences, and as was the case in the aftermath of the 2020 elections, it took on racial overtones like many other issues raised in the tense and divisive times. Those who played the race card in the attempts to kill the filibuster to clear the path for the Biden agenda contended the filibuster was created as a parliamentary procedure for blocking anti-slavery and civil rights legislation and is a "relic of the Jim Crow era."

A little history sometimes clears the air of hyperbolic pollutants. For example, the filibuster tactic can be traced back to the Roman Republic and a debate in the Senate over tax collectors pitting Marcus Cato against rival Julius Caesar in 48 BC. It's an interesting tale but not relevant here other than to document its longevity and original purpose.

The history of the tactic in our modern Republic, from accounts of the Senate historian and National Geographic, does not suggest that it was intended as a tool of segregation or racism but was employed to influence many diverse issues in the nineteenth, twentieth, and twenty-first centuries.

The filibuster—not labeled that until 1841—was used in the 1st Congress in 1789 during the debate about selecting Philadelphia as the new capital. In 1811, a filibuster was used in the House to thwart the passage of a trade embargo against Great Britain. In 1837, a Senate filibuster was employed to prevent the "expungement" of censure of President Andrew Jackson over the elimination of the national bank. Jackson won.

In 1917, after Senator Robert LaFollette of Wisconsin filibustered a bill to arm merchant ships during World War I, with pressure from President Woodrow Wilson, the Senate adopted Rule 22, which provided for cloture to shut off debate with a two-thirds (sixty-six of one hundred) vote of the Senate. That number was reduced to three-fifths (sixty of one hundred) in 1975.

Dave Hoppe, the long-serving staff to Senate and House Republican leaders, including Senate Majority Leader Trent Lott, wrote in the *Wall Street Journal* on April 11, 2021: "For the first 47 years after Rule 22's enactment in 1917, there were only five successful attempts to cut off debate in the US Senate. A few senators felt so strongly about their right to extended debate that they vowed never to vote for cloture, even for legislation they supported."[27]

In 1957 and 1964, Southern segregationists used the filibuster to fight civil rights legislation, but they were unsuccessful both times, thanks in part to bipartisan consensus. In 1964, President Lyndon Johnson made civil rights a top legislative priority.

Johnson "worked with Senate Majority Leader Mike Mansfield (D) and Minority Leader Everett Dirksen (R) to maneuver the bill through the challenges of senators who planned to filibuster," Hoppe wrote. Instead of Mansfield attempting to ram the legislation through the Senate, he committed to its chief opponent, Senator Richard Russell of Louisiana, that there would be "an honest facing of the situation and a resolution of it by the Senate itself." The debate commenced in February 1964, and in the following months, the filibuster continued with long debates and numerous amendments considered.

Hoppe observed:

> *A total of 543 hours, 1 minute and 51 seconds were consumed by the longest filibuster in Senate history. Most importantly, the Senate and the country saw an open process that allowed the minority every opportunity to debate and offer amendments. They saw the leaders of both parties in the Senate work to gather the 67 votes then needed to cut off debate and pass a bill that extended civil rights to black Americans across the US.[28]*

The filibuster has been abused, as have most legislative procedures over the past two decades. Now, a senator is no longer required to stay on the Floor and speak against a measure. But abuses can be fixed. The procedure is one crucial distinction between the Senate and the House, which is and should be more reactionary and spontaneous. As George Washington described it to Thomas Jefferson, the Senate should be more deliberate. It is, he said, like a saucer intended to cool the tea before consuming it.

Hoppe concluded:

A bipartisan consensus seems like a distant dream in this divided country," "but the filibuster is central to achieving it. Ramming legislation down the throats of the minority by a narrow margin or a single vote breeds animosity, distrust, and unrest ... By giving the minority time to be fully heard and negotiated with, passage of legislation with bipartisan support creates a path for a more stable, peaceful democracy[29,30]

The filibuster debates generate a high velocity of hypocrisy and hyperbole. If you want to get both sides of the story, you could listen to President Joe Biden and Senator Joe Biden. The President joined fellow Democrats in opposing the filibuster in 2020 when it threatened his legislative ambitions. Yet, for many years, Senator Biden supported and defended the filibuster when serving in the minority in the Senate. President Biden's recent approach to the filibuster has been influenced by the fact that senators can now merely threaten a filibuster rather than engaging in one for days or weeks to kill legislation.

You can also get both sides of the story from Senate Majority Leader Chuck Schumer of New York, who, in 2017, when President Trump wanted to kill the filibuster, said, "The legislative filibuster is the most important distinction between the Senate and the House. Without the sixty-vote threshold for legislation, the Senate becomes a majoritarian institution, just like the House."[31]

In 2021, Schumer joined Biden in a campaign to kill the filibuster to pass what they called "voting rights legislation." The Leader did pause in his vehement opposition to the filibuster, however, to use it to block a majority of senators from passing sanctions on the Russian gas pipeline to Western Europe. When asked at a press conference about filibuster reform on May 28, 2020, Schumer said, "Everything is on the table."[32]

So, the future of the filibuster continues to float untethered in the high winds of political parochialism. Alterations in the ability to use the procedure may be made as the debate drones on, but because it is one of the few distinctions left between the House and the Senate and more expansively between it and most other democratic legislative bodies throughout the world, its life in the world's greatest deliberative body does not seem threatened.

The longest *individual* filibuster records were set by Oregon Senator Wayne Morris, who talked against an oil bill for twenty-two hours, and in 1957, by South Carolina Senator Strom Thurmond, who spoke for twenty-four hours against a Civil Rights bill.

Another long filibuster occurred in 1964 against the landmark Civil Rights Act. It began on March 30 and ended on June 10, when after a fourteen-hour speech against the bill by Senator Robert Byrd of West Virginia, the Senate voted on cloture, which at the time required sixty-seven votes.

One of the most dramatic incidents in Senate history occurred on that roll call, according to a 2010 article for Historynet.com, by Peter Carlson:

> *A Senate clerk called the roll. "Mr. Aiken."*
>
> *"Aye."*
>
> *"Mr. Ellender."*
>
> *"No."*
>
> *"Mr. Engle."*
>
> *Two navy corpsmen wheeled Sen. Clair Engle of California down the center aisle. Engle was dying of brain cancer, and his voice was too weak to be heard. Slowly, painfully, he lifted his hand and pointed to his eye.*
>
> *"Mr. Engle votes aye," said the clerk.*
>
> *The "ayes" won. For the first time in history, the Senate voted to break a filibuster on a civil rights bill. Nine days later, the Senate passed the landmark law that essentially ended legalized segregation.*[33]

Carlson also recalled another classic filibuster twenty-three years later:

> *In 1987 Republicans defeated seven cloture votes to kill a Democratic campaign finance reform bill. When Democrats brought up the*

bill again in 1988, Republicans launched another filibuster. "We are ready to go all night," said Republican Whip Alan Simpson of Wyoming. "We will have our sturdy SWAT teams and people on vitamin pills and colostomy bags and Lord knows what else."

During the long night, Republican senators boycotted a roll call vote, and, in their absence, Democrats voted to command the Senate sergeant-at-arms to "arrest the absent senators and bring them to the Chamber." Sergeant-at-Arms Henry Giugni found Republican Robert Packwood of Oregon in his office and arrested him. Packwood insisted that he be carried into the Senate chamber—and at 1:17 a.m., he was. Despite the theatrics, the Republicans still killed the bill. "The events of the last 48 hours," noted Republican Warren Rudman of New Hampshire, "were a curious blend of Dallas, Dynasty, The Last Buccaneer *and* Friday Night Fights."[34]

Decades later, at the beginning of the 113th Congress in 2013, Senate Majority Leader Harry Reid of Nevada pushed for filibuster reform. He contended that the procedure had been badly abused.

Cloture votes have increased from fifty-six in the 108th Congress to 115 in the 112th Congress, ballooning to 168 in the 115th Congress (2017–18).

Those who argue against maintaining the filibuster contend, accurately so, that it is not used the way it was intended. Senators no longer talk for hours; they merely threaten to do so, and the Senate moves to other business.

Those who favor the filibuster insist it is one of the few leverage points available to the political minority or an individual senator. Minority rights were badly eroded in the 112th Congress when Majority Leader Reid circumvented the minority by bringing legislation directly to the Floor of the Senate, bypassing the committees where minority Members had some influence. He bypassed the committees sixty-nine times, according to columnist George Will.

The majority party also circumvents the minority through the amendments. The Senate has traditionally given its Members participation in the legislative process through amendments. Reid, however, prevented amendments from being offered by offering them himself. The Leader has the right to offer such amendments before other senators and, by doing so, "fills the amendment tree"—a procedural construct that defines what can be amended, how many, and in what order.

The most recent illustration of the abuses created by improper reading of the Filibuster Rule was the 2021–2022 Senate Democratic Majority's decision to use a budget procedure called "reconciliation" to circumvent the use of the filibuster to stop consideration of the multi-trillion-dollar proposal from President Biden. Reconciliation was designed to force various committees and both Houses to agree on taxing and spending levels. Instead, in the 117th (2021–2022) Congress, it was used as a Christmas Tree (a bill with lots of branches) to add spending and taxes that would not have been tolerated had a filibuster been allowed. In other words, some rules are being used to modify other rules by brute force. The Founders' heads must be spinning.

The House has not had a filibuster since 1842 but operates differently with a similar result: the exclusion of Members of the minority party from the legislative process. The House Speaker controls the Floor through their control of the Rules Committee, the "traffic cop." It decides what legislation will be brought to the Floor and under what circumstances. The need for a Rules Committee is clear. With 435 Members, some control must be exercised. The Rules Committee can accommodate the rights of the minority to participate in the Floor debates but too often restricts both the time for debate and the substance of the amendments allowed to the point of autocracy.

The growing control of the leadership on both sides of the aisle has affected access to the legislative process by the rank-and-file Members. Reasonably restricting debate and amendments on the Floor of the House is necessary for a large legislative body, but an unintended outcome is that it is also an obvious way that Members have been prevented from legislating,

For the public to engage in policy debates and express views to Congress, it must know what is going on within the houses of Congress. Unfortunately, the media's oversimplification of congressional action has created an environment in which complex issues are not fully understood and are often distorted.

As recently as the 1960s, battles over President Lyndon Johnson's fight to create the Great Society serve as an illustration. Whether or not you agree with his philosophy, you cannot deny that Johnson exercised extraordinary leadership by proposing food stamps, the regional economic development commissions, the Office of Economic Opportunity, the Legal Services program, Headstart, and numerous other educational programs. Moreover, his party had overwhelming majorities in both the House and Senate. Yet most of his proposals were subject to major battles within committees and even on the Floor of each House, where debates lasted for weeks on many items.

It was not unusual for the minority Republicans to defeat or change certain sections of various proposals and even force the legislation back to the committee for more consideration.

Why?

Because the oppressive party discipline and media influence that often dominates legislative action today did not fifty years ago. Members of one party routinely broke ranks to vote with the other party to make changes. That began to change a decade later when the new, more liberal, change-oriented young Democrats in the House started to dethrone powerful conservative Southern Democrat committee chairmen, whose stature depended upon a seniority system that did not serve the interests of newer Members.

The elevation of liberal Massachusetts Congressman Thomas O'Neill to the Speakership, followed by the autocratic Jim Wright of Texas and eventually the return of Republican control of Congress and the elevation of Georgia's controversial Newt Gingrich to the Speaker's chair, all contributed to the accumulation of power in the leadership. (Note: Democrats had maintained total control of the House for forty years, and incoming Republicans knew no other way to manage the House.) Every Speaker since then, except for Ohio's John Boehner, has maintained iron-handed control over the process. Boehner's attempt to disperse more power among the Members failed.

The disbursement of power in the legislative process is a delicate balance. Leadership often feels compelled to streamline and limit the flow of legislation to the Floor and restrict the time spent on it. But giving Members as much access as possible is critical to the purpose and principles of a Republic.

The rules of the House and Senate should be subject to constant scrutiny and review. Procedures, processes, and organizational operations put in place one hundred years ago—or fifty or even ten years ago—can easily be so outdated that they no longer serve the interests of the majority or minority. Unfortunately, the House and Senate spend too little time reviewing and reforming themselves.

With the leadership of House Speaker Paul Ryan, the 115th Congress created two special committees on the budget and appropriations processes and modernization of Congress, but with very little time left in that Congress to reach any conclusions.

House Speaker Nancy Pelosi, in the 116th (2019–2020) Congress, created an equally bipartisan select committee on the modernization of Congress, but, of course, its jurisdiction was restricted to the House. There was no Senate involvement. That select committee did, however, produce many bipartisan reforms for consideration by the full House, most of which were ultimately adopted. The select committee was again reconstituted in the 117th Congress but folded into a full committee in the 118th. The bipartisan, bicameral joint committee first introduced in 2015 was discussed for several years but did not move forward because of the growing hostility between the two bodies and the two parties.

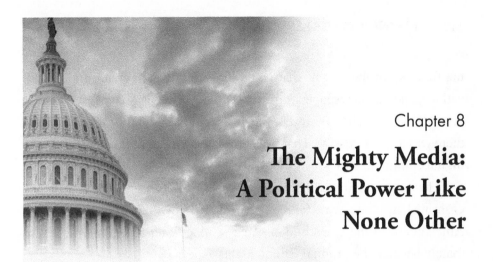

Chapter 8

The Mighty Media: A Political Power Like None Other

Then is no more powerful player in politics than the media. Not money. Not lobbyists. Not even political parties.

The media is a collection of platforms: newspapers, magazines, network news, radio news, cable news networks, digital "online," and "social" media. Combined, they are a formidable communications industrial complex of unparalleled influence over our political lives.

To understand how your government works, you must understand the media and their influence. You should also know a little about how the media have evolved over the last two centuries relative to our experiment in self-government. Their history is essential because it repeats itself. What they are doing now, they've done before—but in an older print context. They are now in uncharted waters, with new digital technology, visible partisan polarization, growling-in-your-face incivility, and aggressive movement away from objective journalism. In some respects, they are harkening back to print media alignment with political parties and ideologies at the very moment when an objectively informed citizenry may be more critical than ever. So let's set the scene by looking back before going forward.

THE PRINTED WORD

The print media were the first on the block, historically speaking. The Founding Fathers felt strongly about certain basic freedoms, among them the freedom of the press—that is, the freedom of individuals and organizations, such as newspapers, to express their opinions, advocate one way or another, and generally report the news and the gossip of the times (and there was a lot of gossip). That freedom now includes radio, television, and digital communications.

The founders thought this *right* so critical to our liberty that they enshrined it, along with four others, in their own amendment, the First Amendment to the Constitution. Among nine other amendments, it ultimately became the original Bill of Rights.

It reads:

> *Congress shall make no law respecting an establishment of religion, or prohibiting the free exercise thereof; or abridging the freedom of speech, or of the press; or the right of the people peaceably to assemble, and to petition the Government for a redress of grievances.*

The new Republic's first political newspapers were intensely partisan, with strong ties to political movements, the precursors to what would soon become the first political parties of the times. In 1789, Thomas Jefferson and James Madison were behind the creation of the *Gazette of the United States and* its publisher, John Fenno. The purpose was to advance the cause of what was then called the Democratic-Republicans. Alexander Hamilton launched a dueling (a characterization that may be of questionable taste, given Hamilton's fate at the hand of Aaron Burr in 1804) publication, the *National Gazette.* He worked with publisher Philip Freneau in 1791 to advance the Federalist cause and support the Administration of George Washington. Hamilton was also involved in creating the *New York Evening Post* ten years later.

These publications became the instruments and the chroniclers of the budding new political parties in America. They used anonymous sources and contributors who wrote under pseudonyms. The publications were rich with gossip. Hamilton was a prime target, with his rumored alliances and reported upbringing as what was known then as a "bastard child." It was not uncommon, as well, for newspapers to have lucrative government contracts.

However, American newspapers' birthright and genetic make-up can be traced back to the appointment by Britain's King George II of William Cosby as the twenty-fourth Colonial Governor of New York and New Jersey. (Our storytelling draws from the excellent book about the origins of the American free press, *Indelible Ink,* by Richard Kluger.)[35]

Cosby arrived in America in 1732 and, years later, probably wished he had never made the trip. Nevertheless, it did not take long for Governor Cosby, described in *Indelible Ink* as "vile and of the foulest reputation," to alienate some of the most influential and politically astute members of New York society, including a young attorney named James Hamilton and a powerful politician named Lewis Morris.

Alexander and Morris soon began a campaign to get Cosby recalled to London. They created an anti-administration newspaper called the *New York Weekly Journal* with a capable young printer named John Peter Zenger.

There were about seven other papers in the colonies at the time, but the Zenger paper stood out because of its relentless campaign against Cosby. The Governor brought the full weight of his administration down on the *Journal.* The government hauled Zenger before three grand juries and imprisoned him in November 1734 for over a year. While he awaited trial, it remained an open question whether Zenger didn't post bond and remained in jail for the publicity and public sympathy it engendered. Zenger was charged with seditious and malicious libel of Cosby and the government, thereby undermining the government's ability to govern.

The trials produced a historical debate over whether a government could be libeled even when the accusations were true and whether freedom of speech and the press would become pillars of the colony's political life. They also reinforced the sanctity of the jury system, which colonial magistrates would circumvent with what they called "special verdicts" that gave them final authority to determine guilt or innocence. Zenger was found not guilty on August 4, 1735. His revered attorney, Andrew Hamilton of Philadelphia, whose words after the trial extolling the freedom to protest by voice or pen the misconduct of government, are among the most exhilarating in the annals of American politics and jurisprudence.

Hamilton said,

> *The question before the court and you gentlemen of the jury is not of small or private concern. It is not the cause of a poor printer nor of New York alone, which you are now trying. No! It may in its consequence affect every freeman that lives under a British government on the main of America. It is the best cause. It is the cause of liberty, and I make no doubt but your upright conduct this day will not only entitle you to the love and esteem of your fellow citizens, but every man who prefers freedom to a life of slavery will bless and honor you as men who have baffled the attempt of tyranny and who, by an impartial and uncorrupt verdict, have laid a noble foundation securing to ourselves and our posterity. And our neighbors that to which nature and the laws of our country have given us a right—and liberty—of exposing and opposing arbitrary power (in these parts of the world at least) by speaking and writing truth.*[36]

And the rest, as they say, is history and a history worth remembering.

Papers gradually dropped their overt party affiliations but retained their posture as partisan and ideological publications. As a result, larger cities often had both a Republican-leaning paper and a Democratic-leaning paper.

The face of American journalism changed in other ways. Toward the end of the nineteenth century and the beginning of the twentieth, the era of journalistic muckraking dawned, in no small part due to the Presidency of Theodore Roosevelt, the progressive Republican who went after the corporate trusts. Roosevelt transformed the relationship between politicians and journalists.

Historian Doris Kearns Goodwin colorfully and comprehensively describes the period of the muckrakers and these three in her book, *The Bully Pulpit: Theodore Roosevelt, William Howard Taft, and the Golden Age of Journalism:*

> *Roosevelt's flagging hopes of confronting the trusts, purging corrupt political machines, and checking abuses by both capital and labor were rekindled by the January 1902 publication of McClure's magazine. In this celebrated issue the "groundbreaking trio" of Tarbell, Steffens, and Baker produced three exhaustive, hard-hitting investigative pieces that ushered in the distinctive new period of journalism that would later be christened "the muckraking era." First off, Ida Tarbell revealed the predatory, illegal practices of Standard Oil; Lincoln Steffens exposed the corrupt dealings of Minneapolis Mayor Albert "Doc" Ames; and finally, Ray Baker described the complicity of union members manipulating and deceiving their own fellow workers.*[37]

Baker became a close confidant of Roosevelt, who, as New York City police superintendent, Governor of New York, Vice President, and President, dissolved the presumptive lines of separation between the press and the politician. He used the media and allowed it to use him to pursue their mutual interests, which were considerable.

"It is hardly an exaggeration to say that the Progressive mind was characteristically a journalistic mind, and that its characteristic contribution was that of the socially responsible reporter-reformer," historian Richard Hofstadter observed. "Before there could be action, there must be information and exhortation. Grievances had to be given specific objects, and these the muckraker supplied. It was muckraking that brought the diffuse malaise of the public into focus," Goodwin quoted Hofstadter in *The Bully Pulpit*.[38]

As we will discuss later, the muckraking phenomenon remains with us today.

It's essential to remember that over the past 250 years, newspapers at various periods have strived to achieve objectivity in reporting, exercised political independence and ideological neutrality, and constructed firewalls between editorial commentary and straight news. But in other periods, including this one, newspapers have had economic, political, or ideological alliances that influenced news judgments.

It is also important to note the significant economic and technological advancements that have changed the face of the news business and journalism. The economic and social climate and digital communications have caused daily newspaper numbers to decline steadily and for newsrooms to contract. There were about 1,220 daily newspapers in the United States in 2020 (PEW), down from 1,480 in 2000 (according to Statista's website), 1,331 in 2015, and far lower than the 1,748 in 1970 they'd reported.[39]

"While the pandemic didn't quite cause the reckoning that some in the industry feared, 360 newspapers have shut down since the end of 2019, all but twenty-four of them weeklies serving small communities," David Bauder reported in the Associated Press in July 2022.[40] Another growing phenomenon is the absorption of newspapers by chains.

"Less than a third of the country's 147 weekly newspapers and just a dozen of the 150 large metro and regional daily papers are now locally-owned and operated" based on a Medill School of Journalism study, according to Bauder.[41] In addition, the number of newspaper journalists decreased from 75,000 in 2006 to 31,000 in 2022. Again, according to PEW, seven publicly traded corporations own 25 percent of all daily newspapers.[42]

Many of the survivors have been in trouble financially.

Total newspaper revenue, according to Medill, was approximately $50 billion in 2006 and was down to $21 billion in 2022. Journalism.org also reported that daily newspaper circulation has gone from 63 million in 1973 to 56 million in 2000 to 28.5 million in 2018. At the same time, digital readership had grown from 8 million in 2014 to 11 million in 2018, according to the Medill School of Journalism.[43]

Papers struggle with the high costs of doing business (newsprint, ink, delivery, and labor) and compete with cyberspace's speed, making news delivered in a newspaper no longer the most up-to-date medium available. In addition, societal changes are reducing the public appetite for traditional news, particularly among younger readers. Of the total adult population in the United States, 41 percent of women and 46 percent of men still read a daily newspaper, but only 29 percent of those eighteen to thirty-four years of age, compared to 49 percent over thirty-five and 57 percent over fifty-five, according to the Newspaper Association of America.[44]

Pew said in a 2018 report that:

> *Newspapers are a critical part of the American news landscape, but they have been hit hard as more and more Americans consume news digitally. The industry's financial fortunes and subscriber base have been in decline since the early 2000s ... The estimated total US daily newspaper circulation (print and digital combined) in 2017 was 31 million for weekday[s] and 34 million for Sunday[s], down 11% and 10%, respectively, from the previous year.[45]*

Newspapers have tried various ways of expanding their corporate empires by acquiring radio and television stations and even more unrelated subsidiaries. For example, the *Washington Post* used to own a private education company. Fortunately for the Post, in 2019, it got an infusion of revenue from new owner Jeff Bezos, one of the wealthiest people in America. Less than four years later, however, profits were declining, and Bezos was reportedly tired of newspaper ownership and casting his eye toward the Washington Commanders football team.

Newspapers have continuously and aggressively expanded to the internet, with a wide variety of cyberspace platforms and points of access for their readers. They attempt to duplicate the interactive character of websites, blogs, and popular podcasts so a reader feels more of a contributor to the process, not just a passive consumer. They now do video stories, stream panel sessions and interviews, and develop other special events for streaming, creating, and reporting the news.

As we know, cyber products are splattered with ads that speak, move, wiggle, squiggle, and interrupt your reading—and sometimes relate their message to your buying habits, location, or recent activities, exposing an uncomfortable familiarity and invasion of privacy. But they continue to grow.

Editorially, the landscape has changed as well. As we mentioned, much of the mid-twentieth century was marked by a return to objective journalism and clear demarcations between news and commentary, news and advertising. But newspapers have been evolving again, particularly since the Watergate scandal, which led to the resignation of President Richard Nixon in 1974. The scandal made the media more inclined toward political advocacy, adversarial journalism, and investigative reporting, with less straight news and more opinionated writing. Marketing professionals call it an appeal with "a sharper edge." But unfortunately, objective reporting, transparency, credible sourcing, verification of information, editing, and headlines are all elements of quality, balanced journalism being compromised or abandoned on some platforms.

Former President Barack Obama, in a YouTube interview on December 9, 2020, by Pen America's Ron Chernow, said, "The lines have blurred now between propaganda and what we would consider journalism in a way that has been described as truth decay." He further said, "You've got an epistemological problem where people don't know now entirely what's true and what's not, and the old authorities and curators of what is factual are greatly weakened."[46]

"The lines have blurred now between propaganda and what we would consider journalism in a way that has been described as truth decay." —President Barack Obama

The practice has only gotten worse since the Obama interview.

The media is undergoing a historic realignment to no-holds-barred subjective advocacy and adversarial journalism. The trends run both toward progressive and conservative ideologies, with some media moving farther to the left and the right along the political spectrum, making it difficult for readers, listeners, and viewers to get a balanced view of their world and the information they need to form opinions and make intelligent decisions.

RADIO, TELEVISION, AND THE DIGITAL AGE

Broadcast—radio and television—is the second branch of the traditional media, an industry born of technology and an unquenchable consumer thirst to "see it now," the historic watchwords for Edward R. Murrow's ascendency in early television news.

Radio

Broadcast journalism has its roots in the early twentieth century, transitioning from a primitive experiment in wireless communication to a major American industry in the 1920s. RCA, Westinghouse, and General Electric were instrumental in the creation of the legacy networks we know today: The National Broadcasting Company (NBC) in 1926 and, a year later, an upstart network, The Columbia Broadcasting System (CBS), emerged with its network of radio stations across the country.

In the Golden Age of Radio, during the 1930s, the staples were music and entertainment, but programming also included news and opinions, the latter first introduced at the University of Chicago round tables and the American town meetings aired on NBC.

It didn't take long for political figures, such as Senator and presidential hopeful Huey Long of Louisiana and President Franklin Roosevelt of New York, to see the advantage of communicating through this somewhat mysterious medium. Long introduced his flamboyant broadcast style as early as the 1920s, when a friend who owned a Shreveport radio station gave him free airtime. According to the Journal of Radio Studies, he talked for several hours, sometimes remotely from a hotel room, where he lounged in his pajamas.

Roosevelt institutionalized political dialogue with his famous fireside chats during the Great Depression, offering millions of Americans information and hope. "The President wants to come into your home and sit at your fireside for a little fireside chat," is how Robert Trout introduced the President on CBS airwaves in 1933, according to the White House Historical Association.

American Catholics discovered the power of broadcasting following the defeat of Catholic Al Smith for President in 1928. Church leaders realized the critical need to educate the public about Catholicism. According to the author Scott Farris, writing in the *Washington Post,* "The bigotry aimed at Smith dismayed and outraged American Catholics, who began aggressively using the new media of radio and film to familiarize their fellow Americans with the true tenets of their faith. By the 1960s, Catholics were a powerful force in popular culture and presidential candidate John F. Kennedy's faith was as much a positive as a negative."[47]

According to radio historian Ken Mills of Minneapolis, the talk radio format can be traced back to 1945, when WMCA disc jockey Barry Gray held an on-air telephone conversation with big band personality Woody Herman. Early talk radio began with more milquetoast programming, but it didn't last.

Talk radio reinvented itself with the advent of television. Talk's new format featured more provocative and controversial discussions and interviews, more focused on current events and issues. The personalities at the microphone were often obnoxious voices, such as Morton Downey, Long John Nebel, Bob Grant, Wally George, and Joe Pyne. The vitriol reached a peak in 1984 when Alan Berg, the self-proclaimed "wild man of the airwaves," was shot by members of a neo-Nazi domestic terrorist group.

Modern-day talk radio, according to historian Mills, evolved in the late 1980s and 1990s as AM stations looked for inexpensive ways to compete with FM, satellites, and corporate entities with political agendas that began buying up radio broadcast licenses. The new era made big stars of the late Rush Limbaugh, Don Imus, shock-jock Howard Stern, and current host Dr. Laura Schlessinger.

Television

Television was a natural extension of radio but required technology far more sophisticated and expensive than its predecessor. The technology can be traced to experiments conducted in Russia, England, and the United States in the first decades of the twentieth century. Still, most of the credit goes to Philo Farnsworth, a twenty-one-year-old American inventor who captured images as radio waves and projected them as pictures onto a screen in the 1920s. His first image was, appropriately enough, a dollar sign.

News began to surface on local television stations as early as the late 1930s and 1940s before World War II put the technology on hold. Early pioneers were Lowell Thomas, Richard Hubbell, and John Cameron Swayze.

But by 1945, the news on television was back in the game, according to David Shedden, of the Poynter Institute, on April 4, 2006:

> *Beginning in 1947, 20th-Century Fox/Movietone produced the daily Camel Newsreel Theatre. It was sponsored by the R. J. Reynolds Tobacco Company. The NBC Television Newsreel program started in 1948. In 1949 the Camel News Caravan with John Cameron Swayze began.*
>
> *The Camel News Caravan was one of the first NBC news programs to use NBC filmed news stories rather than movie newsreels. Television news was becoming more independent and relying less on radio and newsreels.*
>
> *John Cameron Swayze, who worked in radio for many years, had done voice-over work for the Camel Newsreel Theatre before becoming the television anchor of Camel News Caravan. Although his journalism credentials were thin, he created an on-air personality that viewers liked.*

He made eye contact and understood the visual role that
anchors play in presenting the news. He could memorize scripts
using his photographic memory—an invaluable talent in the years
before the teleprompter.[48]

David Sarnoff, who built Radio Corporation of America (RCA),
made one of the first investments in television technology and hired
a Russian scientist to make it a reality. Television made its public
debut at the World's Fair in 1939, and it included a speech by none
other than radio personality himself, President Franklin Roosevelt.
RCA began broadcasting that year, and in two years, the Columbia
Broadcasting System (CBS) was putting two newscasts on the air for
New York viewers.

Full-scale commercial television broadcasting was underway in the US
by 1947, and a few years later, a third network, ABC, came on the air. The
early shows ranged from entertainment with Milton Berle to news with
Douglas Edwards.

The rise of television was meteoric. There were 12 million TV sets in
homes by 1951, and four years later, half of all homes had a black-and-
white set. According to Nielsen's National Television Household Universe Estimates, there are 119 million TV homes in America and about
1.4 billion globally. Those audiences attracted local and national news
programming worldwide.[49,50]

ENTERTAINMENT WAS KING

Despite the increase in news content, television remained an entertainment
medium, featuring specials such as the rebroadcast of the movie Peter Pan
with Mary Martin; regular comedy programs such as I Love Lucy with
Lucille Ball and Desi Arnez, and The Honeymooners with Jackie Gleason;
variety shows, such as The Ed Sullivan Show and Your Show of Shows,
and talk shows, such as The Tonight Show—first with Jack Paar and later
with Johnny Carson, Jay Leno, and Jimmy Fallon.

But politics seeped into TV entertainment with the long-running *All in the Family* show, featuring Archie Bunker as a bigoted, small-minded jerk living in a world of rapid and dramatic social change. *M*A*S*H* was the entertainment industry's introduction to anti-war messaging.

"Entertainment" on TV has been used as a tool for reshaping political views to an ever-increasing degree ever since.

THE EMERGENCE OF TELEVISION NEWS

Political news coverage expanded substantially in 1952 with Walter Cronkite's coverage of the national political party conventions on CBS. It didn't take long for the competition to up the ante. In 1955, NBC introduced co-anchors Chet Huntley and David Brinkley on Nightly News. Cronkite took to the air on the daily CBS Evening News in 1962 and ultimately became who pollsters described as "the most trusted man in America." Imagine that; a network news anchor is seen as the most trusted man in America!

How profoundly TV news coverage could impact politics became apparent two years earlier during the presidential debate between Richard Nixon and John Kennedy. Nixon's physical appearance on television, with his five-o'clock shadow and profuse perspiration, was so bad, and Kennedy's so good in comparison, that pollsters speculated the optics contributed to Nixon's loss in November 1960. It may have been a foreboding omen of the greater influence of cosmetics over substance.

Television news began adopting a sharper, more provocative, and less objective tone with the explosion of the Civil Rights movement in the mid to late 1960s and the growing national unpopularity of the Vietnam War. However, the new tone was not so new. It had its roots in the work of former war correspondent Edward R. Murrow, whose *See It Now* program on CBS gained national acclaim and ridicule when it took on Senator Joseph McCarthy and his Un-American Activities Committee's investigations of communist infiltration of government and the media in the 1950s.

Walter Cronkite shocked the nation on his CBS broadcast on February 27, 1968, when this icon of steely news objectivity and neutrality publicly criticized the war after a protracted visit to Vietnam following the Tet Offensive, as reported on the Alpha History website on the Vietnam War Updated 2019:

> *For it seems now more certain than ever that the bloody experience of Vietnam is to end in a stalemate. This summer's almost certain standoff will either end in real give-and-take negotiations or terrible escalation; and for every means we have to escalate, the enemy can match us, and that applies to invasion of the North, the use of nuclear weapons, or the mere commitment of one hundred, or two hundred, or three hundred thousand more American troops to the battle. And with each escalation, the world comes closer to the brink of cosmic disaster.*
>
> *. . . To say that we are mired in stalemate seems the only realistic, yet unsatisfactory, conclusion . . .But it is increasingly clear to this reporter that the only rational way out then will be to negotiate, not as victors, but as an honorable people who lived up to their pledge to defend democracy and did the best they could. This is Walter Cronkite. Good night.[51]*

One could argue this change, where a newsman becomes a policy advocate, was a significant shift in journalism's treatment of politics and governance, Murrow, notwithstanding.

Aggressive political journalism in all media continued into the early 1970s with early investigative reports in *The Washington Post* of criminal behavior connected to the break-in at the offices of the Democratic National Committee's Chairman, Lawrence F. O'Brien Jr., in the Watergate Hotel in 1972.

The scandal permeated the airwaves. One highlight of the Watergate investigation for the media came with the extensive hearings in the Senate by the Select Committee on Presidential Campaign Activities. The Senate created the committee in 1973 to investigate the scandal with authority to investigate the break-in at the Democratic National Committee. The hearings took popular soap operas off the air, but no one seemed to mind. Americans remained glued to their televisions throughout the hearings, and participants became instant celebrities. Watergate eventually brought down Richard Nixon, who was never a media darling. It also sped the transition in the relationship between journalism and politics from one of healthy skepticism to unhealthy cynicism.

It took a former movie actor to turn things around by forcing a sense of balance to the power struggle between politics and the press. The Governor of California, Ronald Reagan, was a master communicator with a natural flair for political theater that he could manipulate television as much as it tried to manipulate him. He and those around him were highly skilled and proficient at messaging and staging. Moreover, Reagan was a charismatic and sometimes mesmerizing public speaker whose words, gestures, and facial expressions could turn an exceedingly complex subject, like strategic nuclear arms negotiations, into a simple primer on national defense. Some consider him one of the greatest communicators in American politics.

On the network news stage, the previous Walter Cronkite objective-reporter model lasted for many years, producing made-for-television anchors and correspondents who were celebrities as much as journalists, capable of producing objective news reporting while bringing in higher viewer ratings and more ad revenues. Moreover, they were as American as apple pie on the screen: stately, senior, well-traveled sages whom audiences trusted. It was a period in which viewers put a lot of faith in what they heard on the radio and saw on television.

Some anchors were experienced journalists who polished an image of intelligent, common-sense thinking, fair and honest reporting, and news judgments in which the public had confidence and trust. So it was, in many respects, both economically and professionally, a golden age, although critics today would say a golden age with blinders.

Yet, behind the scenes, the monopoly on political news was beginning to crack as science and technology were giving birth to a new digital age, and the metal of the American anchor was starting to rust.

One of the first spoilers was Dan Rather, who forced Cronkite out of the anchor chair at CBS. Rumor had it that Rather was so full of himself that he refused to go on air unless Cronkite's anchor chair was removed from the set.

Dan Rather may have lowered the bar of objective journalism just too far. He finally met his Waterloo in 2005. He was convinced that a young George W. Bush had gotten favorable treatment by the National Guard during the Vietnam War. So, as a news anchor, he pushed that narrative. He and his producers at the "magazine" news show *60 Minutes* manipulated and, in some cases, fabricated the facts to reinforce their conclusion. Eventually, the truth came out. Rather was forced to resign along with several of his colleagues.

The Rather incident is important in the history of news because it was not only a case of "gotcha journalism" gone awry but what seemed like the beginning of the end for the image of the saintly anchor. But the incident was certainly not groundbreaking. More than ten years earlier, for example, NBC was caught in a fabrication and cover-up of a *Dateline* broadcast scandal involving a rigged explosion of a Chevy pickup truck to demonstrate the danger of the truck's gas tank location in a side collision. The flim-flam in the 1992 show came to light through competing media coverage of a suit filed by General Motors. NBC's admission of fault brought down the executive producer, segment producer, and correspondent of *Dateline*.

Both the NBC and CBS scandals revealed how policy news reports could create a believable storyline by threading together facts with speculation and information with innuendo to nudge viewers toward a desired conclusion. It is a method of news construction featured in the 1981 movie *Absence of Malice*. In the film, information and evidence concocted by a federal prosecutor and an ambitious reporter were found to be "accurate, but not true." That tactic is among those that citizens need to be particularly alert to because they can drive political decision-making and, ultimately, public policy with profound consequences.

Other anchors have come and gone, and some brought down the way Rather was. For example, NBC Nightly News anchor Brian Williams played fast and loose with the facts about a story he reported out of Iraq. As a result, he was demoted to the network's sister cable station when they were found untrue. Among conservative cable anchors, Eric Bolling and Bill O'Reilly, while not strictly news anchors in the traditional sense, similarly fell from grace because of allegations of sexual behavioral misconduct. Another widely popular anchor, Glenn Beck, lost his perch because of unacceptable toxicity.

Others lost the coveted primary anchor chair in part because they couldn't generate the ratings needed to pay their hefty salaries. CBS anchors Katie Couric and Scott Pelley were relieved of their jobs, along with others who failed to exude the gravitas, imagery, and persona of their contemporaries like Peter Jennings, Bob Schieffer, and Charles Gibson, who epitomized the character and journalistic and broadcast excellence of pioneers Cronkite, Huntley, Brinkley, Frank Reynolds and two ground-breaking anchors Max Robinson, the first Black anchor, and Barbara Walters, the first woman.

As viewers know, the networks, both over-the-air and on cable, continue to embrace a news-making model that is personality and hot-button issue-driven, generating more heat than light. It's a brand of journalism that deliberately stimulates emotion rather than intellect to attract more "clicks" and "eyeballs." Yet, as a possible sign the model is once again being rewritten, Fox News canceled the popular *Tucker Carlson Show* for various cases of abuse, even though his was a highly rated evening show for the network.

THE THIRD BRANCH OF THE MEDIA

While ABC News was rising to power against NBC and CBS in the 1970s, another new technology was creeping up on the over-the-air broadcasters, as cable TV wire was buried underground or strung along telephone poles in New York City. In 1979, political junkies caught their first glimpse of the Floor of the US House of Representatives on C-SPAN. And on June 1, 1980, viewers were getting their first look at the twenty-four-hour news channel CNN, anchored by husband-and-wife team David Walker and Lois Hart.

Cable Television Had Arrived

At first, cable TV was limited to large cities. However, soon cable was being tunneled across the entire landscape, reaching much smaller communities, such as Galesburg, Illinois, a small, blue-collar community of 43,000, where Mike was a journalist at the time. The new technology was greeted by the guffaws of some community business leaders, who thought cable was pure folly and a terrible investment.

Today cable and satellite carry over 900 national and regional networks and are wired into more than 85 percent of American homes.

It is hard to calculate the impact of cable news shows on the flow of political information to Americans and, maybe more importantly, to people all over the globe.

Cable television has offered Americans thousands of hours of entertainment. For politics, though, its most significant development has been the twenty-four-hour news cycle pioneered by CNN. The network partly thrived because it was especially effective in providing live and ongoing coverage of major events like the Gulf War and the explosion of the spaceship Challenger.

But later, CNN did something else. It reinforced a perception among millions of Americans that network news—cable or over-the-air—like its relatives in the newspaper industry, had a pronounced liberal bias.

Survey research bore out the bias, which for years had documented that most journalists considered themselves liberal and acknowledged an affiliation with, or an affinity for, the Democratic Party. Pick a survey. In 1981, researchers interviewed journalists and found that 94 percent voted for Lyndon Baines Johnson in 1964, 81 percent voted for George

McGovern in 1972 and Jimmy Carter in 1976. A survey in 2016 found that 96 percent of the political donations of media figures went to Hillary Clinton. Another survey in the *Atlantic* in 2016 found that four in five journalists willing to acknowledge a party affiliation said they were Democrats. The vast majority of those who claim party affiliation say they are liberals.

By reinforcing the ideological liberal distinctions in journalism, real or imagined, CNN may have inadvertently given rise to a new era in cable television: the introduction of Fox News. Its conservative format, in turn, spurred another cable network, MSNBC, as a liberal counterweight, creating both confusion and conflict with its sister broadcasting entity, NBC News.

While cable channels can make dubious claims to be venues for serious journalists, for the most part, they have changed the news business by giving rise to a fast-growing, influential group: infotainers, the cross-breeders of news information and entertainment. They include talented comedians who make news funny to quasi-journalists who go beyond the bounds of good journalism doing the same thing. *The Comedy Show's* Jon Stewart was one of the pioneers in infotainment, as were Stephen Colbert and Bill Maher, and radio and cable infotainers Rush Limbaugh, Tucker Carlson, and Sean Hannity on the right and Chris Matthews, Rachel Maddow, and Lawrence O'Donnell on the left. The infotainers appear on talk radio and television, write books, blog, operate websites, Tweet, and want you to "like" them on Facebook and follow them everywhere else. They have created a new genre that mixes and matches the basic genetics of politics, news, and entertainment.

THE DIGITAL AGE

If cable television changed the dynamics of news' impact on politics, the internet completely uprooted it.

Blogs and podcasts caused an early upheaval, but there have been so many other potent factors, like the explosion of news-oriented websites, so-called citizen journalists, and the use and abuse of a whole new universe of social media by both politicians and journalists.

If you want to be cute, you can trace the history of social media back to cave dwellers. However, in contemporary times, what got us to this dizzying kaleidoscope of digital playpens has been a steady lineage of technological developments from the invention of the Guttenberg printing press to the first selfie in 1839 and the first telegraph message in 1844 to the telephone in 1890, and to the first supercomputer in 1940, to the WELL in 1985, to Listserv the following year. Finally, the defense department unveiled the worldwide web in 1991; universities adapted in short order, and public use quickly followed.

The rest, as they say, is history.

Among the first political and social activist entries in the social media realm was the liberal site, MoveOn.org in 1998, which started organizing political campaigns across the country.

Globally, one of the major turning points in movements organized on internet sites was the Arab Spring uprisings across the Middle East in 2011, *Face the Nation* host Margaret Brennan recalled. She told Mark Berman in a 2022 Forbes interview:

> *I remember flying into Cairo and the chaotic scene in the center of the city, as there was this social media-based organized protest movement that used Facebook as its platform to galvanize support among young people to come out and protest the government. That was the first time, I think, we all saw social media having that impact in that way.*[52]

It is hard to quantify today's political impact of Google, YouTube, X (Twitter), Facebook, Wikipedia, Reddit, Instagram, and TikTok, among others. In its early days, X (Twitter) magnified the extent to which politicians and media celebrities thrive on each other's forty-character comments that twenty years ago would have been an insult to intelligent political dialogue. More recently, sites such as YouTube, Facebook, and Threads, (launched in 2023) have imposed what critics believe are restrictions on free speech and political content by banning some users whose postings or videos they find offensive. Such bans raise profound questions about private companies' rights and conflicting moral obligations to monitor and regulate (or not) activity in their domain. When Elon Musk bought Twitter (X), he placed a new emphasis on free speech but got criticized for his new policies and management.

New platforms on social media circle the globe of ideologies from far-right anarchists all the way around to far-left anarchists and most cloisters of political thought and activism in between. The content ranges from urban myths to actual investigative reporting. They often cater to people with like minds, who are more forgiving of factual error than ideological apostasy. Algorithms analyzing how you engage on the platform determine the type of content you will see next, a form of curation that happens whether you want it to or not.

The platforms represent revolutionary advancements in personal engagement, providing interactive forums where readers can access news and information, comment, share opinions, ridicule political opponents, rally the troops, and provide policy and other information aimed at specific political niches—all for a fraction of the cost of mainstream media productions.

While many platforms have become legitimate voices of political movements and sources of information, there are those, such as TikTok, that collect vast amounts of data with no transparency as to where it goes or how used. In 2023, Congress launched investigations of TikTok amid allegations that the site collects massive amounts of personal information on users, which the app's Chinese owners can access. In 2023, the CEO, Shau Zi Chew, a forty-year-old Singaporean, was excoriated by Members of Congress on both sides of the aisle under threats to shut the app down in the United States or demand its sale to American investors.

Or YouTube, which through sophisticated algorithms, may open doors to dark places users don't want to go. And then numerous sites spew a lot of garbage, from vile white supremacist sites advocating hatred to ultra-left sites that advocate violence and wish suffering upon political opponents.

One might conclude that you must browse the web more carefully than walking your dog in a poorly lit park after dark. It would be best to watch where you step and keep an eye on the shadows.

There is a wide and almost endless digital communications landscape in front of us, with a vast array of information and opportunities to expand our horizons. There aren't many times in human history when "progress" can be described in such sweeping and life-altering dimensions. Our focus, however, is limited to the consumers' use as it relates to Congress and political issues and events, where there are many pitfalls.

THE NEED FOR MEDIA LITERACY AND VIGILANCE

First, some used to say what happens on social media stays on social media, but that is no longer true—and maybe never was. Social media content travels faster than you can delete it or deny it. Deleting a tweet can sometimes be more damning than explaining it. Social media has bolstered the damaging belief in media that politicians are guilty until they prove themselves innocent, and for some, their guilty even after they are proven innocent. Misinformation takes on a life of its own. Social media also thrives on information, true or not, that occurred so far in the past, it is often irrelevant to any reality other than the perplexing public passion to air politicians' dirty laundry. Social media's long memory and instant recall can make a valued contribution to public oversight, but it can also do senseless damage to people and events. Knowing the difference can make a difference.

A second inherent problem with social media is the greater degree of over-simplification and exaggeration that it adds to public discourse already saturated with both. Congress is a place where the simplicity of sound-bite banter and the glittering generalities of political campaigns must end at some point to allow policymakers to deal with the complexities of legislating and developing public policy. But, unfortunately, over-simplification of the process and the incessant exaggeration that goes along with partisan posturing doesn't end. An engaged citizenry must see through the partisan fog and demand focus on where and how sensible public-policy consensus can be achieved.

The third dynamic is the preponderance of misinformation and fake news on social media. The problem, as one media professional explained it, is described here: "I think most people know that a lot on the internet is fake news. They are just tired of fact-checking and researching So, they find a couple of sources they consider trustworthy and just passively consume that content, blindly believing that none is false. The problem, of course, is a lot of those sources aren't trustworthy at all, but the followers don't find out until it's too late." That statement is borne out by a 2022 article in PRWeek. Natasha Bach reported that a survey by public relations firm DKC "found that a large majority of both groups—91 percent of Gen Z and 84 percent of Millennials—don't trust at least one major type of media outlet. They are especially distrustful of news they read on social media, even though this is often their primary sources of news." She said, "48 percent of Gen Z respondents called social media their 'go-to' option for news, but 54 percent of them (the respondents) also said they generally do not trust it."[53]

And that leads to the fourth dynamic, getting to the other side of issues and beliefs that may contradict what you think, but are legitimate points of view that are important in providing a broader perspective on the world around you. Berman said in his story that Facebook and X (Twitter) are "where people tend to surround themselves virtually with those individuals who only share their common beliefs. And while some stories might contain a nugget (or two) of truth, they may lack any relevant details."

"When I open Twitter (X), I always see the same people and I wonder what the other side is thinking but it is very hard to get to the other side," a frequent user of X (Twitter) and Facebook told us.

The one-sided nature of so many sites today is reflected in mainstream media, as we discuss in the next chapter, where respectable journalists no longer feel obligated to tell you both sides of a story or describe both sides of an issue. Instead, it is yet another dumbing-down exercise that may harm the citizens' ability to think independently and make intelligent decisions about public policy debates. "If we are to guard against ignorance and remain free, it is the responsibility of every American to be informed," Thomas Jefferson said. The problem, of course, is keeping informed when information is withheld or distorted.

All of this becomes more relevant each day. The influence of digital news sources is growing. According to the Pew Research Center in 2021: ". . . 86 percent of US adults say they got news from a smartphone, computer, or tablet 'often' or 'sometimes'. . . 60 percent who say they do so often." Television was often the source by 40 percent, well above the percentages for radio and print. "About two-thirds of US adults say they get news at least sometimes from news websites or apps (68 percent) or search engines, like Google (65 percent). About half (33 percent) say they get their news from social media, and a much smaller portion say they get news at least sometimes from podcasts (22 percent). Underneath these numbers lie stark differences by age," the study concluded, "with those under 50 showing very different use patterns than their elders. Americans ages 50 and older use both television and digital devices for news at high rates, while the younger age groups almost fully turned to digital devices as a platform to access news."[54]

"Social media has become a hotbed of misinformation and conspiracy theories," Goeas and Lake wrote in *A Question of Respect*. "Driving the likes and views is a business model that employs algorithms designed to exploit human weaknesses and spawn outrage. Outrage stimulates the same pleasure centers in the brain as hard drugs. Social media-related businesses exploit this vulnerability for profit."[55]

The data on digital use reinforces what we already knew. Traditional outlets, such as major dailies and network news, may still drive public opinion, but they have competition and economic challenges that didn't exist in their worst nightmares three decades ago, and yet now, social media serves as a significant source of mainstream journalists. Moreover, the competition is a greater challenge because many platforms are more unbridled, undisciplined, uncertified, unedited, and unruly than the mainstream media.

We would like to believe and hope, because democracy depends on it, that serious journalists continue to adhere to the more traditional role of their profession—that they would serve as chroniclers of history in the making and serve as a check and balance, a watchdog. And an honest broker that gives us the tools we need to make up our minds, to ensure that we are literate and vigilant and better able to govern ourselves. But . . .

"HAVE YOU CONSIDERED THAT ALL YOUR FEARS MAY BE 'MEDIA DRIVEN'?"

Chapter 9

Journalists As Advocates and Adversaries

Media has changed dramatically in recent years, but what has not changed is the critical role they play in the life of the Republic. We still can't live with them or without them.

The transformation taking place in professional journalism and the business side of media is historic. We have entered a new age in which the media have significantly rewritten the fundamentals of journalism. Advocacy, partisanship, and ideological preferences have rendered objectivity a relic of a lost generation of iconic journalists.

We will delve more deeply into the changes, but citizens must be better media-educated: more intelligently and dispassionately about what we see, hear, and read. In short, it is incumbent on each of us to become media literate if we wish to follow and participate in civic affairs and public-policy decisions. Moreover, we must know and understand more if we wish to have more control over the impact of government in our lives and have greater influence over those who are supposed to represent our interests in Washington and state capitals across the country. The media is just that impactful to an effective democracy.

WHAT IS MEDIA LITERACY

The National Association of Media Literacy Education defines media literacy as "the ability to access, analyze, evaluate, create and act," on what you take in.

The Oxford Research Encyclopedia on Media says:

> *The concept of media literacy has been circulating in the United States and Europe since the beginning of the 20th Century to acknowledge the set of knowledge, skills, and habits of mind required for full participation in a contemporary media-saturated society. The concept continues to morph and change as a result of rapid changes in digital media, mass media, social media, popular culture, and society.*

That's putting it mildly. Since the opening decades of the twenty-first century, media consumption has undergone a revolution of greater significance than at any time since the invention of the Guttenberg press. Think of the media's current environment:

- A new world of technology;
- New platforms for instantaneous delivery of news and entertainment;
- A new expanded universe of information that makes everybody believe they're an expert on everything;
- Dramatically changing economics, ownership, and competitiveness of the media business;
- Tectonic political, social, cultural, and demographic shifts expanding the English language, redefining the news business, and making media rethink its business model, from the corporate offices to the reporters on the beat; and
- The explosion of artificial intelligence and what the future holds in its use by the media (It is too early to tell if it is a legitimate source of information and a substitute for reporting, or will it expand media chaos?).

All that has and will continue to diminish news literacy. As consumers of this avalanche of information, we're failing miserably. According to the 2020 Edelman Trust Barometer survey, only one in four respondents practice what it referred to as "good information hygiene; news engagement; avoid echo chambers; verify information and do not amplify unvetted information." Ouch.

GETTING THE FACTS RIGHT THE FIRST TIME

The new age of journalism is the evolution of a profession that challenges our ability to sort through what we're fed about candidates or public policy issues. It's like eating fresh trout but ignoring the bones. If you're not careful, you're going to choke on it.

We found one of the sharper bones in an interview media mogul Arianna Huffington did with news critic Howard Kurtz in 2011. She told Kurtz that *Huffington Post* editors don't concern themselves so much with accuracy, instead focusing on getting the story out first. "We let the news self-correct itself," she said.

> The new age of journalism is the evolution of a profession that challenges our ability to sort through what we're fed about candidates or public policy issues. It's like eating fresh trout but ignoring the bones. If you're not careful, you're going to choke on it.

That description of the new age of internet journalism—self-correcting news—was a surprise back then to a great many consumers who assumed, justifiably, that the news they were getting was the news they could trust: factually correct, double-checked, balanced, complete, and untainted by the prejudices of whoever was delivering it. The idea of professional journalists leaving accuracy up to unfolding events *was* news. The financial influences of the business were overtaking the journalistic imperatives in news delivery.

It turned out that *Huffington's* strategy would spread to traditional media. Today, it seems that being first often outweighs being accurate.

One story stands out among many as a classic example of this phenomenon. In January 2019, some Catholic high school students from Covington, Kentucky, were at the national mall in Washington, DC, waiting for their bus after attending an anti-abortion rally. They encountered a Native American activist and a group known as Black Hebrew Israelites. Their interaction got intensive media coverage.

Major national broadcast and print news outlets, apparently without any reporters present at the site, portrayed the students as villains, alleging they were belligerent and mocked the Native Americans. It was a faster-than-a-speeding bullet rush to judgment, based almost entirely on what turned out to be a deliberately doctored amateur video that went viral. The result can only be described as media profiling: the teens were Catholics, anti-abortion, and some wore Make America Great Again (MAGA) base-ball caps, so obviously, they were up to no good.

The youngsters were later subjected to death threats and ridicule and even criticized by their bishop. When the full video was aired, however, it was the Native American activist and the Black Hebrew Israelites who were harassing the teens. As it turned out, the students acted relatively maturely and respectfully, despite being confronted with intimidation.

The bishop apologized. Most news outlets corrected their mistakes but did not apologize or provide a sufficient analysis of how, when, and why the coverage went off the rails. *The Washington Post* editors went a mite further: In a considerable understatement, they admitted they did not have all the facts.

Here's another example. That same month, a black Hollywood actor named Jussie Smollett told Chicago police he had been assaulted by racists who put a noose around his neck. The media were all over the alleged incident, immediately reinforcing his accusations and sparking new outcries of racial injustice. Facts were fluid or non-existent during weeks of such coverage. Joe Biden, a candidate for President, didn't hesitate to pass judgment without the facts: "What happened today to @JussieSmollett must never be tolerated in this country," Biden said. "We must stand up and demand that we no longer give this hate safe harbor, that homophobia and racism have no place on our streets or in our hearts. We are with you, Jussie."

The incident was an elaborate hoax designed, financed, and acted out by Smollett to enhance his acting career. To their credit, it was the Chicago media, working with Chicago police, that eventually exposed the fraud. Smollett was charged, but the new Cook County state's attorney, whose motives remain in question, dropped the charges. Nevertheless, Smollett was re-indicted on similar charges in February 2020 and found guilty in December 2021. In early 2022, he was sentenced to 150 days in jail, but appeals continued into 2023.

Those egregious examples of this practice of shooting from the partisan hip stand out for their brazenness and the damage they did to American journalism and the damage journalism then did to an informed public. Unfortunately, those events also helped seal the nation's fate for a foreseeable future of politics frozen in partisan polarization. The media soon embraced more dubious patterns.

Narrative journalism or advocacy and adversarial reporting replaced objective news reporting—providing several sides of an issue or situation so readers could make up their minds. Objectivity was put on life support.

Here are two even more ominous examples of the media pushing narratives in these cases—even though they had evidence that their stories were not legitimate. The first involves a massive campaign by Democrats and their media collaborators to convince the American people that candidate Donald Trump actively conspired with Russian President Vladimir Putin to rig the 2016 US election in Trump's favor.

The lengthy investigations of Trump's alleged collusion produced unsubstantiated, but at the time, persuasive news reporting of a conspiracy. The drumbeat reverberated across the country with unrelenting news coverage and commentary. Leaks flowed from the pours of both the Justice Department and congressional investigations. At one point, the head of the House investigation, Congressman Adam Schiff of California, said he had inconvertible evidence of Trump's guilt. He didn't. The hysteria was driven by preconceived notions, the assumption that someone was guilty until proven innocent, and a transparent attempt to drive Trump from office.

It was a true-life spy thriller, complete with secret agents, leaks, money laundering, and conspiracy theories that went so far as to claim Trump was a Russian operative. It also produced one of our history's most ill-con-

ceived and partisan impeachment trials. Some of the nation's most prominent law enforcement and high-ranking intelligence officers contributed to
the narrative and were eventually exposed. Unfortunately, the FBI (Federal
Bureau of Investigation) is still smarting from its poor behavior.

After years of keeping the country on edge, independent investigations
found no clear evidence that Trump was complicit. A subsequent investigation by the Justice Department allowed to proceed under the Biden Administration, produced evidence of a conspiracy, including a trail of what appeared
to be laundered money back to the campaign of Trump's opponent, former
Senator Hillary Clinton. But no conclusive legal action has been taken.

The second transformative event followed immediately. While the
Democrats were winding down their conspiracy that Trump had stolen the
2016 election from Clinton, Trump began sounding an alarm that the 2020
election would be stolen from him.

That accusation ballooned into the second historical example of a "don't-
bother-me-with-the-facts" practice of journalism, this time by right-wing
media that promoted the stolen election narrative mostly on the slim and selective evidence provided by Trump and his legion of election-fraud advocates.

President Trump wasted no time after the 2016 presidential election to
claim that millions of people had voted illegally. He insisted that had the
voting not been laced with fraud, he would have won the popular vote and
the Electoral College count by a landslide. The popular vote count was
almost 63 million for Trump and nearly 66 million for Clinton. But Trump
won in the Electoral College by 304–227, which is what counts.

Trump even appointed a presidential advisory commission on election
integrity in May 2017 to prove his allegations. When that effort failed, the
President began building the expectation that if he lost the 2020 elections,
it was the result of massive fraud. When the results were in on election
night, he said, "This is a fraud on the American public. We were getting
ready to win this election. Frankly, we did win this election."

That led to what may have been an unprecedented campaign to overturn an American election. Trump advocates filed sixty-two lawsuits. He

attempted to persuade state and federal officials, including his own Department of Justice, to overturn the results, up to and including apparent efforts to fire Acting Attorney General Jeffrey Rosen.

When the dust settled (in some respects, it never has), there was evidence of invalid and fraudulent ballots cast—there always is in any national election. But investigation after investigation and court case after court case, especially in battleground states—Georgia, Arizona, Pennsylvania, Michigan, and Nevada—revealed no clear evidence of collusion, conspiracy, massive fraud, or even enough mistakes to come anywhere near deciding the election in Trump's favor.

Despite the findings, the Trump's fraud furor culminated in a historical attack on the nation's Capitol on January 6, 2021, in a vain attempt by hundreds of Trump loyalists, some more radical and violent than others, to prevent Congress's procedural process of certifying the Electoral College count, declaring Joe Biden the President.

Many right-wing and more conservative media outlets refused to acknowledge Trump's defeat. Bret Baier's Fox News' Special Report was an exception to most other Fox shows that bought into the rigged election bombast and, by doing so, contributed to the toxic atmosphere that day and the eventual congressional investigations and criminal trials.

The election-fraud controversy led to another dramatic event, the $1.6 billion defamation lawsuit filed by Dominion Voting Systems against Fox News, alleging that the cable network "sold a false story of election fraud in order to serve its own commercial purposes, severely injuring Dominion in the process," according to a copy of the lawsuit obtained by and reported by *The Associated Press* shortly after the filing in March 2022. Suits were also filed against other organizations and individuals, including Newsmax and One America News Network.

The Dominion lawsuit generated many revelations about Fox's internal politics and the privately held beliefs that the election was not rigged, even though their coverage pulled viewers in a different direction. In April 2023, the parties settled the lawsuit for a reported $785 million and, in part, led to the firing of Fox's popular and lucrative talk-show host Tucker Carlson.

These departures from journalistic ethics and objectivity are important to citizens who follow politics. Drawing premature and inaccurate conclusions because of preconceived notions is a scourge on the political system and many who involve themselves in it—the body politic. Unfortunately, it happens far too often. Consumers of news cannot outrun that kind of pack journalism. The public can't turn it off and must exercise restraint in drawing conclusions the media too often do not. Responsible news literacy means never assuming what you consume is true or factual. Almost always, some facts are not revealed, and information is withheld. Allow for the potential veracity of a point of view with which you are not entirely comfortable. Be skeptical and keep your mind wide open.

These kinds of changes in the media's farther drift toward advocacy and propaganda, which accelerated during the Trump era, have changed the face of American news media and the journalism profession. Unfortunately, they have reinforced other movements of our time toward censorship, revisionist history, political and social intolerance, and ideological polarization.

None of these incidents, however, holds a candle to another transformation of genuine historical significance for American journalism and how you get the information you need to be more engaged in self-government. At the heart of it is what we referred to earlier, the abandonment of objectivity as a journalistic standard of performance.

Some journalists and academics have argued that "objectivity" never existed. That may be true for them but not necessarily for a wide swath of the public. The term represents a standard of journalistic excellence and a code of conduct on which consumers have long depended. Objectivity is being scrapped in favor of a new paradigm that frees the media to tell us *what* to think, to persuade rather than to inform, and to deny readers, listeners, and viewers contrary perspectives that, to the writer, may not seem relevant but are. It has been coming for years, spirited by brutal political extremes and a growing intolerance for diversity of thought.

BALANCE VERSUS EQUIVALENCE

Professor and columnist Jonathan Turley expressed concern in a series of columns on the website Res ipso loquitur between August 2, 2021, and February 2023: "The problem is that journalists themselves are now asserting advocacy journalism as a moral normative imperative—and few editors will risk confronting such bias even if they are inclined to do so . . . the growing intolerance for dissenting views is stifling and alarming." Turley wrote that former New York Times reporter Nikole Hannah-Jones, creator of the 1619 Project, said. "All journalism is advocacy."[56]

The new definition of journalism has made its way into academia. Turley cited Stanford Communications Professor Emeritus Ted Glasser, who said he's not a big fan of objectivity because it inhibits the ability of journalists to pursue "social justice." Turley also cited Northwestern professor Steven Thrasher who scolded a *Chicago Tribune* reporter who wrote, "It was too soon to draw conclusions" about the police shooting of suspected gunman Adam Toledo.[57]

NBC News anchor Lester Holt said in a 2021 speech that "fairness was overrated."[58] He voiced support for a growing trend in American journalism to abandon the notion of balanced reporting, which many consider telling both sides or all sides of a story, providing facts and contrary opinions, and letting viewers make up their minds. As a result, major newspapers and legacy broadcast media have released their journalists from the obligations of the old truth-telling style.

Holt's misguided epiphany has been championed for years by Margaret Sullivan, a columnist with *The Washington Post*, who contended the old idea of representing "all points of view equally is absurd and sometimes wrongheaded" and that reporters must be advocates and evangelists for what they deem is right and just in an atmosphere where those judgments are very hard to come by.[59]

Wesley Lowery, a controversial journalist who gained notoriety among his colleagues when arrested for disobeying police in Ferguson, Missouri, said, "Americans view-from-nowhere, 'objectivity'-obsessed, both-sides journalism is a failed experiment. We need to fundamentally reset the norms of our field. The old way must go." He said journalists should not report the news but give it a "moral clarity."[60]

National Public Radio (NPR) has extended the new concept of advocacy to permitting its journalists to abandon journalistic neutrality and participate in a limited way in protests that "express support for democratic, civic values that are core to NPR's work, such as, but not limited to: the freedom and dignity of human beings, the rights of a free and independent press, the right to thrive in society without facing discrimination on the basis of race, ethnicity, gender, sexual identity, disability or religion."[61] Those are, of course, broad, glittering generalities that have endless meaning.

The range of support for some new variables on the muckraking journalism of a century ago is wide, stretching from veterans such as Holt to student journalists. For example, Taylor Blatchford wrote in the journalism newsletter of the Poynter Institute in 2021, "Today's student journalists are more likely than ever to challenge what it means to be an 'objective' reporter—as well as whether this journalistic standard is truly necessary."[62]

A journalist who worked for the *New York Times* and *The Washington Post* put it more crassly. "Younger people recognize the power of having their own brand and audience, and the longer you stay at a job that restricts you from outside opportunities, the less relevant your brand becomes," Taylor Lorenz told Business Insider. Lorenz considers herself an "influencer journalist," according to Andrew Stiles in Washington Free Beacon. But, to their credit, several of her journalistic colleagues criticized her comments, calling them "cringey."[63]

The branding of journalists, particularly since the advent of broadcast, has been around for some time. But there is little question that branding is on the rise and easily recognizable across a wide spectrum of the profession, from Jim Acosta at CNN to Laura Ingraham, and Sean Hannity at Fox to Chuck Todd of NBC, plus a legion of bloggers and print journalists, trying to make a name for themselves and establish a marketable niche in the trade.

The new version of advocacy journalism empowers national professional journalists whose frames of reference—more urban lifestyles, different values, cultural cores, politics, etc.—are far removed from millions of consumers who live in the vast stretches of America they refer to, sometimes with elitist pomposity, as "fly-over country," and have values and lifestyles that are foreign to journalists. While journalists may think their perspectives and opinions based on their knowledge and experiences are valuable assets, which their consumers need and deserve, they are not in many circumstances. They may be harmful. In Mike's experiences as a communication professional in congressional leadership, not all reporters covering Congress were consistently well enough informed and had enough knowledge of the issues, politics, and the power players to substitute their judgments and opinion for those of experts and experienced hands on the front lines.

The 2022 survey of American journalists, done periodically since 1971, give news consumers information about professional journalists today that may help them better understand what they consume. For example, the Newhouse School of Communications at Syracuse University found that just under 23 percent of journalists think journalism is going in the right direction; the number of women in the profession has doubled since 1971 and now stands at 41 percent; practically 96 percent of working journalists have college degrees, and they earn a median average salary of $74,000.[64] Another Statista report indicates the median age of journalists has gone from the early thirties, twenty years ago, to forty-seven in the most recent survey, five years older than the American workforce, suggesting strong familiarity with the baby boomer generation.

The important party affiliation of journalists has seen both stagnation and significant change. In 1971, 35 percent of journalists professed alliance with the Democratic Party, topping out in the 1992 survey at 44 percent but declining back to the normal range—36 percent—in 2022. However, a dramatic decline was seen in alliance with the Republican Party, steadily declining from 28 percent in 1971 to just 3 percent in 2022. The big increase came in allegiance in the reported Independent affiliation, steadily moving from 32 percent in 1971 to 51 percent in 2022. Finally, journalists were asked what was "the most pressing problem facing journalism today." You could guess what came in first: public trust.[65]

Recently, a very prominent journalist, and from our perspective, a highly unlikely advocate of objectivity, spoke up in its support as a standard and guiding principle of journalism.

Former Executive Editor of *The Washington Post*, Martin Baron, wrote in March 2023:

> *Let's take a step back. First a dictionary definition of objectivity. This is from Merriam-Webster, "expressing or dealing with fact or conditions without distortion by personal feelings, prejudices or interpretations." Baron said we expect objectivity from judges, juries, police officers, prosecutors, doctors, medical researchers, government regulators, bank loan officers, and scientists, so why not journalists? "Most in the public, in my experience, expect my profession to be objective, too. Dismissing their expectations—outright defying them—is an act of arrogance. It excuses our biases. It enshrines them. And most importantly, it fails the cause of truth." Increasingly, he wrote, "journalists—particularly a rising generation—are repudiating the standard to which we routinely, and resolutely, hold others."[66]*

That learned opinion was shared by Walter E. Hussman, Jr., former publisher of the *Arkansas Gazette* for more than forty-five years. A few months earlier, in the *Wall Street Journal*, he quoted another editor who made this case: "Stephen Engelberg, editor in chief of ProPublica, echoed Mr. Downie's mystification: 'I don't know what it means.' While they may not understand objectivity, the public certainly does. A Gallup/Knight Foundation survey released in 2020 found that 68% of Americans 'say they see too much bias in the reporting of news that is supposed to be objective as 'a major problem.'"[67]

The core value subscribed to by the *Gazette* is a "complete separation of news and opinion," Hussman wrote.

Journalism has always been an exercise in professional judgment—some good and some bad—based on perceptiveness, sageness, and wisdom that come with age and experience. Journalism has never demanded a perfect balance between two sides of an issue or circumstance. Some judgment has always been demanded in the search for relevance, validity, and veracity. But what is being done to reporting today is the extreme of those practices in a time when extremes seem to be the wrecking ball of our democracy. The abandonment of the principle of objectivity and its bizarre reasoning may be the demise of news and information delivery, as we have known it for a century. It has already had an impact on public opinion. According to the *Washington Examiner* in 2020, "A 2018 Gallup poll found that only 32 percent of Americans say the media 'is careful to separate fact from opinion' compared to 58 percent in 1984; 45 percent see a 'great deal of political bias in news coverage,' up from 25 percent in 1989."[68] This view is exacerbated by the practice of pack journalism, the practice of journalists to follow in their colleagues' footsteps, repeating what they read and hear in other news outlets, including social media, without confirming the accuracy of the content. If you read it or hear it from many outlets, it must be right. Right? Not necessarily.

Another consideration for journalists is defining who should be considered a professional journalist. The profession should insist on some degree of formal education or apprenticeship, experience, and professional recognition that gives news consumers confidence that what they are getting is not amateurish, unedited, or absent the disciplines of standards of professional conduct. Standards should be set without consideration of a journalist's personal views but with professional qualities that help ensure a trustworthy product.

THE CONSUMERS

We are in a world of "what ifs" as opposed to "what is." That makes media literacy an essential base of knowledge needed before clicking on a website, opening the daily newspaper, watching, or listening to radio and television broadcasts, and then using that information as a basis for exercising political responsibilities, especially voting.

We are in a world of "what ifs" as opposed to "what is."

Informed citizens will be open-minded and self-educate while exercising caution before drawing conclusions. So how do you get from here to there? First, media literacy should be taught in schools under high academic standards, given priority at home, and pursued as an adult.

Second, there are ways to become more media literate and many places to go for help, including sites like FactCheck.org.

Here are some of the keys to becoming more news literate.

LEARN WHAT YOU CAN ABOUT THE SOURCES OF NEWS

In the previous chapter, we reviewed some news sources in the electronic smorgasbord of 21st-century technology. Finding credible and trustworthy sources and then exercising the mental discipline to seek a balance in those sources can be difficult and frustrating. It is blissful to listen to what you want to hear and read that reinforces your beliefs. But that's not being media literate.

To be media literate, we start with trust—not just in sources we usually agree with. Trust is a key element in determining what those with whom you may disagree read, watch, and listen to. Unfortunately, for years, the public trust needle for news sources has gone the wrong way, dangerously close to the red zone on the barometer, where you'll find politicians, Wall Street bankers, lawyers, and used car salesmen.

In the 2021 Edelman Trust Barometer, most people said government leaders (57 percent), business leaders (56 percent), and journalists (59 percent) are purposely trying to mislead them by saying things they know are false.[69]

According to Edelman CEO Richard Edelman, "This is the era of information bankruptcy. We've been lied to by those in charge, and media sources are seen as politicized and biased."[70]

In a 2020 Gallup poll, only 9 percent of respondents said they trust mass media "a great deal" and 31 percent a "fair amount." A disturbing 33 percent said, "none at all."[71] The following year, Gallup found that "21 percent of respondents said they had 'a great deal' or 'quite a lot' of confidence in newspapers and only 16 percent . . . reported the same of television news," wrote Professor Jonathan Turley in June 2021.[72] "What is interesting is that media figures do not appear to care about the destruction of their profession. The public now ranks the United States as dead last in terms of trust in the media. Yet reporters continue to saw on the limb upon (which) they sit," he concluded.[73]

Most independents have not expressed confidence in the media since 2004 and for Republicans since 1998. However, a majority of Democrats do continue to have confidence in them.

A 2016 study by the American Press Institute in cooperation with the Associated Press concluded, "Public confidence in the press by many measures is low. In this survey, for instance, 6 percent of people say they have a great deal of confidence in the press, 52 percent say they have only some confidence, and 41 percent say they have hardly any confidence."[74]

Research commissioned by the Knight Foundation's Trust, Media and Democracy Initiative, conducted by Gallup in 2018, produced similar conclusions:

- "Most US adults, including more than nine in 10 Republicans, say they personally have lost trust in the news media in recent years. At the same time, 69% of those who have lost trust say that trust can be restored.
- Asked to describe in their own words why they trust or do not trust certain news organizations, Americans' responses largely center on matters of accuracy or bias. Relatively few mentioned a news organization's partisan or ideological leaning as a factor.
- Accuracy and bias also rank among the most important factors when respondents rate how important each of [the] 35 potential indicators of media trust are to them. Transparency also emerges as an important factor in the closed-ended ratings of factors that influence trust: 71% say a commitment to transparency is very important, and similar percentages say the same about an organization providing fact-checking resources and providing links to research and facts that back up its reporting."[75]

The difficult question is, how do you determine which sources are the most trustworthy? There is some research on the subject, but even the research can create false positives, especially in the new era of more ideologically focused news coverage.

Here are a few recommendations from veteran journalists and public affairs professionals:

1. Does the news source have a reputation for biased or slanted reporting or editing?
2. Is there an agenda underlying the coverage? Does it fit under the definition of *agenda* or *pack journalism* or engage in the constant repetition of stories that deliver the same message (pursuing the belief that if you hear it or read it often enough, it becomes true)?
3. Does the reporter have experience that would add credibility to what they are covering?
4. Does the reporter or correspondent express personal opinions without citing an expert(s)?
5. Who owns the news outlet? Does that owner (s) have other financial or ideological interests that may suggest conflicts of interest, potential conflicts, or other entanglements that may affect business and journalistic judgments? Is the news outlet transparent about its potential conflicts?
6. Does the reporter detail their information sources so you can judge their reliability, expertise, and self-interests?
7. Are stories covered by the outlet done so without a lot of hype and hyperbole, worst-case-scenario sensationalism, exaggeration of the importance of the subject, and theatrical drama that would draw them more hits, clicks, and eyeballs but fall short in factual content and clear-eyed perspective?
8. Is coverage usually balanced, exposing you to different points of view and perspectives and giving you the information and latitude needed to decide what conclusions to draw?

9. Does the information make sense? Is it logical, practical, and realistic? Are there plausible elements missing from the reporting? Are you left with questions about the story that the journalist did not answer—especially the who, what, when, where, and how?

10. Does the story include opinion or philosophical slant or spin?

One final thought retired Associated Press correspondent Dave Espo reminded us: "Pay very careful attention to the words that are used by a politician when he or she is denying a story. Saying explicitly that something isn't true is very definitive. As an alternative, do they avoid a flat denial? Do they attack the source, say the other side does the same thing, or say that whatever they were accused of isn't that important? These are all things that tend to confirm the story. They are hoping to divert your attention from the facts."

There are a lot of potholes on the road to finding trustworthy news that is fairly presented and of value in making judgments and forming opinions about policy matters. Some are wider and deeper than others. To be an informed citizen, you must learn to spot them. It is all that more important to go to news outlets that have a different ideological slant, such as MSNBC and Fox News. Often you can be assured that when looking at headlines or listening to newscasts coming from opposite points of view, the truth will reveal itself somewhere in the middle.

MORE WAYS TO COMBAT THE PROBLEM

Here are some areas deserving of those blinking caution lights. Let's begin with Factcheck.org, a project of the Annenberg Public Policy Center with a list of literacy tools:

1. Consider the source and be watchful for websites that look legit, such as abcnews.com, which is not the internet address for ABC News.

2. Read beyond the headline before passing the story along. They don't always tell the story.

3. Check the author. Unfortunately, they are often made up in the world of fake news.

4. Check the support. Bogus stories may cite official—or official-sounding—sources, but the source doesn't always warrant credibility, or what the source propounds isn't supported by other sources.

5. Politicians and others in the public eye make claims that are seemingly backed up by news stories. Still, a closer look at the circumstances says otherwise. Factcheck uses, for example, stories that Ford Motors moved a plant from Mexico to Ohio because of Trump's election, but the story about the move from August 2015 involved only the transfer of some assembly operations. It had been scheduled for a year. Trump, who was elected in November 2016, ignored the discrepancy in the dates and took credit for something he was not involved in.

6. Is this story a joke? Satirists and comedic websites also generate fake news to increase clicks, which increases revenue. So, too funny to be real? Ask that question.

7. Check your biases: Confirmation bias leads people to put more stock in information that confirms their beliefs and discounts information that doesn't.

8. Consult with the experts: FactCheck.org, for example.

Another tool is a reliable website that studies the political bias of news outlets, such as AllSides or Ad Fontes Media, both media literacy companies. They provide analyses of the bias exhibited in the news, sometimes separating the news section from the opinion section.

"Unbiased news doesn't exist. Everyone has a bias: everyday people and journalists. And that's OK. But it's not OK for news organizations to hide those biases," Julie Mastrine, AllSides marketing director, told Jake Sheridan of the Poynter Institute on Nov. 2, 2021. Readers can be manipulated if they do not know about the source's bias.

Both of those companies produce charts that categorize media outlets. AllSides has four categories along the political spectrum: Leftist, Leaning Left, Centrist, Leaning Right, and Right. For example, in the Left column, you will find CNN opinion, Mother Jones, MSNBC, HuffPost, and New York Times opinion. In the Leaning Left, ABC, CBS, CNN news, NBC, and The Washington Post.

In the Center, AP, Axios, Christian Science Monitor, Reuters, Real Clear Politics, and The Wall Street Journal news section. Leaning Right are Fox News news segments, New York Post, Newsmax news section, New York Post news, and Wall Street Journal opinion section. Farther Right are the American Spectator, Blaze, Breitbart, Daily Caller, National Review, and the Federalist.

Charts, of course, are not entirely accurate. The news may easily fall between these arbitrary categories along the political spectrum, and in some outlets that may lean one way or the other, there is a representation of alternative views. It is also important to remember that these companies do not make important judgments about news accuracy, reliability, or sourcing. However, these sources can be very helpful in enhancing the literacy of news and opinion consumers.

ANONYMOUS SOURCES: BE SKEPTICAL AND EVEN CYNICAL

There are generally three overarching ground rules for talking to the press:

1. On the record, where everything said is quotable;
2. On background or deep background, where what is said is quotable but not attributable, unless by agreement before publication; or
3. Off the record, where nothing said is quotable or attributable but can be used to educate the journalist further, lead to other information and sources, or confirm information.

There are, of course, variations of those rules.

The latter two serve as platforms for anonymous sources, which have become an overused and sometimes abused staple of modern reporting. For example, *The Washington Post* and the *New York Times,* during the Trump Presidency, seemed to compete on how many anonymous sources they could cite in a single article. Some counts went as high as twenty-five. It was a silly exercise intended to convince readers the story was well documented—silly because the number of sources cited doesn't necessarily testify to the quality or accuracy of the reporting, nor does the number of sources predictably increase credibility. Credibility is really the key to good journalism.

Usually, the most reliable sources are the principals, those directly involved in the incident or subject matter, or individuals with direct, first-person knowledge of a situation (they were present when the incident occurred). But even principals have agendas and may not have all the facts or information at their command.

Others less reliable are those who have indirect information (sometimes just hearsay), and still others who got information from their uncle's brother's sister's supervisor in the heating plant with access to air ducts, who overheard a person who may have been involved.

Readers and viewers are usually told little about those sources' credibility or degree of knowledge. Instead, the media use vague terms, such as "someone with knowledge of the situation," or "someone briefed on the incident," or "someone familiar with the subject," which could mean almost anybody. Nor do readers know what editors or producers know about the validity of those sources.

Anonymous sources may be individuals with an ax to grind or a grudge to reconcile; people with personal or political agendas; financial interests; or people schilling for another person or organization. There are many reasons why information from an anonymous source may be tainted or compromised. For the sake of an informed citizenry, we believe the media should use anonymous sources sparingly and carefully. Regrettably, that is not always the case. More to our regret, in the past, the use of those sources would depend upon the consumer's trust in the good judgment of reporters and editors who used them and have verified information through other sources, preferably those willing to speak on the record. That trust factor is not always there.

Journalists and their editors should know and be as transparent as possible about what prejudices their anonymous sources bring to a conversation and the degree of risk of trusting them. But in this age of aggressive adversarial journalism, in which the pursuit of an agenda and beating the lightning-fast competition, objective reporting may not be the highest priority.

Anonymous sources may be courageous whistleblowers or neutral observers with a range of knowledge of value to readers and listeners. Some stories, important to the public, could not be told without sources with a sense of civic responsibility who simply cannot or will not assume the risks of public exposure. Nor could they be told without reporters who practice standards of ethics and journalistic best practices designed to protect consumers from the provocateurs, schemers, and scoundrels wagging their tongues behind the curtain.

Recognizing the difference between reliable and unreliable sources is the viewer's or reader's responsibility. Unfortunately, such information consumers often don't get to judge for themselves in an atmosphere of significant proliferation of anonymously sourced stories.

The Watergate scandals of the early 1970s produced one of history's most dramatic examples of anonymously sourced reporting. News consumers went for more than thirty years not knowing the identity of Deep Throat, the moniker given to a primary source of information and collaboration for the famous Bob Woodward and Carl Bernstein investigation of the June 7, 1972, Watergate break-in, which ultimately led to the resignation of President Richard Nixon. The anonymous source, who turned out to be FBI Deputy Director W. Mark Felt, was the source of guessing games and wild speculation. He had an ax to grind (he had been bypassed for promotion), but his guidance to the *Post* proved reliable and lethal for Richard Nixon's Presidency.

The use and abuse of anonymous sources exploded during the Trump Presidency. As mentioned earlier in this chapter, one of the most controversial anonymous source scandals involved the alleged Trump conspiracy with the Russians to impact the 2016 presidential elections in his favor. The accusations were repeated so often and convincingly that most Americans believed them true, and many probably still do.

Realistically, the FBI was involved. Multiple FBI agents, including Director James Comey, were accused of being—and some were eventually exposed as—leakers and anonymous sources in the frenzied campaign to drive Trump from office. A special counsel, Robert S. Mueller, was appointed to investigate whether Russians infiltrated the election process and whether Trump colluded with them. Mueller and his team spent over $31 million of taxpayers' money and investigated the charges over eighteen months. But, unfortunately, his most important conclusion, that Russians did attempt to influence our elections, was regrettably cast aside.

"The end of the collusion illusion should also cause the media to do some soul searching about rushes to judgment," the *Wall Street Journal's* editorial pages editorialized after the report was made public.[76]

Bob Woodward, of Watergate fame, said he did not find collusion in his research. "Of course, I looked for it, looked for it hard."

Brit Hume, former ABC correspondent, and Fox analyst, called it "the worst journalistic debacle of my lifetime."

Famed *Nightline* founding anchor and longtime ABC correspondent Ted Koppel said in an interview with former journalist Marvin Kalb, "I'm terribly concerned that when you talk about the *New York Times* these days . . . about *The Washington Post* . . . we are talking about organizations that I believe had in fact decided as organizations that Donald J. Trump is bad for the United States."[77]

Former *Rolling Stone* writer Matt Taibbi wrote a damning article on media inaccuracies, bias, unverified information, agenda-driven reporting, and the refusal of media to acknowledge their mistakes. "Of course, there won't be such a reckoning (there never is)," he wrote. "We broke every written and unwritten rule in pursuit of this story, starting with the prohibition on reporting things we can't confirm."

"What is most insidious are those who did have access to classified intelligence and led Americans to believe that they had seen what we could not: actual evidence of Trump-Russia collusion," wrote *The Washington Post* columnist Mark Thiessen on March 28, 2019.[78]

Was he referring to former Intelligence Committee ranking Member Adam Schiff, D-CA, about whom a colleague, former Member Trey Gowdy of South Carolina, said [Schiff], "leaks like a screen door on a submarine". Maybe it was former CIA Director John Brennan, who promoted the collusion narrative and called Trump a traitor (Brennan later recanted). It could have been Comey and other former FBI officials, all of whom may well have been regular anonymous sources.

Justice Department Special Counsel John Durham, in May 2023, added to the consternation and accused the FBI of overreacting to available information about the alleged Trump-Russia collusion. He called FBI actions "seriously flawed" and lacking "rigor, objectivity and professionalism."[79]

With all these sources throwing information, or misinformation, at the public, what is a thinking citizen to do?

The news literacy lesson is to assume there is more to what an anonymous source says than meets the eye or the ears.

FAKE NEWS

Former President Trump popularized the term "fake news" as a description of news stories and commentary that he found to be inaccurate, not to his liking, misleading, or simply false. In a bit of irony, he also popularized the use of fake news.

The term fake news, however, can be traced back hundreds of years to sixteenth-century England as *false news.* In the US, it appears to have emerged in 1805 in newspapers in Richmond, Virginia, and fifty years later in Cincinnati.

Fake news is the deliberate fabrication of information or allegations generally disseminated as news. Here are some formal definitions/explanations:

Cambridge Dictionary: "False stories that appear to be news, spread on the Internet or using other media, usually created to influence political views or as a joke."

Collins (Harper Collins) Dictionary: "False, often sensational, information disseminated under the guise of news reporting."

Merriam-Webster Dictionary: "The reason *fake news* is unlikely to be entered in our dictionary anytime soon is that it is a self-explanatory compound noun—a combination of two distinct words, both well known, which when used in combination yield an easily understood meaning. *Fake news* is, quite simply, *news* ('material reported in a newspaper or news periodical or on a newscast') that is *fake* ('false, counterfeit')."

Famed author Michael Crichton saw it coming in a September 15, 2003, speech before the Commonwealth Club in San Francisco, he offered this warning:

> *The greatest challenge facing mankind is the challenge of distinguishing reality from fantasy, truth from propaganda. Perceiving the truth has always been a challenge to mankind, but in the information age (or as I think of it, the disinformation age), it takes on special urgency and important ... Every one of us has a sense of the world, and we all know that this sense is in part given to us by what other people and society tell us; in part generated by our emotional state, which project outward; and in part by our genuine perceptions of reality. In short, our struggle to determine what is true is the struggle to decide which of our perceptions are genuine and which are false because they are handed down, or sold to us, or generated by our own hopes and fears.*

The founder of the accuracy website Snopes, David Mikkelson, advised against the Trump approach in 2016. "The fictions and fabrications that comprise fake news are but a subset of the larger *bad news* phenomenon, which also encompasses many forms of shoddy, un-researched, error-filled, and deliberately misleading reporting that do a disservice to everyone," he wrote on Snopes.com.[80]

A serious escalation of fake news came with the growing activism of Trump's political following. It proved a valuable tool in expanding and hardening Trump's support and cementing in peoples' minds the false notion that the 2020 election was stolen in several states.

Fake news about evolving news stories is a significant challenge. But what happens when the country faces an evolving, life-threatening pandemic and essential information is flooded with fake news? Conspiracy theories, false information, and lies on social media from the full scope of the political spectrum continue to damage the accurate and balanced dissemination of information about COVID-19 vaccinations, tests, treatments, its prevalence in various states, close-downs, inoculation advice for different age groups, etc. So, again, it is left to news consumers to exercise their judgment and cautionary skepticism regarding what they read, hear, and see.

Also, warranting those blinking caution lights are:

- Inaccurate information;
- Unsubstantiated information;
- Misrepresented or exaggerated facts and information;
- Agenda-driven (adversarial or advocacy) reporting; and,
- Unreported news.

The public questioned much of what they were told about COVID-19 by the media, health experts, government, and even their neighbors. As a result, they did not have the contextual information needed to decide how to react, mask, inoculate, keep children home, stay away from work, or not.

It is too early to see in-depth studies on the impact of fact and fiction on the coronavirus. Still, one of the first massive studies of fake news, by the Massachusetts Institute of Technology, completed in early 2018 by a research team headed by data scientist Soroush Vosoughi and reported on in *The Atlantic* by Robinson Meyer in March of that year, said:

"It seems to be pretty clear that false information outperforms true information," the researchers concluded. "And that is not just because of bots (robots). It might have something to do with human nature." The MIT study of 126,000 stories over ten years found that "truth simply cannot compete with hoax and rumor. By every common metric, falsehood consistently dominates the truth on Twitter (X). . . Fake news and false rumors reach more people, penetrate deeper into the social network, and spread much faster than accurate stories," according to the research. "A false story reaches 1,500 people six times quicker, on average than a true story does. And while false stories outperform the truth on every subject . . . fake news about politics regularly does best."

The researchers said while the study focused on X (Twitter), the results apply to other platforms, such as Facebook, YouTube, and other major social networks.

The Washington Times reported in June 2019 that in a separate survey by international French market research firm Ipsos, conducted in twenty-seven nations, "big majorities are encountering news reports that appear legitimate but are often skewed with agenda, disinformation, misinformation or sensationalism."[81]

The *Wall Street Journal* assembled a committee to help reporters navigate fake content, according to Lucinda Southern, writing for DIGIDAY, focusing on "deep fakes," falsehoods generated by artificial intelligence.

Finally, the seriousness was magnified by a PEW Research study reported by Jessica Campisi in *The Hill* newspaper in June 2019: "In a survey of more than 6,000 Americans, 68 percent said made-up news and information affects their confidence in government institutions. . . . Fifty-four percent said they think that fake news has a big impact on Americans' confidence in each other, while 51 percent cited an effect on political leaders' ability to get things done." Many said they see it as a bigger problem than "racism, terrorism or climate change."

Examples of fake news are easy to find. Readers will remember from the Introduction the outlandish falsehoods spread about Congress and its Members: Members of Congress don't pay Social Security and are entitled to full retirement benefits equal to their full salaries after one term in Congress. Or another widely circulated claim: In just one year, thirty-six Members were accused of spousal abuse; eighty-four were arrested for drunk driving, and seventy-one could not get a credit card because of bad debts. None of the allegations was true or even close to factual. Yet they circulated as authoritative on the web for years.

Following the attempts to prevent Congress from ratifying the Electoral College results of the 2020 election, right-wing outlets quickly suggested the invasion of the Capitol was nothing more than a peaceful tour of the building, reinforced by strong Trump supporters in Congress. At the other end of the information spectrum, left-leaning outlets claimed that pro-Trump Members of Congress conducted tours of the Capitol for the rioters just days before they invaded the place.

AND THEN THERE IS JUST BAD JOURNALISM

There is a thin line between airing or publishing a knowingly false story and airing a story from an unreliable source or the internet without verifying the facts.

Both were evident in the Dan Rather incident on CBS, discussed in the previous chapter. He used forged documents, known to be phony by his producer, to accuse President George W. Bush of dodging service in Vietnam.

In another case, bad journalism will not be denied an explosive headline. Around 7 p.m. on June 19, 2021, the Stonewall Pride Parade was just getting underway in Wilton Manors, Florida, when a white pickup truck struck and killed one man and injured another.

Ft. Lauderdale Mayor Dean Trantalis didn't hesitate to place blame. He told local media, "This is a terrorist attack against the LGBT community.

This is exactly what it is. Hardly an accident. It was deliberate. It was pre-meditated, and it was targeted against a specific person (Congresswoman Debbie Wasserman Schultz, who was participating in the parade). Luckily," he bloviated, "they missed that person, but unfortunately, they hit two other people."

Before reporting his words, the mayor and the media should have consulted with Justin Knight, the president of the city's Gay Men's Chorus, who said the driver of the pickup was a chorus member waiting to participate in the parade. "Our thoughts and prayers are with those affected by the tragic accident," he said through a spokesman. "Our fellow Chorus members were those injured, and the driver was also a part of the Chorus family."

SPIN: IT'S A DIZZYING GAME THAT THROWS YOU OFF BALANCE

Another element of the misinformation phenomenon is the contributions of official government agencies, departments, and their public relations and communications professionals. It's called spin, shaping the message to suit your needs.

The government should produce reliable and accurate information essential to an educated public, a source you should be able to count on. But government public relations specialists and the estimated $400 million marketing machines inside government agencies, to no one's surprise, also produce slanted, sometimes misleading, and promotional materials ranging from simple press releases to elaborate Hollywood-style films. Moreover, you can be confident their product is one-sided, specifically designed to persuade rather than inform.

However, voters and elected officials should call them to task when an official entity distributes literature that crosses the border between bias and spin. It is a dangerous practice. *The Washington Post's* Paul Farhi wrote about it in November 2018, when the White House distributed a film of an incident in which CNN correspondent Acosta, a virulent Trump antagonist, was shown to be rebuffing an effort by a White House press office aide's attempt to take a microphone out of his hand. But the video "was altered to exaggerate the aggressiveness of Acosta's actions," Farhi wrote. "If this is the case, the video may belong in a category rarely employed by democratic governments: visual propaganda."[82] That may be a stretch. Visual propaganda is not rare, but the seriousness of tape doctoring or distorting is.

MEDIA ARE BUSINESSES

Scott Pelley, the dethroned anchor of CBS Evening News, in an interview with one of the more biased media critics on the air, Brian Stelter, formerly of CNN, called journalists public servants. Presumably, Pelley was using the term in the same vein as the people who serve on library boards, city councils, police officers, firefighters, legislators, mayors, or governors.

The news media are, like government, schools, organized religion, and charities, an institution vital to the framework of our system of governance. However, unlike those who serve in government, journalists are business professionals, and more to the point, the outlets for which they work are first businesses, not public servants. It is an important distinction and reflects a change from the public's long understanding of the media's role. Even the romantic image of the struggling little-town newspaper owner/writer/publisher was reinforced in the early days of television. Moreover, law and custom established "news" as a public service required as a condition for obtaining broadcast spectrum, so the media perpetuated that image.

Jerry tells the story of hosting a briefing by a prominent TV news anchor for a large group of congressional wives. The anchor was asked why a story did not show up in the broadcast. The spouses were complaining about bad-news versus good-news stories. After several failed attempts to dance around the question, the frustrated anchor finally told them they didn't get it; they are not a charity or public service; they are a business, and they broadcast what will keep eyes glued to the TV long enough for viewers to see to the commercials. That answer did not go over well, but it was the truth. Their product is advertising first, interrupted by newsreaders, and talking heads bloviating about events in the news, which meets their public service obligation.

News media are profit-oriented, profit-motivated, competitive enterprises, sometimes lost in the hierarchy of bigger businesses and conglomerates, which make many decisions in the interests of shareholders, audiences, and subscribers but not necessarily in the interest of spreading public information about politics and policy.

Good examples of the conflicts between making money and public service are news outlets' agreements to secure exclusive coverage of events, interviews, and many other marketable products, such as books.

Media literacy means keeping in mind the sometimes conflicting influences that drive what media executives do, how they think, how they respond to stimuli, and when their interests supersede yours.

TALKING HEADS AND EXPERT COMMENTATORS

Be skeptical about the so-called experts who appear on television or radio shows and are frequently quoted in newspapers and magazines. Make sure their credentials qualify them to comment on current events. Keep a skeptical eye on their affiliations and past experiences. Does their background suggest a strong bias or conflict of interest? Few experts appear in print or broadcast media without personal and professional agendas, which may cloud their judgments. Some get paid for their presentation expertise; that means what they say and how they say it could be filtered through the lens of good ole' capitalistic self-interest. That proved troublesome when officials of the World Health Organization (WHO) got constant coverage on their pro-Chinese (it wasn't our fault) version of the origins of the COVID-19 virus. Later, it was found they had financial relationships with the Chinese government and the laboratory suspected of being the source of the virus. The conflicts of interest in the lab's benefactors and the source of the virus have remained controversial.

MEDIA IN DENIAL

Amplifying the problems discussed thus far is the stubborn failure of too many in the media to admit there is a problem that deserves attention and maybe ultimately reform. To wit, CNN's Jake Tapper, who said the CNN coverage of the Russian collusion controversy was mistake-free, or the former Washington Post columnist Margaret Sullivan, who was dismissive of the criticism and insistent there is every reason for journalists to be proud of their coverage. There are many more. Executive editors of the New York Times and The Washington Post have insisted journalism hasn't changed its coverage model.

CLOSING THOUGHTS

Millions of people who don't live, eat, and dream politics or make their living in adjunct fields, like lobbying or the news and entertainment industries, or academics—and even many that do—face considerable challenges in their attempt to keep abreast of current events and monitor the actions of those elected to serve the public in the halls of Congress.

This challenge is especially true in times of great political divisions, high levels of anxiety and public distrust, a disintegration of civic institutions, and few trustworthy news and information sources. These conditions represent high seas for the small boats trying to keep informed voters afloat. The boat analogy is apropos because the breadth and depth of American politics are not a river or a lake; they comprise an ocean.

Media literacy is one way to calm the waters and ensure you are sailing in the right direction. The good news is literacy is mostly good old-fashioned common sense, reason, and rationality sans emotion. We all have it.

Special interests know how and when to lobby.

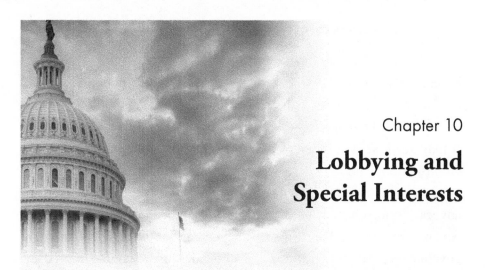

Chapter 10

Lobbying and Special Interests

T here are few political terms more derogatory than, dare we say it in front of the children, special interests.

Even the words themselves—*special* and *interests*—sound undemocratic.

Who are these evil interests? And what makes them so special?

Loosely defined, special interests are those individuals and organizations that advocate for one or more issues of concern to them. They can be as large as a corporate giant like General Electric, which has interests in trade, energy, taxes, transportation, environment, education, and health care, or they can be a single-issue non-profit organization like the Alzheimer's Association, which focuses on private and public funding for research and treatment, insurance coverage, a resource for caregivers and experts on the economics of the condition. Or they can be a labor union with concerns about several issues, such as pension contribution laws and rules that govern organizations in the workplace.

Did you know, for instance, that the American Association of Retired Persons (AARP), representing seniors (if fifty can be called *senior or retired*), is one of the largest associations and tops Fortune magazine's list of the most influential special interests in Washington, DC? Few people do.

The Boy Scouts of America is a special interest. So are barbers, bakers, basketball players, beauticians, bingo players, buglers, bureaucrats, bricklayers, bar owners, caterers, churchgoers, circus performers, car dealers, cab drivers, cooks, can manufacturers, cable operators, and chaplains—and that doesn't even get us through the Cs. It may surprise you they are all represented in Washington, and most employ lobbyists.

The Founding Fathers could not have envisioned the sophistication that advocacy efforts have attained. Still, they codified the practice in the First Amendment of the Bill of Rights, which guarantees the right to petition the government to redress grievances. The Founders didn't go into much detail about how such redress could be sought, but they made it clear that it was a right they wanted to be protected.

In a sense, every one of us is a special interest.

If you own a car or a refrigerator, travel on an airline, watch television, go to church, get sick, hunt, invest in a mutual fund, or have a hard time breathing, you are a special interest, and there are probably associations and organizations representing you at both the state and the national level.

The fact is a $4.7 trillion government, with thousands of programs and hundreds of thousands of rules and regulations, affects just about everyone. At one time or another, we all need relief or assistance from the federal government or more than 87,000 state and local government agencies, not to mention sundry other jurisdictions, including counties, regional transportation authorities, cities, towns, townships, sanitary districts, school districts, and water districts.

Generally speaking, *special interests* do not refer to concerns so much as to the groups representing them; in fact, the phrase typically is shorthand for *special interest groups*. They're also called single-interest, public-interest, advocacy, lobbying, and even pressure groups. The important reason they exist is to influence political decisions and public policy.

THE GOOD, THE BAD, AND THE UGLY

Special interest groups despite their overriding negatives, can be a necessary component in a pluralist democratic republic. (As mentioned previously, the term defines everything and everybody from churches, Girl Scouts, relators, and environmentalists to the chamber of commerce and unions that are organized to influence decision-makers at all levels of government). They provide lawmakers and executive agencies with information they wouldn't get otherwise. They also provide assessments on the political, economic, social, and environmental impact that legislation or policies are likely to have. For example, in the years Mike lobbied for corporations, charitable organizations, non-profit groups, and sometimes even individuals, he provided information to policymakers that they would not have gotten elsewhere.

Mega tax bills often have many provisions with which representatives or senators would not be aware, such as international trade provisions that would harm domestic production, or tax breaks that would favor one industry or company over another and create a competitive advantage.

Pension legislation, or the lack of it, would often threaten the retirement benefits of employees, or bail out one pension plan and not another, or create financial burdens for an industry to bail out another industry's bankrupt pension plan.

A major infrastructure bill would create a stampede of lobbyists who wanted to convince appropriators that their industry had higher priorities than others or why their sector had a more legitimate claim to funding. The examples are endless. In an age of mega-bills, lumping many together, representatives and senators and their staff members can't possibly be aware of all the provisions and the short and long-term unintended consequences of each.

Special interests in Washington or your state capital are not monolithic; they are not one entity or structure. The strongest adversaries of special interests are often not government agencies or the media but other special interests. Businesses fight labor; the coal industry fights nuclear and renewable fuels companies; nurses squabble with doctors; and big-government liberals fight limited-government conservatives. Pro-abortion advocates battle pro-lifers. Gun enthusiasts fight gun controllers. For each special interest advocating one position, other special interests advocate different or opposite positions. They often cancel each other out and force the process toward compromise or gridlock.

Special interests positively influence a democratic republic as massive as ours. But they can also be a destructive and oppressive negative influence. They deprive or override average citizens of their influence and access using special interest money and access, both to policymakers and by motivating large bodies of constituents that they employ or represent.

There is, and has been for some time, great concern and agitation over their involvement in the political process, raising fundamental questions about money in politics, about the basic injustice of some special interests being more powerful and influential than others, and about access to government that average citizens don't have. They are portrayed as governance's villains, creatures who rule in the Washington "swamp."

Before delving into some of those traits, however, let's pop the hood and look more closely at the mechanics of these engines of influence.

THE MAIN PLAYERS

There are six kinds of special interest groups, all with similarities with their counterparts:

1. Corporate

Thousands of companies and corporations of all varieties maintain a presence in the nation's capital, whether through a Washington office with full-time employees or through a contractual relationship with one or more law firms, lobbying firms, or trade associations. Private companies, ranging from the newer commercial giants like Amazon and Apple to classic American industries such Burlington Northern and Weyerhaeuser, find being in Washington necessary to protect their interests or advance public policies that are good for their stockholders, customers, and employees. Most present their cases before the legislative and executive branches and regulatory and quasi-governmental agencies.

While journalists often rail against special interests with hyperbolic and sometimes hypocritical indignation, the companies for which they work—*The Washington Post*, the *Wall Street Journal*, Sinclair, Gannett, *Chicago Tribune*, ABC, NBC, CBS, CNN, and Fox—are all represented by Washington lobbyists and trade associations (or both), advocating on their behalf over everything from content piracy to taxes, postal rates, protection of sources, privacy, public funding, and any issues that can have an impact on their ability to hire people or produce a product and make a profit.

2. Associations, Organizations, and Labor Unions

These fall into two categories defined by their membership or issues. Some, such as the National Association of Manufacturers, the Chamber of Commerce, the American Medical Association, the National Federation of Independent Businesses, the AFL-CIO, and the United Auto Workers, all represent professions, occupations, industries, and individual companies/corporations that have a stake in government actions. Their membership defines their priorities.

Others, such as Common Cause, Citizens for Responsive Politics, the American Heart Association, and the National Rifle Association, represent and specialize in more clearly defined causes or issues. They are self-perpetuating movements that rely on individual donors' loyalty and commitment to fund their efforts.

In most cases, larger associations do not exist for the sole purpose of lobbying. For example, while an association lobbies at the federal, state, and local levels, it may also conduct research, offer membership education programs, gather public opinion research, and host conventions and conferences where members can exchange information.

Associations such as the National Retail Federation or the National Association of Realtors provide a means for local "mom and pop" businesses to band together and raise a collective voice as loud as big corporations. They also provide their members and the public with valuable information on economic trends, the impact of international trade, analysis of trends in their businesses, best practices, training, and how to deal with new laws and regulations.

Some special interests attempt to wrap themselves in the cloak of altruism by contending they're *public interest groups*. It's a branding strategy aimed at convincing outsiders their objectives are more honorable—and, by extension, the objectives of anyone who disagrees with them are not. For example, the motives of an organization whose mission is campaign finance reform are no purer than those of the Realtors. They both advocate their interests based on their interpretation of the public interest. People who run those organizations respond to the demands of those who pay their salaries.

The so-called public interest groups do not like to be called "special interests." They prefer to think of their interests as somehow different. But they lobby Congress and the Executive branch as aggressively as any other special interest. They are particularly effective at influencing public opinion through the media; they have media access that few others do, sometimes making up for what they may lack in financial resources.

3. Single-Issue Organizations

These are not-for-profits in terms of membership, financial support, and tax status, in some cases. They distinguish themselves by representing just one issue or a closely-knit set of related issues. While a labor union may have positions on various topics, including trade, minimum wage, health care, and workplace conditions, the single-issue organization focuses all its energy on one, like abortion, gun ownership, a specific form of tax reform, or saving the whales.

Single-issue organizations may have a shorter lifespan than others. When their issue has been resolved or relegated to a lower priority by the organization's backers, they may disband or gravitate to another similar issue. One classic example of this phenomenon is the March of Dimes, which was so successful in helping to wipe out polio—its original purpose—that it shifted focus to birth-related issues affecting mothers and babies.

4. Lobbying Companies, Multiple Advocacy, or Consultant Organizations

Many organizations and associations have full-time employees representing their interests in the state capitals, Washington, DC, and even in some foreign countries. However, they also hire additional professional advocates or lobbyists to represent them. These professional advocates might be associated with law firms, public affairs firms specializing in government and public relations, large or small lobbying firms, or independent contractors.

Over 2,000 firms in Washington, DC, lobby on behalf of their clients for a variety of reasons: The firm may have extraordinary expertise or an area of specialty—many firms employ former Members of Congress and committee staff with unique knowledge about pertinent issues and programs and valuable access to committee staff and Members—or the client may find that hiring the lobbying firm is less expensive and faster to get started on its behalf than creating an in-house team.

Some professional advocates have long-term contracts. In other cases, relationships are brief and involve a single, clearly defined task. If, for example, railroads find their livelihood threatened by negative publicity surrounding a rail accident that could lead to punitive action in Congress, they may need the help of outside pros, such as crisis communications experts and lobbyists, to improve their image, fight other special interests that advocate for greater rail safety, and ultimately adverse legislation.

5. Coalitions

Corporations, associations, foundations, and single-interest lobbies occasionally form coalitions to advocate an issue or action in their common interest. Coalitions are usually temporarily financed and structured to meet

a specific mission or common goal. Typically, a coalition will hire independent staff and solicit what might be referred to as *dues,* even though contributions are based on what each Member can afford or is willing to devote
to the effort. An executive director generally manages them and answers to
a board of directors or advisors, usually composed of the biggest contributors. Coalitions sometimes operate out of the office of a consultant, lobbying firm, public relations firm, or law firm hired to handle the campaign.

6. Governments

The world of special interests is also populated by state governments,
public or private colleges, universities, regional governing authorities,
cities, counties, townships, associations of governors and attorneys general, and other bodies of elected officials or units of government. Governments also employ lobbyists and hire outside public affairs specialists. In
addition, there are foreign governments represented in Washington—most
of which also depend on paid lobbyists to speak on their behalf. Not to be
left out, the federal government itself employs a vast legion of lobbyists in
every major agency. They don't call themselves lobbyists, of course. They
are "legislative liaisons." The law says they are not supposed to lobby Congress but just answer questions and provide information. But that law is,
well, a joke easily circumvented.

BY THE NUMBERS

According to opensecrets.org and the Center for Responsive Politics, there
were about 11,000 registered lobbyists in Washington, DC, in 2019, down
from 11,500 in 2018. Open Secrets estimated there were 12,600 registered
lobbyists in 2022.[83] Those registered lobbyists are supported by an equal
number of staff members and supervisors who do not have to officially
register with the Executive and Legislative branches of the government.

There is also a much larger community of policy professionals, lawyers, grassroots operatives, public relations professionals, and senior business executives who are also not registered but are integral to advocacy. In

addition, there are more than 2,000 corporations, over 8,000 non-profit and trade associations, and thousands of governments or quasi-governmental agencies that have Washington representation.

All these special interests realize that direct pressure may not be, and often is not, enough to solve their problems. They know there is strength in numbers and power in public opinion. That's why many, particularly when in trouble, seek help. They invest heavily in indirect advocacy—grassroots (general population) or grasstops (people with influence in a community) mobilization, or both; survey research; and public relations. All three forms of advocacy have evolved in recent years into highly sophisticated means of influencing public opinion and public policy.

An effective grassroots operation can educate thousands of people with a few clicks on a keyboard and motivate them to write, email, tweet (now post), Skype, Zoom, or call their representative and senators; write letters to the editor of the local newspaper; dial into radio call-in shows; blog; participate in town-hall meetings or tele-town halls; and engage in other activities designed to influence the actions of their elected officials and staffs.

The term *grasstop* describes campaigns that aim to educate and motivate public officials, opinion leaders, and prominent local citizens. The goal is for these individuals to call and pressure Congress to take a particular action and begin word-of-mouth advocacy that gets those in their circle of influence involved in the campaign.

Intensive public relations campaigns are critical too. They can include paid and unpaid advertising, the creation of websites, and pitches to journalists to encourage coverage of pertinent issues and the development of a positive brand for an individual, an organization, or an issue. In support of these initiatives, opinion polling and survey research provide data and themes for their messages.

An individual needing help with a problem usually can get it from an elected official. But an individual's efforts rarely change laws or keep laws from being enacted. This task takes many individuals working together, and even then, it is difficult to make major changes in public policy.

A coordinated lobbying campaign can produce results. No elected official has the time, staff, or mental capacity to learn, retain, and understand all the intricacies of hundreds of issues that influence the lives of constituents and, more broadly, the country. However, advocates with knowledge of and experience with the myriad issues policymakers face can be a valuable source of information and insight if the policymaker is thoughtful enough to manage and evaluate the information available and verify the worth of the sources.

As noted earlier, the Founding Fathers established the right to petition the government in the First Amendment. They made it clear that it was a citizen's right they wanted to be protected.

In the days before the volume became unmanageable, citizens were encouraged to submit written petitions directly to Congress, where the House set aside time to address them. Benjamin Franklin led one of the first petition drives and advocated the abolition of slavery. It was one of our new government's first real grassroots/grasstops lobbying efforts.

Consider the disputes between Alexander Hamilton and James Madison that led to the formation of the Federalist and Republican parties.

Early in the life of the Republic, the Continental Congress was so broke throughout the Revolutionary War that it paid General George Washington's Continental Army with bonds, essentially IOUs. Believing the government would never redeem the bonds, most soldiers sold them to speculators at a fraction of their face value. These speculators held onto the bonds until 1787, when they began lobbying the new federal government for payment in full. They essentially forced open the decision-making process.

Hamilton favored paying the face value to whoever held the bonds. Still, Madison objected because his State of Virginia had gone into debt by redeeming bonds paid to soldiers from Virginia. He argued veterans deserved to be repaid and should receive half the value of any redeemed bonds. Hamilton won out when, at a private dinner arranged by Thomas Jefferson, Madison dropped his demands in exchange for a commitment on the part of the federal government to pay off Virginia's debt and build the new Capital city on the banks of the Potomac River.

Lobbying on a more broadly organized level eventually became a fixture in the governing process, but advocacy has always been integral to political decision-making. You probably won't be surprised to learn that with increased lobbying—and abuses—the calls for regulations and restrictions became commonplace. Major efforts to regulate lobbying at the federal level didn't occur until 1876, when a resolution approved by the House required lobbyists to register with the clerk of the House.

Where there is money, power, and politics, there is abuse, exploitation, and greed. Advocacy has never been immune. It is subject to abuse, sometimes on a grand scale. The excesses of the business monopolists peaked during what Mark Twain called "the Gilded Age" in America, from the post-Civil War Reconstruction to the turn of the century.

> Where there is money, power, and politics, there is abuse, exploitation, and greed.

The term *Gilded Age* described an economic and political system in which conditions looked glittery on the surface but were badly corrupted and corrosive underneath, undermining the foundations of our system of government.

Members of Congress and other public officials were wined and dined, bullied, and bribed by the great barons of rail, steel, and oil. Burton W. Folsom, in his work, *Entrepreneurs vs. the State*, painted a vivid picture:

> *In 1866 Thomas Durant wined and dined 'prominent citizens' (including senators, an ambassador, and government bureaucrats) along a completed section of the railroad. He hired an orchestra, a caterer, six cooks, a magician (to pull subsidies out of a hat?), and a photographer. For those with ecumenical palates, he served Chinese duck and Roman goose; the more adventurous were offered*

roast ox and antelope. All could have expensive wine and, for des-
sert, strawberries, peaches, and cherries. After dinner some of the
men hunted buffalo from their coaches. Durant hoped that all would
go back to Washington inclined to repay the UP (Union Pacific) for
its hospitality.[84]

The scandals of the time came to a head when the period's muckraking journalists reported that Credit Mobilier stock was being handed out freely on the Floor of the House of Representatives, and Members of Congress were being given special deals on stock and land purchases. Those revelations eventually led to a period of profound reform, including the enactment of the Civil Service Act, the Interstate Commerce Act, the Sherman Anti-Trust Act, and lobby registration.

With each new scandal, from Teapot Dome to Abscam to Jack Abramoff, have come calls for greater regulation of the relationship between legislators and lobbyists.

The Jack Abramoff scandal was one of the most dramatic in history. In 2004, Abramoff, a lawyer/lobbyist who indulged in fancy clothes and expensive cigars but maintained the reputation of a family man, committed to church and community, pleaded guilty to a series of corruption charges stemming in part from his representation of Indian tributes in four states and a series of business deals that went sour over a decade of flamboyant living and influence peddling. He was sentenced to forty-eight months in prison. Ultimately, twenty-four of his associates were convicted of corruption and bribery, including several Members of Congress and congressional staff.

As a result, Congress placed another new set of restrictions on the activities of lobbyists. These new rules dramatically increased disclosure requirements and the paperwork they must maintain and file. In addition, the new laws imposed harsh criminal sentences and fines for violations of the rules and imposed new restrictions on Members and staff in their interaction with lobbyists.

The Congress considered but rejected provisions that would have restricted the ability of Members of Congress to solicit campaign contributions from lobbyists, given yet unresolved constitutional issues over the extent to which campaign contributions constitute a form of freedom of speech.

What was enacted turned out to be a confusing labyrinth of rules and regulations that, on the one hand, prohibit a lobbyist from buying a Member lunch so they can talk about the merits of legislative issues. But those rules permit that same lobbyist to buy that same Member the same lunch *if* the lunch is part of a campaign fundraising event to which lobbyists and other participants deliver personal or Political Action Committee (PAC) checks for anywhere from $250 to $1,000, or more. Each source's campaign contributions may not exceed the maximum for that election cycle, now $2,800.

PETITION THE GOVERNMENT FOR REDRESS

The absurdity of some new rules speaks volumes about the conflicting nature of freedoms we cherish to speak and act freely and to exercise a constitutional right to influence our government versus the real and perceived corruptive nature of money in politics and the unfair advantage of the in-crowd. It also speaks to the contradictions inherent in politicians restricting their ability to raise money essential to election and re-election.

Every citizen, whether individually or through a union or association or an employer, has the right to petition the government to influence what goes on in Washington. Naturally, that will inevitably involve the, sometimes titanic, competition and conflict between and among special interests.

The practice of professional lobbying needs improvement. The lobbying associations could do much more to establish and enforce codes of conduct. They do exist, by the way. More research is needed on the influence of campaign contributions on the governmental process and alternatives to that system, including more constitutionally compatible limits on contributions and transparency, as well as the kind of organizations that can funnel large amounts of money into politics with little oversight or public disclosure of the sources of such funds.

Business Insider's Joe Perticone reviewed spending on lobbying tracked by OpenSecrets.org and found that the third largest spender in the 2018 cycle was the Open Society Policy Center, a group formed and funded by liberal activist George Soros. The Center spent $31.5 million influencing public policy. In 2022, the biggest spenders among specific organizations were the National Association of Realtors at $84 million, followed by the US Chamber of Commerce at $81 million. Among the other big spenders were multiple organizations in the pharmaceutical and health industries at $380 million and the insurance industry, which spent $158 million in 2022, according to statista.com.[85]

It should be remembered there are variations and subtext to the world of special interests and the amount of money spent and people involved. More precise distinctions are needed, especially regarding who is and who isn't a lobbyist. Today, the distinctions are highly misleading and, in some cases, a charade.

Public servants, the politicians who serve you, also need a more well-defined code of conduct in dealing with special interests without jeopardizing the Members' ability to meet their responsibilities to you and the country and without diminishing the ability of legitimate advocates to advocate change in government.

More importantly, the public needs to be better educated and have better access to educational tools that open the enormous complexities of public policy issues and reach a consensus on them in a politically charged environment. There is no shortage of information about issues of all kinds; social media and communications media are full of it, but the problem is the lack of tools to turn information into knowledge.

The following is a simplified hypothetical scenario that we hope illustrates the complexity of the process and the risks of rushing to judgment about the merits of issues. Unfortunately, this scene is not uncommon in Members' congressional and committee offices.

A congressional staffer newly employed by a Member of Congress is visited out of the blue by a college classmate the staffer hasn't seen in years. The classmate says he stopped by to welcome the staffer to Washington and life on Capitol Hill.

After briefing one another on what's been going on in their lives since the last time they shared a pitcher of beer, the visitor tells his old friend he's a lobbyist for the XYZ Communications and Technology Corporation.

More out of politeness than interest, the staffer asks what issues he focuses on.

"Net neutrality," the visitor replies.

"Not familiar with it," the staffer says.

"It's pretty significant," he says and manages not to sound critical of his friend's ignorance, not entirely sure the staffer really knows little about the issue. Net neutrality, a concept adopted by the Obama Administration, was repealed by the Federal Communications Commission in 2017. However, the DC Circuit Court upheld the core of the repeal in 2019, leaving it up to Congress or the states acting independently to reinstate, modify, or permanently dislodge net neutrality.

With a little prodding, the visitor does what a good lobbyist should *not* do: He proceeds with a one-sided, subjective explanation of the issue, claiming that net neutrality's reinstatement would severely hamstring the internet's usefulness, threaten to produce unfortunate precedents that will critically limit the nation's competitive telecommunications edge, discourage investment, deny providers the ability to offer services that distinguish them from one another and give other communication providers an unfair advantage.

Sounds downright un-American.

Exactly the kind of issue the Congressman is interested in.

The new legislative aide leans toward the lobbyist's point of view but declines the lobbyist's pitch to get the Congressman to commit to the issue. Instead, the staffer promises to look into the issue.

Wise decision. The staffer then does what a good legislative aide ought to do—contact the offices of Members who know a lot about the policy and the politics of the policy. Then they talk to constituents who may have an interest in or knowledge of the issue and then talk with other private entities with a different viewpoint than XYZ Communications.

Following a closer look at net neutrality, the staffer discovers it remains among Congress's most contentious issues. Opposing sides are well entrenched, and it is controversial back home. The staffer quickly learns that net neutrality is a riddle wrapped in a mystery inside an enigma, to paraphrase Churchill's description of Russia.

Content providers argue that allowing DSL (digital subscriber line) providers to charge for access would be tantamount to providing them with near-monopolistic authority over the internet. By duplicating the content of providers and making it free to their customers while charging the providers for delivering it, DSLs could drive the competition out of the market. Software manufacturers argue that charges for DSL access would discourage innovation and development. And this scratches the surface of the complications involved in resolving the issue. There are committee politics, leadership politics, partisan politics, and constituent interests, and the new staff member is still unsure what a DSL is.

What's right? What's wrong? Much of the time in politics, you can't answer those questions until you've looked at a lot of options and heard many different points of view, only to realize that the more you learn about it, the more you need to know. As Billy Crystal said about grieving in the movie *Analyze This*, "It's a process."

So when you hear about special interests, you're not always hearing about fat cats and mega corporations taking advantage of the system. They're around all right, but often, you hear about interests competing against other interests on issues that impact a broad cross-section of the citizenry, or advocates seeking more funding for research into deadly and costly diseases, or local governments seeking help with everything from storm sewers to public safety funding. Thousands of individuals and organizations in Washington and the state capitals nationwide are engaged in advocacy. It's safe to say what they do may ultimately benefit you and them. But unfortunately, the circumstances and conclusions are nowhere near as clear-cut as they are made out to be.

"That group of constituents I'm meeting...
is that feedback or blowback?"

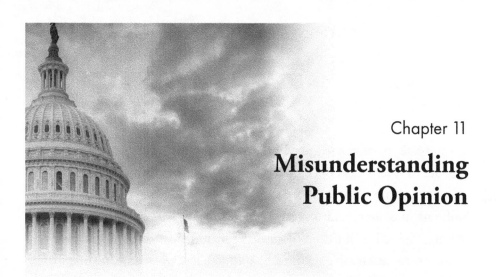

Misunderstanding
Public Opinion

You cannot pick up a newspaper or listen to the radio or TV without hearing about a poll. Some are about candidates: X leads Y by so much. Others about policy: among twenty-four-year-olds, 100 percent are over twenty-three.

The uninformed take such reports at face value and may be led astray because there is more information to analyze in professional polls than a thirty-second broadcast, 140-character tweet, or an 800-word article can communicate. Moreover, the more in-depth data becomes relevant to how legislators decide what they want to legislate.

For more than two centuries, Members of Congress have grappled with whether they were elected to make wise decisions about what's best for their constituents or to vote the will of their constituents, regardless of their views. The representative who does the job well does a little of both, consistent with the precepts of a democratic republic.

Just as the Founding Fathers balanced political principles of governance in designing the Constitution, so must the Congress sometimes balance the good of the nation against the parochial interests of each constituency or balance the judgment of the elected (Members of Congress) with the will of the electors (voters). When those needs and opinions mesh (e.g., recent action on COVID-19), life on the Hill can be very impressive indeed. When they don't (much of the last ten years), individual Members' skills, and sometimes their courage, can be tested to the limit.

When ascertaining what the electors want and where they stand on any given issue, representatives will tell you there is no substitute for personal contact in their states or districts. However, to overcome the difficulty of communicating with 762,000+ constituents in a House district, or usually millions in a state, and to verify whether what the Member hears on the street is reflective of the opinions of a scientifically sampled group of constituents, representatives will often turn to survey research, also known as public-opinion polling—or simply as "polls."

Public opinion reflects what voters think about an issue *at a given moment*. However, because of human nature, it fluctuates, often quite frequently. Therefore, it is not necessarily based on a thorough analysis of the facts and is susceptible to people's emotions about an issue.

Public opinion is subject to change—and can shift with surprising speed. For example, at the Presidential level, President George H. W. Bush trailed Governor Michael Dukakis by seventeen points the day after the Democratic National Convention in 1988. Still, he went on to win a comfortable victory just two months later.

Even before Election Day 2008, on which Senator Barack Obama was elected President, a writer for ABC News asked if the election meant "the veritable death of the Republican Party as they know it?" As Speaker Nancy Pelosi and *former* President Obama would tell you, by 2010, the death of the Republican Party had been greatly exaggerated. A similar analysis was made about the Democratic Party after the 2000 election when President George W. Bush's victory gave the Republicans control of the Congress and the Presidency for the first time since Dwight Eisenhower was first elected in 1952. Polls also misled the public and the press in the 2016 surprise election of Donald Trump over Hillary Clinton and again in the surprising strength Republicans showed in House and Senate elections as Donald Trump went down, defeated by Joe Biden in 2020.

But this year's (2020) problems are still alarming, both to people inside the industry and to the millions of Americans who follow presidential polls with a passion once reserved for stock prices, sports scores, and lottery numbers. The misses are especially vexing because pollsters spent much of the last four years trying to fix the central problem of 2016—the underestimation of the Republican vote in multiple states—and they failed.[86]

The point is that public opinion can change—and if the public feels threatened by a bad economy, terrorism or war, or an attention-getting and emotional news story, they can change their opinions in a hurry. For example, let's say you get a telephone call from a pollster asking your opinion on this question: *Do you favor saving current Social Security benefits for older people no matter what we must do?* If you're like most Americans, you would answer, "Yes."

But what if a week or so later, you are called about the following question: *Do you favor preserving Social Security benefits as they are today, even if it means not building highways, cutting funds to your schools, and cutting back on emergency room care?* You may say, "No."

Public opinion research could validly report different answers on the broad issue of support for Social Security. People react to a stimulus when offering their opinion. Public opinion is a top-of-mind reaction, highly influenced by the question's wording, the environment, and the time it was asked.

Over time, the challenge of distinguishing public opinion and public judgment (value-based stable beliefs) has increased as public opinion has become ever more readily available. In addition, the nation's population has become more technologically empowered and better informed about daily events. At the same time, an opinionated public has created the need for even more sophisticated methods of gauging how that electorate feels about issues.

Historically, when representatives were unsure of their constituents' opinions, they knew where to go for guidance. Society was less complicated and less nuanced then. Community leaders were easier to identify.

Interest groups were fewer in number and less complex. The purveyors of news and information were just a few broadcasters and the local newspaper editor. Personal relationships were simpler, and so was the economy. Members of Congress knew their constituents, who relied primarily on hard work, ingenuity, neighbors, and local government to resolve the issues that concerned them. A Member could learn much of what they needed to know merely by talking to local unions, church leaders, storekeepers, busy-bodies, local politicians, and service organizations, such as the Rotary, Kiwanis clubs, and Chambers of Commerce.

As recently as 1958, the American Association of Retired People (AARP), the Semiconductor Industry Association (SIA), and Greenpeace did not exist. Nor did thousands of other trade groups, social and political associations, and global corporations employ thousands of lobbyists trying to steer the course of a multi-trillion-dollar government that operates and manages hundreds of thousands of federal programs with millions of rules and regulations.

America had about 150 million residents in 1950, compared to more than 333.9 million, according to 2021 census data. In the ensuing seventy years, the nation's population more than doubled, but the number of seats in the House of Representatives has remained constant at 435.

Despite improvements in transportation and communication, the challenge of keeping up with constituent interests and needs has become immense. In addition, district size, demographics, social and educational diversity, aging, and a host of other factors have combined to make public opinion polls an essential source of information about the electorate's will.

On Capitol Hill, polls are ubiquitous, yet multiple pollsters consistently provide differing results to similar questions. If polling is a statistical science, how can this be?

Most professional pollsters freely admit the biggest danger associated with surveys is that their results are misinterpreted and what they reveal can be exaggerated, over-dramatized, and over-applied. Polls produce a snapshot of attitudes at a given moment prompted by a given question addressing an issue that has been simply defined. They require precise design, scientific analysis, and an understanding of their limitations to be of any real value. Unfortunately, some in the media have neither the capability nor the inclination to apply such rigor to the process.

> Polls produce a snapshot of attitudes at a given moment prompted by a given question addressing an issue that has been simply defined.

Individual politicians use private polling to measure public attitudes but rarely share the high-quality information they obtain, and they don't solicit feedback in fundraising letters when it is serious research. So when a politician or an interest group publishes the results of a poll, take it with a big grain of salt. Such a release may be designed to influence attitudes, not reflect reality.

MARGIN OF ERROR

Many people are familiar with the term margin of error, which helps define a survey's accuracy. Generally, the more people you survey, the more accurately the survey will reflect the entire group being studied. It's like the elementary school experiment where you flipped a coin one hundred times to demonstrate that the closer you got to one hundred, the closer the heads-to-tails ratio was to fifty-fifty. The margin of error is usually represented as a percentage—the higher the percentage, the less reliable the poll. However, arriving at an acceptable margin of error is the easy half of the science.

Even more significant is what's known as the survey sample. For survey results to be accurate, the sample must reflect the demographics of the population whose opinion is being sought. Say, for example, 60 percent of your sample consists of women and 40 percent men, but the ratio of the population you survey is 53 percent women and 47 percent men. As a result, the results are likely to be skewed because women will have been *over-sampled*—that is, too many women were included.

A PEW Research from November 20, 2020, analysis, "Understanding how 2020 election polls performed and what it might mean for other kinds of survey work" by Scott Keeter, Courtney Kennedy, and Claudia Deane, illustrated other prospective problems with the 2020 survey work:

- Pollsters had more difficulty communicating with Republican voters, one of the reasons being greater distrust among Republicans of polling institutions, particularly those affiliated with or run by news media;
- Systematic underrepresentation of "some kinds of conservatives . . ."; and
- Miscalculation of the expected turnout, particularly among Trump voters.[87]

Errors in sampling are the cause of most variations in surveys asking essentially the same question. For example, a survey will yield inaccurate results if it over-samples one of the political parties, ideologies, genders, generations, racial or ethnic groups, or other variables.

Successful pollsters must ensure samples accurately reflect the population considered relevant to the poll. In an election campaign, for instance, the sample would ideally consist exclusively of people casting ballots. But pollsters cannot be sure that a person they interview will vote. After all, in the most highly contested Presidential elections, 33 percent of all eligible voters don't vote. Likewise, in an off year, when congressional elections also take place but no Presidential contest, more than 50 percent of registered voters may not cast ballots.

One of the biggest polling challenges is figuring out who will vote. To address this problem, many pollsters insert a series of questions designed to identify *likely voters*. But even the best-laid plans go awry, as they did in 1998 and 2000 when pollsters who didn't bother to distinguish between *likely* and *unlikely voters* were more accurate than the ones who focused on so-called likely voters.

Identifying likely voters is not a pollster's only concern. They also must assess the validity of polls conducted through live interviews instead of automated polls where people respond to questions using their telephone keypads or articulating a number or keyword decipherable by a computer. However, judging from the results of the last several elections, it seems both methods generate similar results, and the automated pollsters can contact more households.

Pollsters are also finding it difficult to survey significant sectors of the population. For one, an increasing percentage of the electorate (54 percent in 2019) has only a cell phone (and no landline telephone), so it is difficult to obtain accurate phone numbers for such voters. Add to the challenge that area codes no longer define precise geographic locations, an essential in estimating where voters will vote and which contests they can influence. Even if a pollster can reach a voter, many are not willing to participate. Both trends have driven canvassers to experiment with online polling, which in some cases has proven reliable and in others less so.

Still, whatever method is used, the pollster's competency and integrity often determine the poll's accuracy.

So, the next time you read about polling results, begin by looking at the information about the survey, usually at the bottom of the story. Suppose the survey involved the public, regardless of age, gender, political party, ethnicity, employment status, and qualification to vote. In that case, you will learn how *all people* reacted. But if you're looking for some sense of how people will vote and who will win, the survey should only involve people who fit the description of those likely to vote. Furthermore, if the number surveyed is below 500 or the survey has a margin of error of more than 4 percent, then don't make any bets on the survey's ability to predict a vote's results.

Polling anomalies aren't always random errors or the inability to forecast a certain demographic group's participation level. Instead, the polling process can be easily manipulated by intentionally over-sampling a key demographic. For example, a partisan surveyor or one on the payroll of politicians can make a candidate appear stronger than the opposition—creating an impression of political strength or momentum—simply by over-sampling the candidate's party members.

PUSH-POLLING ABUSE

Equally disturbing is a practice known as push-polling, which isn't polling at all but an attempt to prostitute the process by asking a leading set of questions intended not to measure voter opinion but to sway it. In his book, *Playing to Win*, CBS news analyst Jeff Greenfield cites the infamous but classic push-poll used by the 1950 campaign of George Smathers against then Florida Senator Claude Pepper. The question by the so-called pollster supporting Smathers was: "If you knew that Claude Pepper's brother is a practicing *Homo sapiens*, his sister is a known *thespian*, and that he openly *matriculated* when he was in college, would you still vote for him for Senate?"[88] Pepper lost that race by 60,000 votes but was elected to the US House in 1962 and served there for the next twenty-six years. The purported survey was a campaign gimmick, not a legitimate test of public opinion. (There is some dispute about whether this happened or is a political urban legend from the 1950s; nonetheless, it illustrates the point nicely.)

Properly conducted and interpreted opinion polls taken over time and reflecting the same sample provide trends that allow sophisticated policymakers to perceive temporary and permanent changes in the public's attitudes. In the wrong hands, however, polls can produce interesting headlines and generate a great deal of heat—but very little light.

Public opinion surveys can measure movement along the policy evolution journey. Public opinion is a weathervane, a means of telling which direction opinion is heading, a gauge of attitudes toward a range of issues that occupy Congress. Opinions can change by new information that exposes a conflict in values or even by the day of the week a survey is taken. For example, polls conducted on a Friday night during football season usually under-sample Republicans, who are more likely than their Democratic counterparts to attend high school games.

IMPACT TAKES TIME

Change occurs all the time in Washington, DC—that's one of the reasons the tax code and regulations take up more than 74,000 pages, according to CNN, when you include tax regulations and guidelines that many tax preparers must consult. In addition, the code and the explanatory information are amended every year. Complex or radical change, however, is rare. Moreover, even when it does occur, it can take years to understand how it occurred, how long it will last, or whether it will root itself into a lasting public judgment based on core values, not simply opinion.

To illustrate this distinction, we would like to go back to events we witnessed while working on the Hill.

First, President Reagan and Congress responded to concerns that catastrophic illness costs were bankrupting Americans relying on Medicare. Medicare covers one hundred days of medically necessary long-term care in a nursing home. Medicaid then picks up the slack, but only if most of the patient's life savings have been exhausted.

Second, the solution the Reagan Administration came up with was a premium-based catastrophic insurance plan that would cover 100 percent of expenses after the patient paid the $2,000 deductible—and the coverage would cost only $59 a year.

Third, Congress decided to be even more generous and lowered the annual deductible while tacking on additional benefits. By the time Reagan signed the bill just before the 1988 election, public opinion had indicated the new law was hugely popular—after all, Congress had created peace of mind for the elderly without increasing taxes.

Fourth, the problem was that few people understood how the package would be paid for. They didn't realize that Congress had decided that lower-income seniors couldn't afford the premiums that originally were proposed, so it provided a complex formula that exempted those who couldn't come up with $59 a year and required higher-income seniors to pay as much as $800 per year to make up the difference. And for some, the coverage duplicated what many retirees' union and federal pension plans provided, forcing them to pay for coverage they didn't need and couldn't use.

Fifth, the stunning political blowback was unprecedented. As more and more interest groups railed against what they perceived as a seniors-only tax, popular opinion shifted from strong support to strong opposition. A massive letter-writing campaign ensued and was punctuated by House Ways and Means Committee Chairman Dan Rostenkowski being mobbed by his constituents on national television.

Finally, the act was repealed before it could go into effect.

Supposedly painless reform, lean and clean, had become downright mean. The Congress had relied on public opinion, logic, and math without considering the resistance inherent in major change.

A good Congressman and a smart politician won't substitute what they know about the constituents' views or beliefs with polling research but merely supplement it. Instead, a good representative will spend enough time with his fellow citizens to have an instinct, a strong sense of how they feel about an issue beyond what a poll can reveal.

But scientific research provides an important added dimension and is a critical backstop to one-on-one conversations. It is the science of politics if you know how to use it.

Chapter 12

Ethics—Playing by the Rules, or Not

It could probably be shown by facts and figures that there is no distinctly native American criminal class except Congress.
—Mark Twain

O ne of the most scandalous scandals in congressional history occurred over forty years ago and involved two men who became partners in vice. In July 2020, former Congressman Michael "Ozzie" Myers was arrested in Philadelphia and, according to Devlin Barrett's July 23, 2020, report in The Washington Post, charged with "conspiring to violate voting rights, bribery of an election official, falsification of records, voting more than once in the same election and obstruction of justice."[89]

Myers's arrest came two years and two months after Mel Weinberg died at ninety-three in a Titusville, Florida, hospital.

The two men were bound by dark shadows cast over Congress that stretched back forty years. They met in a hotel in New Jersey, where Weinberg, posing as the Washington representative of fictitious corporation Abdul Enterprises, handed Pennsylvania Congressman Mike "Ozzie" Myers a suitcase containing a $50,000 bribe for introducing immigration legislation to help an Arab sheik. Unbeknownst to Meyers at the time, they were key players in a highly controversial Federal Bureau of Investigation (FBI) sting that went on for two years and became known as Abscam, one of the worst scandals in the history of Congress.

In 1978, Weinberg was a convicted hustler and con artist—among the best in the business, according to associates—who got off with probation after agreeing to set up the sting for the FBI. The hoax was still active when the media blew its cover in 1980.

Then Congressman Myers was convicted of accepting bribes, along with five other Members of Congress and one senator. The FBI had video-taped the transactions in New York, New Jersey, and Washington hotels, as well as on a yacht in Florida confiscated by the FBI in a drug bust and in a million-dollar home in Washington, DC, where a video control center was stationed behind a large wine rack. The scandal was the inspiration for the 2013 film *American Hustle*.

Abscam is worth looking at because it reinforces already well-en-grained perceptions that all politicians are crooks. American satirists from Will Rogers and Mark Twain to Dennis Miller and Stephen Colbert have made lucrative careers from politicians' personal and professional woes, mainly at the expense of the politicians and their families. It is one of those professions that, going in, you must accept the reality that you are guilty until proven innocent, and even then, you are sometimes still considered guilty. Abscam also shed light on FBI covert practices and procedures, which were reformed following its conclusion, and it was another of those incidents that challenged the media's ongoing conflict between objective journalism and the crass appeal of melodrama to the prurient interests of their audience.

It helps in reacting to scandals such as Abscam to remember that most of those who have served in Congress as Members or staff have left the Hill with their reputations intact and records of honorable service. Even in the Abscam sting, there were Members of Congress caught on tape turning down the bribes. How many others were rejected as targets by the FBI under the presumption they could not be corrupted? How many others would have had a case of lapsed ethics had they been approached? We don't know.

There are few professions held to as high an ethical standard or require as much transparency as that of Members of Congress. Most are under constant scrutiny, as they should be. Their words and actions are parsed and dissected by their constituents, the media, their rivals, and social media conspiracy theorists. The mere whiff of scandal can destroy careers. The late Rep. Henry Hyde of Illinois used to say, "The only thing I want to leave Congress with is my integrity."

What is the logic that drives ethical standards in Congress?

The website GovTrack.us has assembled data on alleged congressional misbehavior during each decade from the 1790s. The numbers do not appear to include civil misconduct unrelated to congressional service.

In the first decade of the Republic, there were four charges of ethics violations and two other charges not specified. Incidents remained barely visible on the graphs until the 1860s when there were four charges of ethics violations, one bribery, and twenty-six "others." The 1880s produced one ethics, one campaign, twenty-four bribery, and one "other." The next spike occurred in the 1970s, with eight ethics, four campaigns, six bribery, and four "others." The numbers increased in the 1990s but didn't go through the roof until the 2010s. In the last decade, there were sixty-two ethics-related charges, thirty campaigns, thirteen bribery, sixteen sexual harassment (this charge showed up for the first time in the 2000s with three charges), and ten "other" charges.[90]

It is worth noting that 12,415 individuals have served in Congress. We presume, but cannot prove, that some Members of Congress have also gotten off light in the past because of what used to be the protective, clubby environment on Capitol Hill. During periods when one party controls the Congress, it is easy to imagine misconduct was buried. And realists will agree that standards evolve, and the odds that there were no sexual harassment activities before the 2000s are ludicrous. In reading these statistics, context is critical.

The increased ethics violations could result from various influences on congressional behavior, from politicians who somehow think they are immune from prosecution to a pervasive climate of hate, anger, and distrust in which accusations are tossed around easily and freely, sometimes for purely vindictive reasons.

Expanding the oversight system in Congress with another oversight committee may have encouraged more complaints, formal accusations, and visibility. It could also be that the wider and indiscriminate application of the "appearance" of impropriety standard, the increase in aggressive partisanship, and ideological divisions that have added to suspicion, distrust, and the cancellation of the benefit-of-the-doubt in many political relationships exposed more.

When a Member of Congress is accused of wrongdoing, they face a variety of punishments at the hands of colleagues if guilty. Naturally, few Members of Congress relish the notion of judging their colleagues, but the Constitution requires each Chamber of Congress to:

> . . . *determine the rules of its proceedings, punish its Members for disorderly behavior, and, with the concurrence of two thirds, expel a Member* (Article I, Section 5)

This Constitutional provision serves as the core of disciplinary procedures.

The severest congressional punishment for bad behavior is expulsion, typically reserved for Members convicted of crimes in the judicial system.

Short of expulsion, Congress has also censured Members and, short of that, issued reprimands. Congress has also come up with other forms of discipline, depending on the seriousness of the misbehavior.

There is no tried-and-true measure for what punishment is laid down for what violation. The record over 200 years has been inconsistent, to say the least. Here are a few examples of punishments meted out for different offenses:

Representative Lovell H. Rousseau of Kentucky was censured for assaulting fellow Congressman Josiah Grinnell of Iowa with a cane in 1866, a serious offense. Still, that same year, Representative John Chandler of New York was censured for proposing a resolution supporting a Presidential veto, which was judged unparliamentary language and an insult to the House of Representatives, an offense considered more serious then than now, but still not rising to the level of physical brutality.

Two years later, in 1868, Representative Fernando Wood of New York was censured for using improper language in the House Chamber when describing Reconstruction legislation as a "monstrosity;" language then considered of great offense. Representative Charles Diggs of Michigan was censured in 1979 for mail fraud and false statements. In the twenty-first century, censures have been imposed against Representative Charles Rangel of New York in 2010 for tax evasion and improper use of federal offices and Rep. Paul Gosar, an Arizona Republican who posted a Japanese-style video called an anime depicting him killing New York Rep. Alexandria Ocasio-Cortez and attacking President Biden with a sword.

Reasons for House disciplinary actions have included several for unparliamentary language, two for selling military academy appointments, an assault on Senator Charles Sumner, support of the confederacy, mail fraud, false financial statements and tax returns, and sexual misconduct.

To give the numbers a little perspective, in the decade of the 1990s, the charges listed above produced five resignations, one censure, two reprimands, and no expulsions. In the following decade, there were three resignations, six reprimands, and one expulsion. In the next decade, resignations jumped to sixteen, all according to GovTrack.com.

These numbers do not reflect charges and punishments in the federal, state, and local criminal justice systems. Convictions in courts in the 1990s totaled two, while in the 2000s, four, and in the 2010s, five for related crimes. Despite circulating emails and web posting to the contrary, Members of Congress are subject to almost all federal and state laws.

All in all, since Congress first convened, the House has expelled six Members (the most recent, New York Republican George Santos), censured twenty-five, and reprimanded ten, according to House of Representative's files on discipline, and the Senate has expelled twenty and censured nine.

The Senate once censured a US President. Andrew Jackson was censured in a bitter struggle over the re-chartering of the United States Bank, which Jackson opposed. Henry Clay, leader of the Senate majority's anti-Jackson forces and an unsuccessful candidate for President against Jackson in 1832, brought the censure resolution to the Senate Floor, where it passed on March 28, 1834.

However, nothing done by Congress can't be undone. So, when Democrats took control of the Chamber two years later, the censure was overturned in a rowdy ceremony where afterward, Clay declared the "Senate is no longer a place for a decent man."

The Senate's first censure was that of Thomas Pickering, a Massachusetts Federalist who had served as Secretary of State under President John Adams. It occurred in 1811 when Pickering read in public session a confidential letter from the French Minister Talleyrand regarding the claim that a portion of Florida seized by the US was part of the Louisiana Purchase.

Probably the most notorious was attracted by the 1954 censure of Wisconsin Senator Joseph McCarthy, who attempted to purge the Government and the entertainment industry of individuals he claimed were communist sympathizers.

As we asked earlier, what is the logic that drives ethical standards in Congress?

It boils down to this: Members and their staff are expected to obey the rules to the letter, and they are expected to avoid even the appearance of misconduct, the operative word being *appearance*.

The problem is that judgments as to what constitutes appearance change daily.

The "appearance standard" expands the range of those who make and prosecute accusations, from ambitious prosecutors, judges, and juries to the press, internet blogs, political opponents, and interest groups that make their living questioning the behavior of public officials. There are many forces that have a lot to gain in the downfall of a politician. Anyone with access to the media or the web can allege wrongdoing and potentially drum an adversary out of office without the allegation ever being uttered in a courtroom. And the media can and do perform such exorcisms themselves.

For example, Illinois Representative Aaron Schock, a promising young Congressman who developed a reputation for eccentric behavior and boasted about it, resigned from Congress in early 2015 over the "appearance" of impropriety before any official judgment was rendered. Schock was accused of using government funds to decorate his Capitol Hill office, which, according to *The Washington Post*, featured "bright red walls. A gold-colored wall sconce with black candles. A Federal-style bull's-eye mirror with an eagle perched on top . . . It's based off the red room in 'Downton Abbey,' said the woman behind the front desk."[91]

But Schock also posted photos of himself in exotic locations, gave interviews, and appeared on the covers of social magazines, including shots that featured his fit physique and bachelor status. Much of his questionable behavior was not connected with charges leveled against him, but it reinforced the appearance of his impropriety. So out the door, he went.

THE ROLE OF THE MEDIA IN PUBLIC ETHICS

The role of the media must be a critical element in any discussion of political ethics. The media can be the accuser, the prosecutor, the judge, or the jury, and at times, they are all the above. They make or repeat accusations without exposing their sources, ensuring their information is factual and balanced, or meeting standards that are at least like the rules of evidence and due process required in the judicial system. The media have the least oversight of any institution that wields such power in the public arena.

There are three basic roles the media play in ethics matters:

- The media can serve as a straightforward purveyor of information regarding allegations of misconduct or behavior without attempting to sway public opinion one way or the other, generate outrage, or pass judgment.
- The media can disclose accusations, either reinforce them or dispute them with the selective coverage of events and information, and supplement their coverage by generating public pressure with repetitive and narrative reporting. "How often do you kick your dog, Congressman?" "Critics say your denial wasn't very convincing, Congressman, do you have something to hide?" "Congressman, you attended the same college as the individual who was CEO of one of the firms that contributed the maximum amount to your campaign for re-election and is now believed to have influenced your vote on a new trade agreement with a country in which they have a plant. Do you deny the relationship with the CEO?"
- The media can be an echo chamber for someone else's attempt to bring down a politician.

Not all they push through the pipeline of public opinion is reliable or nobly intended. Media receive and make public information from political adversaries, opposing political parties, aggressive prosecutors, defeated opponents, future opponents, hustling book authors, and others who have an ax to grind with the target of their reporting.

We want to give journalists the benefit of the doubt that the information they are passing along has been verified, comes to us without bias or ulterior motive, and represents an honest and balanced assessment. In this age of polarization, no-holds-barred political grudge matches, and instantaneous internet-driven "news," the use of anonymous sources has exploded.

We think there are general truths regarding the media treatment of "scandals." Two stand out in this discussion:

1. The media's coverage rules changed dramatically since President Franklin Roosevelt's Administration when neither his infirmities nor his alleged liaisons were widely exposed. Society's view of what is unacceptable has changed across the spectrum of personal and political behavior, from buying someone a meal to putting relatives on the payroll to foreign travel. Journalistic standards and the rules of engagement changed dramatically during and after the Vietnam War, the Civil Rights movement, and Watergate when the range of subjects and circumstances considered "off-limits" or irrelevant to the news or the public's so-called right to know shrank precipitously. Today, with the rise of social media and the pressures it puts on traditional media, there's nothing left to shrink. It's hard to think of a topic that's not considered fair game, including the spouses and children of public figures.

2. The media exercise vast latitude in making decisions to cover or decline to cover allegations of impropriety or potentially criminal behavior. Some decisions have been, in our judgment, based on what appear to be partisan and ideological biases. One of the classic examples took place in 2008, when the mainstream media gave intense coverage to rumors of an affair involving Republican Senator John McCain—an allegation that was later debunked—but did not report an affair involving Democratic presidential candidate Senator John Edwards, which we learned the media had known about for a year before Edwards admitted to it publicly.

Coverage during the 115th and 116th Congresses (2017–2020) of the Trump Administration offered many examples of jaundiced journalism. On the decline for years, objectivity went out of favor almost entirely. For example, coverage of Minority Leader and then Speaker Pelosi and Intelligence Committee Ranking and then Chairman Adam Schiff. In their dogged campaign to find President Trump guilty of consorting with the Russians to interfere in American elections, and when that failed, impeachment proceedings were marred by questionable fact-finding, rushes to judgment, and highly partisan committee hearings and votes.

Irresponsible reporting isn't new. The Founding Fathers felt the sting of the pen—from George Washington being accused of senility to Andrew Jackson's belief that published attacks on his wife led to her untimely death and the alleged corruption of Ulysses S. Grant to the alleged draft-dodging of George W. Bush.

Fortunately, however, responsible journalism isn't a rarity either. Today, journalists and their editors and producers have tough decisions about what is real news and what isn't and how to give their consumers the information they need to make decisions. Unfortunately, it may take a journalistic reform movement by responsible members of the profession to restore the integrity and public trust journalism has enjoyed in the past.

ETHICS AND ELECTIONS

Campaigns are an accident waiting to happen. The most basic principle of American jurisprudence is that we are all innocent until proven guilty. The surest reality of political life is that this basic principle doesn't apply. The unwritten but even more universal rule of political prudence holds that, as we've mentioned before, the appearance of wrongdoing is as damaging as actual guilt and political campaigns present challenges for Members and staff. Rules and regulations, federal and local statutes, and the media's and campaign opponents' prying eyes leave little room for error or its appearance. Campaign financing ethics is a grenade with a loose pin.

For a variety of additional reasons, including the high cost of advertising and outreach, the size of districts, early primaries, and year-round campaign operations, campaigns have become sophisticated multi-million-dollar enterprises requiring the skills of professional managers, public relations specialists, legal counsel, pollsters, and a small army of others. Moreover, they are expensive, which creates potential ethical challenges. On average, Representatives must raise $1.2 million for each two-year election cycle if they hope to remain in office. For senators who run every six years, the average cost is $9 million. That's what a run-of-the-mill campaign costs. A heavily contested, hard-fought campaign will likely eat up much more.

The law requires a strict separation between campaigns and the duties of elected office. Members may not use the resources of their elected office for campaign purposes. They may not design or conduct fundraising appeals on official time or use official equipment. They can't mail campaign solicitations from congressional offices or use government postage. They can't ask for donations when voters, lobbyists, or others visit their offices.

All these prohibitions apply to their staff as well.

A Member can designate one staff member as the liaison between the campaign and the elected office, but only for specified purposes, such as coordinating the Member's schedule. Like all other staff members, however, the liaison is prohibited from performing any campaign duties on government time or using government resources to do them.

Keeping arm's length between campaigns and the elected office is vital to the integrity of Congress, but nothing about it is simple. After all, in certain respects, there is no distinction between serving constituents and running for re-election. For example, if a representative attends a church social to talk with constituents in the middle of a campaign year in a county that is not a sure win, is it official business or campaign? Likewise, if a representative invites a group of environmental activists to the office to discuss the restoration of marshland, and the environmentalists have been past supporters, is that official business or a campaign event?

Making decisions about events and circumstances such as these suggests Members fall back on that philosophical axiom of legal counsel: If you have doubts, don't do it.

THE INS AND OUTS OF THE ETHICS RULES

The House and Senate each have an Ethics Committee that governs its Members' official actions and activities. The Ethics Committee in each Chamber is supposed to be impartial in its treatment of cases, and accordingly, each has an equal number of Republican and Democrat Members. In addition, the ethics procedures in the House have another layer of oversight that screens complaints first. It's called the Congressional Ethics Commission.

Here is a sampling of the actual rules Members of Congress must follow:

Gifts

The rules prohibit staff and Members from accepting anything of value from a lobbyist or an entity that employs one. This detail is an important point. For example, the manager of a company's manufacturing plant in the congressman's home district cannot take the congressman to lunch if the company employs a lobbyist in Washington, DC.

The same applies to tickets to sporting events or fancy fountain pens. Another example: a former chief of staff was indicted, after taking tickets to a Wiggles concert for his toddlers, for fraud against the House of Representatives from an associate of notorious lobbyist and now ex-con Jack Abramoff.

A Member of Congress or a staffer can accept a gift or meal with a value under $50 if it's from someone who is not a lobbyist or a foreign representative.

Members of Congress and staff can receive gifts from relatives, even if the relative is a lobbyist, if they are related before the gift is given.

To illustrate this complexity, it used to be that a potential groom only needed the permission of a bride's father to give his love an engagement ring. Not anymore—at least not if he's a lobbyist and she works for Congress. The Ethics Committee must grant written permission for any gift to staff from a lobbyist, even if they are going to marry.

On the other hand, there are no limits on federal, state, or local government gifts, including sporting events at public universities. In addition, informational materials—such as books and DVDs—home-state products of "nominal" value, and commemorative items, such as inscribed plaques, are permitted.

Attending Events

Members and staff may go to a reception that offers food and refreshments of nominal value—milk and cookies, for example—but not if the food constitutes part of a meal.

Congressmen may attend a charity event if invited by the charity. However, attendance is out of bounds if the MC is invited by someone else, such as a neighbor or a lobbyist.

The congressman's spouse or dependent child may attend such an event, but the congressman must pay for a ticket for any other guest, including a sibling, parent, or date.

Privately Sponsored Travel

When Members of Congress and staff travel on someone else's tab, the trip sponsor must complete a multi-page certification form. The person making the trip must then submit this form and a separate request for permission to the Ethics Committee. Staff members also must have advance authorization from their boss. Finally, after the trip, the traveler must file a disclosure form detailing how much was spent on transportation, lodging, and food. These disclosure reports become public records.

Campaign Work

Staff members may perform campaign work—paid or voluntary—on their own time but not on the congressional clock and only of their own volition. It is a felony for an office to compel a congressional employee to perform campaign duties.

Except for travel, an employee may not expend personal funds to cover a campaign expense, even if the expense would be reimbursed. And if the employee is not reimbursed for the total amount of campaign travel, the difference will be considered an illegal campaign contribution.

Constituent Casework

On a citizen's behalf, congressmen and staff are permitted to ask federal agencies about the status of inquiries or applications they may have submitted to the agency.

Congressmen and staff, however, may not ask an agency to make an exception to the law or the agency's regulations. They cannot threaten or make any promise to an agency official. They may not communicate with any official with decision-making authority in a legal or administrative proceeding. They may not contact an agency on a matter where they have a personal financial interest. Nor may a Member or staff show preferential treatment to a supporter, contributor, or friend in casework matters. Everyone must be treated equally.

Member's offices are severely limited in the recommendations they can make for civil service employment positions.

Official Events

A congressional office may not use outside resources to conduct official business. This rule means a Member may not jointly sponsor any kind of event with a private group or anyone else outside of Government, for that matter. And Members are not allowed to accept cash or in-kind support for an official event or meeting. The rules also limit how a Member's name can be used in a private event. For example, a Member can be listed as an honorary co-host, but only if the invitation clearly identifies the event's sponsor.

In addition to the rules mentioned above, the burden of being an elected official also means personal privacy goes out the window. Members and senior-level staff must file an annual financial disclosure report. Senior-level employees must also file a disclosure within thirty days of joining a congressional staff and thirty days after leaving one. The detailed report lists income, assets, liabilities, property and security transactions, certain types of gifts, travel expenses, outside positions, and employment agreements. Financial information regarding spouses and children also must be disclosed.

There are also several post-employment restrictions for Members and senior-level employees (those who earn 67 percent of a Member's salary), but considerably more for those who earn very senior staff salaries (75 percent of what their boss makes). Internet stories about Members creating government contracts that they live on after leaving Congress are false in every respect.

Senior staff have many restrictions awaiting them when they leave congressional employment, including prohibitions against lobbying former colleagues on the Hill for varying periods.

CONFLICT OF INTEREST

While rules are complicated and each situation different, common sense is sometimes all it takes to keep Members and staff from violating the host of conflict-of-interest rules. For example, it only stands to reason that Members and staff must not use their official position or any confidential information for personal gain. Any violation of the confidential information clause is the legislative equivalent of insider trading, which is also prohibited.

Finally, Congress has often adopted additional rules and procedures in reaction to scandals and the ensuing public outrage. But in its haste to meet public expectations, it usually has issued rules that are confusing or absent of clear guidance for how they should be implemented. It often takes years of precedents to clarify their meaning and their application.

An excellent example is the STOCK Act, which was signed into law by President Obama on April 4, 2012. The STOCK Act had languished in legislative limbo since its introduction by Representative Louise Slaughter and former Representative Brian Baird in 2006 until the *Wall Street Journal* analyzed the financial disclosure reports of congressional staff

212 | FIXING CONGRESS

members and found they had invested in stocks of companies over which their bosses or their committees had jurisdiction. The paper surmised that the staffers might have had access to information that the public did not have about those companies or their industries and could have engaged in "insider trading."[92]

The *Journal* article was followed by the publication of Peter Schweizer's book, *Throw Them All Out*, alleging that certain Members of Congress had investments in industries about which they had access to information the public did not have, raising the specter of insider trading. The accusations in the book caught the eye of CBS's *60 Minutes*, which did a program repeating and hyping the book's allegations that former House Speakers John Boehner and Nancy Pelosi and former Financial Services Committee Chairman Spencer Bachus may have engaged in insider trading in the conduct of their financial affairs.[93]

Faced with the specter of scandal in an election year, Democrats and Republicans breathed new life into the STOCK Act, broke through the procedural barriers and the now-normal Washington gridlock, and passed it. Boehner and Pelosi quickly got out from under the accusations because Boehner had his nest egg in a blind trust, and Pelosi, who, with her husband, enjoys considerable wealth, convincingly dismissed the allegations. However, Alabama's now-former Congressman Spencer Bachus did not get off so quickly. His political opponents raised the noise level on the accusations, and some interest groups poured money into a negative advertising campaign in his primary race. Suddenly his safe Alabama seat wasn't safe anymore. The media attention prompted the Office of Congressional Ethics to investigate the matter. Six months after the *60 Minutes* piece, Bachus was cleared of all allegations on what he said was a unanimous vote of the Ethics Committee (votes are not made public). His reputation, however, took a serious and permanent blow, although his constituents reelected him until he retired in 2015.

The STOCK Act, which applies to all three branches of the federal government, doesn't create new laws prohibiting insider trading by

Members of Congress. Members and staff were covered under existing securities laws before the uproar. What the STOCK Act does is reaffirm that Members of Congress and staff are subject to insider trading laws and that they "owe a duty of trust and confidence to Congress, the US Government and the citizens of the United States respecting material, nonpublic information derived from their official positions." It also specified that insider trading covers both the source of information and the benefactor, and that passing along information could be covered even if it is intended as a gesture of friendship rather than a means of financial gain.

The Act does require Members and staff to file, in addition to the financial disclosure statements they were already required to submit, a Periodic Transaction Report (PTR) detailing certain financial transactions in stocks, bonds, and other securities over $1,000 in value. It also prohibits them from engaging in initial public offerings (IPOs) in a manner "other than is available to members of the public generally."

The STOCK Act probably reduced a potential political three-alarm fire to a bonfire. It reminds Members and staff that they must be cautious with what they learn on the job and avoid profiting personally from it. In addition, the new forms they must fill out will probably help the media better monitor financial transactions for wrongdoing. And the STOCK Act allowed *60 Minutes* to pound its chest and boast about how it forced change on the Hill while ignoring its history of ethical transgressions.

According to some experts, the STOCK Act was fraught with the potential of unintended consequences that could snare not only Members and staff but also people in the private sector with whom Members and staff regularly communicated about legislative activity. Some language was vague, untested, and seemingly unwarranted. The law of unintended consequences is often triggered when legislation is adopted for the wrong reasons or in haste.

The Stock Act resurfaced in 2020 when some Members of the House and Senate made large-dollar trades in pharmaceutical industry stocks as those Members received information in congressional briefings on the COVID-19 pandemic. The charges were flying like bees dive-bombing a garden full of zinnias. The appearance of impropriety was enough to condemn Members of both bodies, and, as is usually the case, the circumstantial evidence was persuasive. However, none of the accused was charged after investigations by the Justice Department and the Securities Exchange Commission. Ultimately, charges were filed in 2022 against former Republican Congressman Steve Buyer of Indiana, and he was convicted of four securities fraud charges in March 2023.

AND THAT'S NOT ALL

This is but a snapshot of the ethics rules that guide the activities of Members of Congress and their staff—and an idea of how serious and encompassing many of those regulations are.

The manuals in which they are contained run to several hundred pages, and the Ethics Committees regularly add updates and guidance called "pink sheets" because of the color of the paper. Mastering them all takes time and sound advice from legal counsel.

In the end, however, ethics and morality are not attributes that can be legislated or eliminated by rules. Character ultimately comes from the heart and the influence of values, such as honesty, that individuals bring to the job. One of the more frequently used political lines when politicians react to misbehavior is, "We must guarantee that this never happens again." It is a good line but one without hope of finality. It will happen again, in some future time, and maybe in a slightly different form, but it will. You can take that to the bank.

PASSING THE SMELL TEST

As we've written earlier, the mere appearance of impropriety can be as devastating to a political career as actual malfeasance. It's why staff members sometimes lose jobs and Members lose elections even when they haven't done anything wrong or violated any rules.

Staffers refer to avoiding the appearance of impropriety as "passing the smell test"—an expression that refers to how moms historically gauged whether leftovers have been in the refrigerator too long. Regardless of their fresh appearance, they had to pass Mom's smell test.

It's the same with the rules—even if activities are legal and allowed under the rules, the only reliable gauge of whether they're safe is to consider how the media, the public, and political opponents apply their smell test.

Members have resorted to violence when words inflame rather than inform.

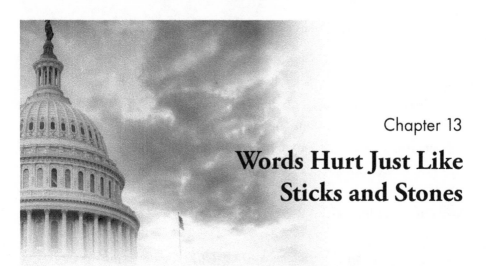

Chapter 13

Words Hurt Just Like Sticks and Stones

I n the time before the American Civil War, polarization sometimes became violent, as when Senator Charles Sumner of Massachusetts was nearly beaten to death by Representative Preston Butler of South Carolina.

Since the Civil War, Members of Congress have periodically expressed their anger with fisticuffs on the Floor of the House and Senate. In 2023, Rep. Mike Rogers, an Alabama Republican, had to be restrained by a colleague from attacking Republican Matt Gaetz of Florida, a notorious agitator, during the rancorous election of Rep. Kevin McCarthy as the new Speaker of the House. Senator Markwayne Mullin, Oklahoma Republican, challenged Teamster President Sean O'Brien to a fight during a formal Senate committee hearing in November 2023. The anger and violence have bled into American politics from one end to the other. Pew Research Center survey research in July 2023 concluded that results were "unrelentingly negative with little hope of improvement on the horizon," Pew reported that 65 percent of those surveyed (8,480)) said they feel exhausted when they think about politics, and 55 percent often feel angry.

Political vitriol and incivility, however, are far more often vented in verbal assaults today. Verbal abuse has been on the rise for decades, and it gets more personal and nastier as the years go by, reflecting more anger and divisiveness in society. That trend was brought home by the outburst of Republican Rep. Joe Wilson of South Carolina, who, during the 2009 State of the Union

Address by President Barack Obama, yelled out, "You lie!" He was admonished for the violation of House rules and later apologized. Contrast that with President Biden's State of the Union Address in 2023, when several Members of Congress screamed "Liar" or "You're a liar," without recrimination.

Politico repeated reports that one Republican Member, Rep. Marjorie Taylor Green of Georgia, yelled liar nine times during the speech, again without recrimination.

> *He wants Americans to work until they die, wants poor people who get sick [to] not be able to see a doctor, not to get the care they need, not to get better, he wants them to die, and he wants an America that consists of nothing but cheap labor for his corporate patrons.* (Former Representative Alan Grayson (D-FL) about Representative Paul Ryan, then Chairman of the House Budget Committee.)[94]
>
> *So, the word is out. He hasn't paid taxes for ten years. Let him prove that he has paid taxes, because he hasn't.* (Senate Majority Leader Harry Reid on the Senate Floor accusing Presidential candidate Romney of paying no income taxes, an accusation Reid bluntly admitted he knew was not true.)[95]
>
> *Mike Pompeo is doing a great job; I am very proud of him. His predecessor, Rex Tillerson, didn't have the mental capacity needed. He was dumb as a rock and I couldn't get rid of him fast enough. He was lazy as hell. Now it is a whole new ballgame, great spirit at State!* (Trump Tweet 3:02 PM, December 7, 2018, as published in the *NYT*)[96]

Democratic leaders caught on. James Clyburn, who was then the third highest-ranking Democrat in the House, compared Trump to Hitler. Speaker Nancy Pelosi said Republicans were enemies of the people who were trying to get away with murder. His allies were henchmen, and Attorney General Barr, she said, was a criminal.

We are never sure what to call it, the kind of language that gets personal, nasty, and untrue to boot. It is excessive partisanship, inappropriate behavior, rude, negative, gridlock, polarization, stridency, intolerance, or ideological extremes. It is all the above. It is incivility. Tragically, today, it is also called *normal*.

Throughout most of American history, Congress and our political system have reflected varying degrees of incivility.

Alexander Hamilton and Thomas Jefferson fought bitterly over the shape and form of the new federal government, and their feuds spread among their supporters and detractors in Congress. The exchanges were tough and sometimes personal. The leading politicians controlled the media, so the incivility reached an ever higher crescendo. Hamilton was the victim of the ultimate uncivil act; he was shot and killed in a duel with political rival Aaron Burr.

Incivility was most prevalent when the whiff of scandal was in the air. Among the examples are the widespread charges of profiteering in the creation of our national currency, which robbed Revolutionary War veterans of their pay, or the divisions over the French Revolution, which led to the passage of some of the most oppressive pieces of legislation ever to be enacted into law, the Alien and Sedition Acts.

Andrew Jackson, a street fighter, a persecutor of Native Americans, and a formidable adversary, believed the death of his wife, Rachel, was caused by vicious charges in his 1828 campaign that she and he were bigamists and she a "whore."

Incivility dominated impassioned disagreements over trade, banking, and taxes when the country was still an infant among the comparatively geriatric nations of Europe and Asia.

Worse behavior erupted over South Carolina's insistence it could nullify federal laws. The decades of bitterness and violence over slavery leading up to the Civil War created one of the worst environments in the nation's history.

Incivility in the nineteenth century precipitated duels and a near-fatal beating on the Senate Floor. Nasty insults were often slung back and forth across the political aisles in the House and Senate. Name-calling was, at times, an art form.

CIVILITY MORE THE NORM

Congress has experienced periods in which bipartisan cooperation and civil behavior were more the norm than the exception. Members across generations distinguished themselves for their adherence to rules of comity (courtesy and considerate behavior) and mutual respect.

The period stretching between the Great Depression and the conclusion of the Kennedy years was a period of relative civil discourse and cooperative governing. But it should also be noted it was a period of global hot and cold wars, followed by prosperity and almost unbroken one-party domination of the Congress.

Yet, even as society became more polarized in the 1960s, Members of Congress could disagree on policy but still do so with personal and professional respect and, indeed, develop and foster friendships across the fences of their partisan political backyards.

The friendship of Democratic House Speaker Sam Rayburn of Texas and Republican Speaker Joseph Martin of Massachusetts throughout the 1940s and '50s, when they both served in leadership, is one example. Speaker Thomas "Tip" O'Neill and Democratic Speaker Thomas Foley retained their friendship with Republican Leader Bob Michel in the 1980s. They were legendary examples of how Members could fight for their beliefs while maintaining a degree of human dignity—and were criticized for it by members of their respective parties as politics was becoming more strident. Foley would privately visit Michel's office regularly to see where they could reach a consensus on national issues.

The same examples could be found in the Senate, a far more collegial body back then, among such leaders as Everett Dirksen of Illinois, Howard Baker of Tennessee, Mike Mansfield of Montana, and George Mitchell of Maine.

That environment was critically important to the enactment of President Lyndon Johnson's Great Society programs, especially the Civil Rights Act.

CONGRESS AND THE PEOPLE'S TRUST

Today's polarization does not approach the formative struggles of our new nation or the horror of the Civil War. But Americans have become increasingly frustrated with the divisiveness, and it is reflected in national survey research that puts the esteem of Congress at chronic lows year after year, regardless of which party is at the controls.

Former House Historian Ray Smock wrote in August 2011, "Despite the brawls of past history I maintain that the civility in Congress, on both bodies, but especially in the House, is at one of the lowest ebbs in congressional history. It is a crisis that should concern all Americans."[97]

Smock said then that we also need a new way to measure civility and dysfunction, different from "the limited historical anecdotes of the past or the feeble attempts of social and political scientists to count things, make charts and declare civility in Congress to be better, worse or about the same."[98]

Research, commissioned by public relations firm Weber Shandwick, published on their website on June 13, 2012, found that 63 percent of Americans think incivility is a major problem that complicates the resolution of significant issues and deters qualified people from entering public service. The firm's 2019 survey showed similar results.[99]

What was interesting to note is that in 2012, 24 percent of those surveyed said social media and the internet contributed to incivility. In 2019, social media was seen as the number one factor at 57 percent, followed closely by the White House at 50 percent, politicians at 47 percent, and the news media at 40 percent. Hollywood celebrities were viewed by 30 percent as factors. The Weber Shandwick survey found that about 90 percent of Americans considered incivility a problem.[100]

The public's disdain for Congress has its ups and downs, but overall, it is mostly down, marked by disenchantment and distrust. The most recent polling data from August 17, 2023, puts the approval rating of the United States Congress at 19 percent, according to Statista.com.[101]

The survey concluded, "Congressional approval, particularly over the past few years, has not been high. Americans tend to see Congress as a group of ineffectual politicians who are out of touch with their constituents... Despite the current Congress having the largest number of women and being the most diverse Congress in American history, very little has been done to improve the opinion of Americans regarding the legislative branch."[102]

CHANGING TIMES

Multiple political events and demographic developments have helped trigger today's polarization. Prior to 1994, the Democrats, with a few exceptions, had complete control over the Congress since the 1932 landslide election of Franklin Roosevelt. But the tumultuous 1960s began to drive wedges in the Democratic Party's coalition and change the face of both parties. Political realignment was still taking place in the 2010s, when the legislatures of Arkansas, North Carolina, Alabama, and Tennessee had Republican majorities elected for the first time since Reconstruction.

The Democratic Party was especially fractured by the Vietnam War, the Civil Rights movement, the explosion in the size of government set off by Lyndon Johnson's Great Society, and the Roe v. Wade Supreme Court decision in 1973 that essentially struck down the states' right to prohibit abortion before the time a fetus could survive outside the womb. These events took their toll on the Republican Party as well, but Republicans had fewer numbers, less power, and were in the minority in Congress.

The most dramatic change occurred in the South. Except for the election of war hero General Dwight Eisenhower, the South had monolithically voted Democratic since Reconstruction in the late nineteenth century. However, the Democratic control in the South began to wane in the second half of the twentieth century.

The Southern realignment first appeared nationally in the 1968 Presidential election when Republican Richard Nixon benefited from the independent candidacy of the former Democratic Governor of Alabama, George Wallace. Wallace's candidacy divided the Democrats in the South and deprived Democratic Vice President Hubert Humphrey of a traditional source of electoral support. Since 1968, the South has become more and more Republican, from state officials to the congressional and presidential levels, only recently showing signs of retreat from that dominance in states such as Virginia and Georgia.

The Southern realignment was not the only indication of a divide among Democrats. You could see this in Congress as a whole. As part of the fissure in the Democratic ranks, party liberals, mainly Members with less than ten years of experience, rebelled in 1974 against conservative committee chairs and forced through a series of rule changes that transferred power from the committees to party leaders. Their elders considered this a significant breach of civility.

The origins of the empowerment of centralized leadership can also be found in the Southern realignment. While Democrats did nominate a Southern Governor, Jimmy Carter, in 1976, the shift in party allegiance continued through the terms of President Ronald Reagan, who was probably the last American President to enter office with a clear and formidable public mandate. The realignment of the parties was reflected in the Congresses that enacted the Reagan agenda of tax and spending reductions and a stronger defense. Reagan and the minority Republican leadership in the House were able to win the passage of major tax reductions in 1981 only with the help of more than forty conservative Democratic Congressmen, mostly from the South.

In the face of those defections on the Democratic side of the aisle and the mid-term elections in 1982 (in the middle of a serious recession) that cost Reagan twenty-six Republican seats in the House, Speaker Tip O'Neill of Massachusetts began reasserting his control over the House and making it more difficult for conservative Democrats to flex their political muscle. O'Neill established tighter control over the committees and the Floor by using the House Rules Committee to block Republicans from offering embarrassing amendments—particularly those offered by Representative Bob Walker of Pennsylvania, Representative Newt Gingrich of Georgia, and other young Turks, who were then insurgent backbenchers. Additionally, these changes included placing the Speaker in charge of the (Democratic) Steering and Policy Committee, giving him (there were no women speakers yet) control over committee appointments for the first time since 1911. The Speaker was given the power to appoint all the Democratic Members of the Rules Committee, to refer bills to multiple committees, and to create ad hoc committees.

These changes had the effect of empowering the party leadership at the expense of the committee chairs. They allowed leaders to "stack" key committees with Members who would vote with them. The committee stacking and proxy voting (allowing Members to vote without being present in committee meetings) further constrained the minority's ability to participate in committee decision-making. The leadership also encouraged party discipline by rewarding Members who demonstrated party loyalty with additional power and other perks, such as bringing legislation they sponsored to the House Floor for a vote.

By depriving conservative Democrats of power if they did not toe the party line, many Southern Democrats were caught between their leadership and their constituents. They found themselves casting votes to support the Speaker that angered their voters and, in some cases, cost them reelection.

Throughout the first term of the Reagan Administration, a limited degree of civility and mutual respect prevailed in many of the deliberations between the President, House and Senate Republicans, and the Democratic leadership in the House and Senate. That cooperation led to the Economic Recovery Act in 1981 and the landmark Tax Reform Act of 1986, among the most significant reforms of the US tax code in the history of the country.

But the working environment was steadily deteriorating. The volatile combination of Republican frustrations with the denial of their minority rights, contrasted by what they saw as increased autocratic rule by Democratic majority leaders, created a highly combustible atmosphere in which younger Republican Members embraced a more aggressive and obstructionist strategy to take control of Congress.

Civil discourse suffered. That growth of confrontation got a substantial electrical charge in 1985 when the Democratic majority insisted on seating Frank McCloskey, a Member of Congress from Indiana's Eighth Congressional District. After a partisan auditing committee of three House Members—two Democrats, and one Republican—declared McCloskey the winner by four votes over Republican Rick McIntyre. That was even though the Indiana Secretary of State, a Republican, had certified McIntyre the winner. The incident led to a historic walkout by House Republicans and ushered in an extended period of increased hostility on both sides of the political aisle. The die was cast.

The Reagan Administration also suffered from politically debilitating events, including a recession. Most notable, however, was the Iran-Contra scandal, in which the Administration was accused of secretly funneling money to rebel organizations in Nicaragua. The scandal made Reagan vulnerable.

Further erosion in the political working environment evolved as the House leadership transitioned in 1987 from Speaker O'Neill to a more strident and—in the minds of Republicans—a more oppressive partisan Texan named Jim Wright.

The seeds of partisan extremes and legislative gridlock were being sown in the fields where policy once bloomed: the Democratic Party was being transformed into a coastal liberal stronghold, while the Republican Party was being transformed as well, filling the void left by the defeat of Southern Democrats and giving up moderate to liberal Republican seats in the North. While the Democrats were becoming more liberal, the Republicans were morphing into staunch neo-conservatives, some of whom might have made Barry Goldwater blush.

> The seeds of partisan extremes and legislative gridlock were being sown in the fields where policy once bloomed . . .

The statistics tell the story.

The number of conservative Democrats, mainly from the South, went from a high of ninety-one in the House to a low of six in the 104th Congress (1995–1996). At the same time, the number of moderate Republicans, mainly from the North and Midwest, went from a high of thirty-five in the early 1970s to a low of ten in the 103rd Congress (1993–1994). The middle ground was narrowing between both sides of the aisle.

In 1994, those insurgent Republicans led by Newt Gingrich of Georgia capitalized on the public frustration with a Democrat President and Congress (caused to some degree by President Clinton's healthcare proposal and crime legislation that increased regulations on certain firearms) and ultimately regained control of the House after forty years in the minority.

They had come a long way since the early 1980s. They did it through a long-term strategy of political insurgency, creating stark distinctions between conservative and liberal leadership, and promoting new ideas that made a perception of a whole new approach to governing.

The strategy proved profitable in restoring Republicans to the majority but costly in terms of its effect on civility in Congress. Many Democrats assumed in 1995 and 1996 that Republican control of Congress was an electoral fluke and that they would regain control in the next election. They didn't, and as the new reality settled in, relations deteriorated even more.

There was a period during the Clinton Presidency when the Democratic President and the Republican House achieved historic welfare reform and a balanced budget (after a good deal of rancorous debate and overriding of two Presidential vetoes), but the days of consensus politics were pretty much over.

As Speaker, Gingrich continued the consolidation of power in the hands of party leaders begun by O'Neill and Wright.

To pass the Republican Contract with America, the 1994 Republican campaign manifesto, in the first one hundred days of the 104th Congress, Gingrich used the power created by his Democratic predecessors to create issue-specific ad hoc task forces to circumvent committees. Legislation was drafted by the leadership and referred to the committees with the expectation of rapid approval. This bypassed the committee members, further weakening their autonomy and short-circuiting traditional procedures in the House.

By the time the 104th Congress (1994) convened, Speaker Gingrich had concentrated power in the leadership, controlled agendas, cut committee staff, reduced procedural powers for committee chairmen, and limited their flexibility on the House Floor. That, and the threat of being bypassed by a leadership task force, completed the neutering of the Committees begun in 1980. Since then, power has remained in the hands of party leaders, even through the return to a Democratic majority in 2006 under Speaker Nancy Pelosi.

Two subsequent political events exacerbated polarization—the attempted impeachment of President Clinton and the closeness of the 2000 election between Texas Governor George W. Bush and Vice President Al

Gore. That election left the outcome in doubt and resulted in legal battles that took ballot counting to the Supreme Court, which upheld Bush's election. Incivility was by then a deeply rooted weed, hard to dig out.

Ohio Rep. John Boehner, elected Speaker in 2011, began reopening and re-empowering the committee process but progress toward returning to what is known as "regular order" (loosely defined as the legislative process as it was intended in the rules, precedents, and laws, in which legislation follows a traditional, modern path through the committee process: Floor consideration, conferencing between the House and Senate and action by the President) was spotty.

WHO TO BLAME?

It is important to note that while some theorists blamed this lack of civility on the boomer generation, others hold the view that there has been a general coarsening of public attitudes among most generations in recent decades. Members of the boomer generation get lots of credit or blame because they prefer to align themselves at the extremes, such as pro-big-government versus small government, pro-governmental-involvement in daily life versus more individual freedom from government, etc. Boomers, born roughly between 1946 and 1964, were the greatest critics of the Vietnam War and its biggest backers. They fought over Civil Rights, abortion, and environmentalism. They did not like to compromise because they each held the view that they were right, and a compromise was the abandonment of deeper beliefs.

As evidenced elsewhere, generational differences play a big role in society and are equally at work in the dynamics of Congress. Members of certain generations tend to reflect that generation, and all Members constantly pay attention to the generational attitudes reflected by their constituents. So what happened in Congress did not occur in a vacuum. It reflected what was happening in the broader society.

Tensions greatly subsided after the tragedies of 9/11, and many experts, researchers, and optimistic politicians thought the resulting unity and benevolence were permanent.

They weren't—not in politics, not among the people.

The incivility was too ingrained in the political culture. Too many politicians and too many in the media had become too invested in its perpetuation. One of the classic lines from the 2016 Presidential campaign did not come from the candidates; it came from Les Moonves, then CEO of CBS Television. He was quoted by Hollywood Reporter's Paul Bond in February: "It (Donald Trump's candidacy) may not be good for America, but it's damn good for CBS," he said. Moonves called the campaign for President a "circus" full of "bomb throwing," and he hopes it continues, Bond wrote.[103]

Other developments were taking place as well.

The world around us transformed from one of geopolitical stability and familiarity with the order of sovereign states to one unable to grapple with global terrorism fomented by fanatical religious, transnational nongovernmental proxy states. These radical changes changed our international behavior, our perceptions of our security, how we were viewed abroad, and how we should respond to a frontal assault on our system of governance and social structure.

What was happening globally could not help but add more instability to the perfect storm occurring domestically: the dissolution of traditional institutions, the hardening of political and ideological views and behavior, increasing distrust of government, and a sense of alienation on the part of segments of society. The political system was further challenged by a technological revolution that divided generations, challenged basic concepts of privacy and individuality, and marginalized once strongly held values and behavioral norms. Rapidly expanding, too, was the influence of what was called the Tea Party Movement on the right of traditional conservatism. The media brushed off the Tea Party as relatively few uncivil and rude troublemakers with no structure or long-term impact, but they could not have been more wrong. It was a movement with credibility among many and depth, drive, and determination.

The 2016 presidential primaries and the general election left the nation more divided. The level of bitterness and anger rose.

Donald Trump rolled through the Republican primaries like a road grader, and the national media gave him the fuel (maybe unintentionally).

He won the Republican nomination with wall-to-wall coverage that was many times more visible than all other Republican candidates combined. Hillary Clinton was a dogged competitor in her primaries, pushing prominent Democrats, such as Bernie Sanders, to the sidelines.

The general election was not a pretty sight. It was peppered with accusations, name-calling, and awful negative ads. In the next four years, the political atmosphere mirrored the climatic atmosphere, a constant stream of raging fires, powerful tornadoes, hurricanes, floods, heat, and high winds. President Trump's four years in office were pockmarked with daily vitriol, unpredictability, and highly unorthodox and antagonizing behavior seldom seen before in any American presidency. Unfortunately, his adversaries responded with equal levels of contemptuousness, engaging in dueling name-calling and partisan rancor.

The public elected a non-politician to the presidency in 2016, a man with no previously elected office background. They wanted to shake up the governing establishment, and they did. The rest of the political establishment did not know how to respond, so they met his bluntness with exceedingly more strident responses. The media, despite having created Trump, also were drawn to his flame like a moth. Every incendiary tweet made headlines, and speeches and messages were searched for the red-hot word or two. Substance was rarely reported in detail.

The behavior and the language of polarization eased somewhat during the onset of the coronavirus pandemic in March 2020 but soon returned to its former ignominy with attacks and counterattacks among Republicans, Democrats, and the press, accusing one side and then the other for being responsible for "murder" as more Americans succumbed to the disease.

Washington Post columnist David Ignatius wrote in June 2019, "We are a country where people are angry at each other, yes, but also feel their core beliefs are under attack. The more each side tries to defend itself, the more the other feels that its identity is demeaned and defamed. That's the death trip that America seems to be on."[104]

As columnist Dana Milbank noted: Professor Jonathan Turley told members of the House Judiciary Committee in testimony on the impeachment of President Trump. "I get it. You're mad," "The President's mad. My Democratic friends are mad. My wife is mad. My kids are mad. Even my dog seems mad, and Luna is a golden-doodle and they don't get mad."[105]

Turley offered the Committee some good advice about the debate that also applies to the broader atmosphere and this "age of rage." Before addressing the constitutional questions of impeachment, Turley, as reported by *The New York Times* told the Committee what was needed in the debate over impeachment was not advocates and adversaries on both sides of the issue but "more objective noncombatants, members willing to set aside political passion in favor of constitutional circumspection. Despite our differences of opinion, I believe that this esteemed panel can offer a foundation for such reasoned and civil discourse. If we are to impeach a President for only the third time in our history, we will need to rise above this age of rage and genuinely engage in a civil and substantive discussion."[106]

Today, calling somebody a liar in politics is just milquetoast. Unfortunately, lying and its twin cousins, exaggeration, and misrepresentation, are acceptable discourse to some players.

A PEW research study found, "81 percent of voters said they could not agree with the other side on basic fact." PEW found that among Republicans and Democrats, more people (53 percent) said they want their representatives to stick by their guns rather than compromise. The number preferring compromise is down 14 percent just since 2017.[107]

Most Americans (59 percent) think "too many people are easily offended these days over the language that others use." Hannah Fingerhut of PEW Research in 2016.[108]

About two-thirds of US adults (65 percent), in a 2021 PEW survey said that "people being too easily offended is a major problem in the country today."[109]

Other institutions, once pillars of American society, aren't doing well either. Young people are losing faith in faith and reassessing their belief in marriage, family, and community. Worship was up during the pandemic. *The Washington Times* reported in May 2020, "One-quarter of U.S. adults overall (24%) say their faith has become stronger because of the coronavirus pandemic, while just 2% say their faith has become weaker," according to research by the Pew Research Center.[110]

Test scores among our educational institutions have been flat-lined or only slightly up in recent years and showed a decline as the country moved to remote learning. Institutions of higher learning have been in constant upheaval, raising tuition while increasing administrative personnel, clamping down on conservative speakers on campus, obsessing over political correctness, the "cancel culture," and sanctioning programs and facilities to which whites are banned.

As the late professor Walter Williams, a prominent columnist and professor of economics at George Mason University, noted, about the destruction of statues and college demonstrations, "I would like someone to explain how tearing down statues of Christopher Columbus, Thomas Jefferson and Confederate generals help the black cause. Destruction of symbols of American history might help relieve the frustrations of all those white college students and their professors frustrated by the 2016 election of President Donald Trump. Problems that black people face give white leftists cover for their anti-American agenda."[111]

Throughout history, governments have used various information controls to justify their policies, be it attacking neighbors, fanning tribal conflict, or stimulating the economy. In recent years in the United States, that abuse has shifted from the government to the media, college professors, and students. Open debate is not tolerated or encouraged. Historical balance and perspective balance in judging the lives of historical figures is not sought even for George Washington and James Madison and their contribution to the country's creation because they once enslaved people.

Two other polarizing dynamics deserve special attention, none more impactful than the media.

THE MEDIA

Everywhere we look we find the media are a significant cause of polarization in government and society. They are an accelerant of the anger and hatred so visible in society. Cable news and the internet's social sites have turned our system of information gathering and dissemination upside down, and they've brought down the traditional media in the process.

The principles of balance, objectivity, factual accuracy, transparency, accountability, and putting public interest over profit are no longer the watchwords of journalistic integrity. They are of the former model, the old way of doing things.

Additionally, there are no longer clear lines between information and entertainment or news and commentary. There's no clear guide to who's a journalist and who isn't. Narrative journalism with the intent to persuade rather than inform is becoming a much more prominent formula in news reporting. Media news dissemination seems to be more closely tied to the profitability of trends in readership and viewership. Strong partisan and ideological alignments drive news judgments to the darker side of journalistic standards and practices.

Many news pieces are based on or heavily slanted by anonymous sources with little assurance that those sources are reliable, unbiased, or even well enough informed to be quoted, as the country learned in October 2020.

It began when the *New York Times,* on September 5, 2018, introduced to the world a highly prized anonymous source said to be high up in the Trump White House, who was of such weight they were allowed by the *Times* to publish an anonymous op-ed piece excoriating the Trump Administration. There was speculation that Anonymous was Chief of Staff John Kelly. The secret source said they were a member of the Trump resistance who claimed access to the President. Anonymous also claimed they could not be more specific about particularly provocative incidents for fear of revealing who they were. As would be expected, the snitch snatched incredible press coverage, promoting an up-and-coming book over the next ten months.

The whole exercise was a public relations coup, but to the American people, it was a dishonorable hoax. Anonymous, as they became known, was revealed in October 2020 to be, at the time of the op-ed, a mid-level advisor in the Department of Homeland Security, who, before leaving the government, served briefly as the agency's chief of staff. Some of the accusations in the op-ed and the book were outlandish and unverified, but that didn't stop the media from giving it national attention without bothering to verify the veracity of Anonymous or the content.

The Washington Post's Phil Rucker helped Anonymous promote his book in November 2019, the day it went on sale, by writing a generous piece repeating the provocative language and titillating stories. Rucker did not indicate whether he knew the identity of Anonymous or had confirmed his claim to close access to the President, the only perch from which some of the stories could have been witnessed. It is bewildering that the *New York Times* would have given Anonymous such rarified access to its editorial pages and news columns and that other news outlets would have done so without verifying the seniority of his position in the White House.

Readers and viewers are asked daily to put their blind faith in the judgments of reporters, editors, and producers regarding their sources of information and how they interpret it. The transformative and historical changes the media has made in their own ground rules and mission in recent years have made public trust a risky proposition.

Traditional media reprint or rebroadcast what is heard and seen on cable news or social media, without fact-checking, sometimes without even a cautionary note that the information is raw.

Here is another good illustration. During the tense weeks when Americans were not sure how long the coronavirus pandemic would threaten lives and paralyze the nation's economy, someone with a sick mind circulated a press release from a company called Bodysphere on April 1, 2020, announcing Federal Drug Administration approval of a new two-minute test the company had developed to detect the critical antibodies that fight the virus. Reuters news service ran the story, apparently without verifying it. The *New York Times* reprinted the Reuters story, apparently without verifying it. The political news service *Axios's* Marisa Fernandez wrote the story without mentioning Reuters or confirming whether the FDA had, in fact, approved the new test. *Washington Examiner's* Philip Klein read the story in the *Examiner*, then did the research and concluded it was a "cruel April Fools hoax."

There's no longer any distinction between information, which we may have too much of, and knowledge, of which there is too little. Substance doesn't sell. Gossip, political intrigue, negativity, and exaggeration are products that sail off the media shelves. Another factor in polarization is the way readers and viewers gravitate toward news sources with which they agree, making it more difficult to communicate with those listening to and reading contrarian sources.

Incendiary and propagandist news practices contribute to the growing disinclination of good people to run for office, in part because they do not want to put themselves and their families through the injurious gauntlet of sometimes highly aggressive adversarial media for two years or more and raise the kind of money that a strong media presence requires.

This harms civil discourse. Media manipulation has harmed the public's ability to make sound decisions and engage in their government while discouraging and sometimes preventing good people from running for public office. It is another crucial factor in why we just can't get along.

RIGID PARTISANSHIP

The excessive partisanship discussed earlier in this chapter plays a detrimental role in our system of governance.

Partisan political campaigns serve a fundamental purpose in our system, but they should be more distinct from governing. Campaigns are supposed to create and then magnify distinctions and divisions. Governing is ultimately supposed to reconcile them into public policy. When campaigns never stop, governing never begins.

Our system of financing political campaigns and the twenty-four-hour, seven-day-a-week nature of those campaigns inhibit civil discourse. The campaign system flows right into the design of governance with no let-up, no dam to slow the partisanship after the election. As a result, it floods the corridors of government, making it extremely difficult for legislators to put aside their party affiliations to govern.

If you recall from earlier chapters on the organization of the Congress, leadership is structured and driven mainly along partisan political lines, just as George Washington feared it would be. There is no question that strong leadership is essential to governing, but the excessive partisanship that thoroughly dominates the legislative process inhibits inter-party cooperation and bipartisan consensus.

In March 2015, *The Washington Post* commentator Chris Cillizza judged then-Speaker Nancy Pelosi as "still the most effective leader in Congress," not because of her ability to govern but "because of her abilities as a pol," because of "an uncanny ability to keep her caucus from throwing even a few votes (House Speaker) John Boehner's way."[112]

In a 2020 *Post* profile, columnist Karen Tumulty wrote an informative and colorful tribute to the highly skilled first female Speaker of the House.[113] The piece ran 4,600 words, but only eighty-six were devoted to public policy.

In other words, Leader Pelosi was judged effective because of her political organizing and partisan forcefulness. She prevented bipartisan consensus and inter-party cooperation rather than contributing to it. She was an effective partisan her entire career in American politics but fell way short of fostering a governing environment, which cannot happen in a one-party rule.

In interviews with retiring Members of Congress before the 2018 congressional elections, Nick Penniman and Marian Currinder wrote for *Real Clear Policy* that the three overriding reasons for quitting Congress were the stifling amount of fundraising required, the overbearing dominance of the partisan leadership, and the dysfunction of the body.

It should be noted that some observers, including notable pundits such as George Will and Michael Barone, have argued that "hyper-partisanship" is not as bad as it seems and that attempts to reform have made matters worse. We beg to differ.

As discussed in Chapter 6, there are several other widely recognized problems with the legislative process, including the increased use of restrictive special rules in the House and the abuse of the filibuster in the Senate. When strong party leadership in the House or Senate blocks amendments and stymies debate, it makes compromise nearly impossible—punishing center-right or center-left Members on both sides.

As the Founders had intended, the Senate is expected to be more pon-derous and frequently finds compromise where a straight up or down vote would have failed.

To put legislative inactivity into perspective, consider three of the most transformative and controversial pieces of legislation from the last century: the Social Security Act in 1935, Medicare in 1965, and the Civil Rights Act of 1964. They all passed with bipartisan majorities: the Social Security Act with a vote of 372–33 in the House and 77–6 in the Senate; Medicare with a vote of 313–115 in the House and 68–21 in the Senate; and the Civil Rights Act with a vote of 290–130 in the House and 73–27 in the Senate. Each of those bills had majority support from both parties, except for the Medicare Act when Senate Republicans narrowly voted against it 13–17. The most modern extreme example is the Affordable Health Care for America Act, officially known as the Patient Protection and Affordable Care Act of 2010 (a.k.a. Obamacare), which only received one Republican vote in the House and none in the Senate.

POLARIZATION

Polarization hurts everyone. It gives fuel to the extremes and disenfran-chises the rest.

There are serious issues facing the country, and the list is growing with every new crisis: health policy, sluggish economic growth, massive budget deficits and government debt, the reform of Social Security and Medicare, energy policy, the deterioration of our transportation system, immigration, postal reform, threats to cyber-security, globalization, and the global war on terror. Those are just a few.

A polarized Congress cannot solve these problems. No serious observer of Congress can believe any of these reforms stand a chance in today's highly charged atmosphere. That cold reality has been reinforced from one Congress to the next for at least two decades. The record of accomplish-ment under both Democratic and Republican majorities has been minimal.

Restoring civility as the core of our public discourse and the develop-ment of public policy does not necessarily mean moderation—Members should be able to discuss profound differences respectfully and in a way that encourages ideas to be fully discussed. Civility doesn't mean compromising principles. But it does facilitate a Member's ability to reach a consensus within the framework of those principles. They can't do that, however, if they don't have a role in governing, or if they don't develop relationships with each other that transcend their partisan allegiances when the greater good demands it, or if they are not put in situations where they can work together.

The ability to participate in lawmaking channels Members' efforts in positive ways. If a minority cannot participate in the legislative process, its only power is to obstruct the majority through dilatory tactics. A minority has no choice but to be negative.

The seepage of incivility in politics and society has been apparent for two decades or more. Any honest discussion of this chronic political and social behavior must acknowledge that reality.

This book was conceived and started long before Donald Trump was a candidate. Crediting or blaming him for the condition we now face is legitimate, but it misses the mark. He exploited a state that had existed for years. He took advantage of a segment of the population long dispirited by a feeling of abandonment and abuse by both political parties. He also exploited the national media, which devoted more attention to Trump than all other Republican presidential candidates combined in 2016.

The media may have been under the naïvely false assumption that his Quixotic run for the Presidency would never materialize into anything but good entertainment and excellent ratings.

But no discussion of incivility should ignore or minimize the behavior of President Trump and his influence over social behavior and attitudes. Voters hired Trump because he was not a skilled politician, and they were exhausted by the professional politician's spin and inability to get things done. Trump violated practically every political norm of the time. His unorthodox treatment of public policy and the policy-making process disrupted what was left of traditional governing and the relationship between the Executive and Legislative. His utter disregard for civil behavior, common decency, and virtually all the traditional values that have defined the American character will be analyzed for years to come. Despite his behavior, he almost won reelection.

He arrived in national politics when many Americans believed the government and the political system needed a shaping up and political leaders of the time a good dressing down. He gladly accommodated them in exchange for their votes. They liked his actions but, in the final analysis, could not stand his behaviors.

It has been baffling how President Trump's behavior influenced that of the media, as we've discussed, and more pertinently, his adversaries, who, instead of embracing the mantra of former First Lady Michelle Obama— "When they go low, we go high"—several of them crawled under the low bar he set, succumbing to the gravitational pull of incivility and confrontation. That die was cast even before Trump was sworn into office in 2016.

Candidate Trump's pre-election behavior was so over the top that powerful figures such as Speaker Pelosi, Senate Minority Leader Chuck Schumer, and media powerhouses, such as *The Washington Post*, *New York Times*, the three major TV network news broadcasts and countless others, all seemed to be in competition to out-Trump Trump in their resistance and outlandish behavior. Seldom has there been a time in history when a President has invited wrath so intensive, his adversaries would attempt to drive him from office from the day he took the oath, contributing with him to polarizing the nation and throwing the government into near gridlock. Hatred and anger became the national media emotions. They punctuated every aspect of political activity.

Incivility reared its ugly head higher across society in the Spring of 2020 with the brutal killing of a Minneapolis Black man named George Floyd by a police officer who had placed him under arrest. His death, and others in the same period, set off protests against racial injustice that turned violent in major cities from Atlanta to Seattle, leaving thirty-eight people dead, hundreds injured, and an estimated $1 billion in destruction.

While the nation reacted to the injustices, the COVID-19 virus was sweeping across the country, creating more fear, anxiety, and anger over the governments'—federal and state—perceived poor response. Those two critical events were interspersed with devastating natural disasters here and around the world and the highly charged 2020 elections, all of which left America dumbfounded and worn out.

Amid the devastation, violence, constant anger, and demoralization, there is one good that came from the experience. It made a lot of people realize that if we are to overcome adversity of any kind, we really need to learn and relearn how to get along.

Uncommon solutions needed to solve unprecedented challenges.

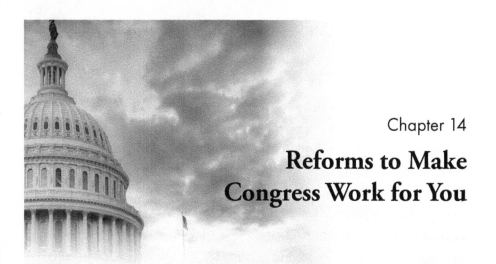

Chapter 14

Reforms to Make
Congress Work for You

As discussed throughout this book, the American system has modified, by accident or intentionally, many of the foundational aspects of the democratic government designed by the Founders.

Do citizens hold supreme power, and are the elected truly responsible and responsive to them? Is anyone taking a long-term view when making decisions in Washington? Have legislative failures led to Executive branch dominance? Is it now time to reaffirm and restore those fundamental values and objectives written into the Constitution that have eroded over the decades?

Most Americans believe our government has gotten seriously off track and is not functioning the way they think it should. The survey research we've highlighted in previous chapters reflects that reality and has for many years. Rarely have our institutions of government been held in such low esteem. The intense turmoil in politics and the uncivil and harsh nature of our discourse and behavior have damaged the very framework of democratic governance.

We have discussed in previous chapters how Congress works—and doesn't—how it is supposed to work, and some of the critical deficiencies that have contributed to its dysfunction and gridlock.

There are procedural and structural solutions, not just those we would recommend but others that have been considered and talked about for years—but not applied.

Some ideas are strategic, designed to fundamentally modernize Congress within the principles of the Founding and, thus, the other branches of government. Others viewed as procedural would make Congress function in a fairer, transparent fashion that facilitates ideas percolating to the top decision-makers and ensures that those decision-makers are responsive to the citizens they are supposed to serve.

STRATEGIC REFORMS

Below are several potentially transformational changes worth considering that would return the United States Congress to its traditional democratic-republic foundation. Some changes must emanate from state legislatures, others from within Congress. Each will only occur if voters demand action.

Let's begin drawing outside the box with an idea for realigning the very composition of the United States Senate. This transformation has been promoted by former Senator Ben Sasse, R-NE, among others.

Before 1913, US Senate Members were *not elected* directly by the voters but selected by their respective state legislatures. The Founders believed the senators must be reflective of the states from which they came, and selection by the state legislatures would secure a balance between the powers of the states and those of the national government. The Founders also wanted the Senate to be a more deliberate and thoughtful body to balance the House, which they correctly assumed would be more spontaneous and responsive to public passions.

According to the Senate historical office, George Washington is said to have told Thomas Jefferson that the framers had created the Senate to 'cool' House legislation just as a saucer was used to cool hot tea.

The selection of senators also avoided situations in which serving in the Senate would lead to lifetime employment. The control of state legislatures shifted with the political fortunes of the parties, and as a result, so did the appointment of senators, who were less likely to stay in office for long periods.

The appointment process kept the Senate revitalized regularly, but it also contributed to the criticisms of the process. Some state legislatures, racked by political gridlock, found themselves unable to agree on who to send to Washington, so there were times when no senator appointment was made for months or years. The gridlock grew more severe as the Civil War approached. For example, a political struggle in Indiana left a Senate seat vacant for two years. Following the war, another seat was left open for four years.

Before the mid-1900s, most state legislatures only met every other year, thus extended vacancies naturally occurred. Today, all state legislatures meet annually, which means most vacant seats are filled quickly to guarantee the state has a voice in pending legislation.

While the Civil War raised havoc with the selection process, talk of popularly elected senators was heard as far back as 1826. Voices continued to get louder through the mid-1800s and reached a boiling point toward the end of the nineteenth century and into the twentieth. It was a series of scandals, growing public demands for change spirited by the new progressive movement for governmental reform, and the muckraking press attacks on the current system that ultimately brought it down.

"Intimidation and bribery marked some of the states' selection of senators. Nine bribery cases were brought before the Senate between 1866 and 1906. In addition, 45 deadlocks occurred in 20 states between 1891 and 1905, resulting in numerous delays in seating senators. In 1899 problems in electing a senator in Delaware were so acute that the state legislature did not send a senator to Washington for four years," according to an article in DailyHistory.org.[114]

They added: "William Randolph Hearst expanded his publishing empire with *Cosmopolitan* and championed the cause of direct election with muckraking articles and strong advocacy of reform. Hearst hired a veteran reporter, David Graham Phillips, who wrote scathing pieces on senators, portraying them as pawns of industrialists and financiers. The pieces became a series titled *The Treason of the Senate*, which appeared in several monthly issues of the magazine in 1906. These articles galvanized the public in maintaining pressure on the Senate for reform."[115]

The proverbial final straw was hoisted on the camel by bribery accusations surrounding the appointment of Senator William Lorimer, R-Illinois. Lorimer, who was called the "Blonde Boss" in Illinois because of his influence in machine politics, was accused of conspiring with some wealthy supporters to bribe a handful of Democratic legislators whose votes were needed to secure his appointment. Two investigations found solid evidence of bribery, but strangely enough, the bribed legislators changed their tune about whether Lorimer was involved when it came time to testify before the Senate. According to Daniel Holt, the Senate's assistant historian, the majority report of the investigating committee was rejected by the Senate, which voted by a bipartisan margin of fifty-five to twenty-eight in April 1912 to invalidate Lorimer's election.

One result of the Progressive's campaign was the passage of the 17th Amendment to the Constitution, ratified on April 8, 1913, which amended Article I, Section 3. It reads in part:

> *The Senate of the United States shall be composed of two Senators from each State, elected by the people thereof, for six years; and each Senator shall have one vote.*

Critics of the Amendment contend it threw the baby out with the bathwater, to borrow an old cliché.

The 17th Amendment contributed to profound changes in how the Senate conducts its business and responds to the public. For example, states were once laboratories of economic and governmental experimentation. Urban states could use one approach to poverty, education, or health care policy. In contrast, non-urban states, because of their size, demographics, and economic characteristics, might focus more on other alternatives. Moreover, because they were closer to the people, the states had a better sense of what would work and not work in their environments. As a result, the odds of them being effective and efficient were higher than when the programs moved to Washington and redesigned as one-size-fits-all policies without adequate oversight.

The Senate has become a second House of Representatives that occasionally addresses issues from a national and often international focus, with less emphasis on the will of the states and more on the passions of individual voters. As a result, state borders have essentially been dissolved, and the distinctiveness and diverse cultural and political character of the states are seriously diluted.

The distinctions intended between the two houses remind us that uniformity is sometimes the enemy of diversity and creativity. Little attention was given to what the change would do to the role of the states in creating national public policy or keeping the creation of policy closer to the people affected by that policy.

In the end, the change, along with many other transformational changes in the Senate and the role of senators, may have had the unintended consequence of leaving individual voters with less influence and less access to their senators when what they wanted was more.

Finally, the move to a popular election of senators, the critics say, was partially responsible for making the Senate much more like the House, more reactive to spontaneous public passions, more partisan, more attuned to re-elective politics, and far less deliberative. It also led to extremely expensive campaigns, such as those in 2020 that saw nearly $300 million spent in North Carolina, according to OpenSecrets.org's' Karl Evers-Hillstrom and Jim Morrill, on October 13, 2020. Even a small state like Kentucky saw nearly $200 million in that state's race.

246 | FIXING CONGRESS

There were costly Senate races two years later in 2022 as well. In Georgia, $260 million was spent. In Pennsylvania, $168 million, and in Florida, $130 million.

Repealing the 17th Amendment would likely generate a debate over increasing the number of senators by one for each state. Hence, every state would have a senatorial selection every national election cycle, every two years in essence.

Former Senator Sasse also proposed a similar strategy of eliminating the necessity for Members of the Senate to run for reelection by limiting senators to one twelve-year term of office. The single term, he says, would make the Senate far more effective and efficient by extracting from deliberations the ever-present menace of fundraising's campaign influence on legislative behavior.

Opponents note the ever-present shadow of political opposition keeps senators focused on constituent interests. What would senators do if they were unaccountable lame ducks from day one? Allowing state legislatures to appoint a senator to a six-year term would normally guarantee a change by the time that term had expired, but not necessarily so. If the senator reflected the state's interest, they could be reappointed. If the state legislature had changed partisan hands or political attitudes, a different person would probably be appointed.

There are numerous other solutions with which citizens ought to be familiar so they can inquire about their worth with their representatives in state legislatures and Congress.

INCREASING THE POWER OF INDIVIDUAL VOTERS

Another reform, outside of conventional thinking in Washington, involves the size of the House of Representatives.

A *non-constitutionally mandated* legislative decision in 1913 radically reduced the influence of the average voter and changed the very character of the House of Representatives for the next one hundred years and beyond.

Before 1913, the number of people living within a congressional district was adjusted every ten years, following the decennial census, to reflect the country's growth. That was accomplished by adjusting the number of seats in the US House. The process, known as reapportionment, is the redistribution among the states of the total number of representatives in the House, so each Member represents about the same number of citizens.

The total number of seats in the House is entirely up to Congress. The current number, 435, was set after 1913 when Congress could not agree on how many seats to add. Throughout the 124 years from 1789 to 1913, Congress added seats every ten years, with one exception, to keep the ratio of voters to a single representative reasonably balanced, a fundamental precept of equal representation.

The first Congress (March 4, 1789) consisted of a House of Representatives of only sixty-five Members, each representing roughly 37,000 citizens. By 1913, each of the 435 House Members represented around 200,000 citizens, almost 5.5 times as many. Today, each Member represents more than 762,000 citizens, or twenty times as many people as those first congressmen. Wonder why today's average citizen feels left out and unheard? Today's citizen, numerically speaking, has less than 5 percent as much influence as their ancestor in 1789.

Today's voters can blame the Apportionment Act of 1929, signed weeks before the Great Depression, for their declining influence with their representatives. Realizing the Electoral College was soon to meet and that uncertainty about the size of the House could create a constitutional crisis, Congress passed legislation that froze the House at the 435 seats established in 1921. In doing so, their inability to solve the size issue reduced the influence of individual citizens, which continues to diminish.

As a citizen, would you have more influence over your Member of Congress if you were one of 37,000 voters or one of 762,000? Or look at it another way; it doesn't take a complex algorithm to understand that representing 200,000 people in 1913 was easier and more effective than representing 762,000 people today.

Survey research suggests that part of the public's anger at the government and their distrust of it is because they feel detached from it and those elected to represent them.

Advocates argue that reducing the population of congressional districts would not only make it easier and less expensive to run for office, but it would also probably increase the number of women, minorities, younger people, and citizens from the ranks of middle-class workers who are now vastly underrepresented in Congress.

Even if we reverted to 250,000 people in each district, the probability of non-professional politicians winning an election goes way up. Lawyers and professional politicians might see their share of seats reduced.

Most current Members of Congress are lawyers or previously held other public offices and are known to some as professional politicians. Representation should allow anyone with a solid reputation and good ideas to be elected without spending years raising money or working their way up the electoral ladder.

Opponents of enlarging the House argue that it may not necessarily benefit those intended. It may also make the House more unwieldy than it is, make it more difficult for Members to get to know one another on a more personal level, and put more power in the hands of the Leadership in assembling coalitions of Members in support or opposition to legislation. More Members would also increase the costs of House operations, from office space to security. To achieve a ratio of 250,000 constituents to every Member, the House would have to be enlarged by 885 new Members over the current 435. That's a House with 1,320 Members of Congress.

There are other ways to look at the calculations for determining the proper size of the House. As reported by FiveThirtyEight.com, Brian Frederick, Chair of Bridgewater State University's political science department and author of *Congressional Representation and Constituents: The Case for Increasing the House of Representatives,* has studied representation ratios and is a strong advocate for reassessing the size of the House. Numerous reports have backed up Frederick's conclusions.

Frederick noted, "Representatives who serve fewer people are more popular, more likely to have contact with their constituents and more likely to get higher marks for their constituent service. Moreover, they often better reflect the views and make-up of the people in their districts," reported FiveThirtyEight. "The reality is that it's easier to represent fewer people than a larger number of citizens on a per-district basis," said Frederick."[116]

Mark Oleszek, author of *Congress & the Presidency,* observed about Frederick's thesis that the size of districts impacts the quality of representation: "[T]he empirical richness of this study makes a valuable contribution to our understanding of how constituency size influences the representation we receive from Members of Congress. Scholars of political institutions are well advised to consider Frederick's argument and the evidence he brings to bear in its defense."[117]

Other academicians have recognized a practical mathematical way of looking at the most effective ratio of representatives to citizens. It is called the Cube Root Rule. In other words, the number, when multiplied by itself twice equals the country's population. With a population of around 334,000,000, the cube root in the US works out at roughly 694. Although the mathematics involved in getting to that number are not essential, the fact that jurisdictions with such a ratio, by accident or on purpose, seem to have better relationships between the elected representatives and the residents is important.

Matthew Shugart, distinguished professor emeritus at the University of California at Davis, reviewed the cube root of thirty-plus countries and found that most Western countries where citizens somewhat approve of their legislature tend to fall near that cube root ratio.

If the cube root standard existed in the US, each congressional district would have around 481,000 people. That is still large but much more likely to be a size in which voters would feel and be more connected to their representative.

Shugart noted that the size of the US House of Representatives was close to the cube root ideal throughout most of US history—until Congress failed to enlarge the House in 1913.

Opponents argue that increasing the size is a solution looking for a problem. Advancements in communications technology enable Members to talk to thousands of constituents with a single phone conference, television broadcast, or website posting, neutralizing much of the disconnect in the larger congressional districts. Others say that it is managing a district as opposed to representing it. Managing encourages incumbents to respond to their primary voters instead of the broader general electorate.

The arguments, pro and con, are extensive and, at times, mind-numbing. Regardless, however, our system fails when these subjects are not even talked about in coffee shops, cloakrooms, and state legislatures.

As a final point for your consideration, many naysayers overlook that large legislative bodies exist in many democracies that work. For example, New Hampshire has 400 state legislators for a population of 1,360,000, which means each representative serves 3,400 neighbors. England's lower House, the Commons, has 650 members representing a population of 67,886,000 or one representative for every 104,440 people. France has 577 deputies in the National Assembly for a population of 67,000,000 or one deputy for 116,117 citizens.

In our neighborhood, Canada's House of Commons has 338 members serving a population of 37,742,154, or one member per every 111,663 citizens. Mexico has 500 deputies serving a population of around 129 million, or one deputy for 258,000 people. Again, each Member of the US House is expected to represent 762,000 citizens. Is there any reason folks feel disconnected?

AUTOMATIC REPLACEMENT
OF REPRESENTATIVES THROUGH TERM LIMITS

For many years, the idea of establishing term limits has been discussed and heavily promoted by the Tea Party factions. In essence, such a proposal would prohibit a senator or representative from seeking reelection once they have served a specific length of time, say twelve years for a senator or six years for a House Member.

Some feel term limits are a last-gasp effort to force more new blood into each legislative body. Others think it is a way to eliminate incumbents who have become too connected to lobbyists and bureaucrats in Washington and have lost touch with their home folks. They are willing to remove a good representative with whom they agree just to get rid of others not as much to their liking.

Adopting such limits would result in higher turnover among elected leaders, but would it also change the nature of the larger Legislative branch? Those familiar with how Congress works know that the federal government's too large and too complicated for newcomers to Congress to have a comprehensive understanding of the hundreds of programs, the thousands of details in tax and healthcare law, and, as the old joke goes, where the light switches are to be found. Most new Members spend a few years becoming experts in the subject matter; others go to the media and make divisive news.

Citizens should ask if the membership changed rapidly, where would the power go? Japan is an example where bureaucrats of the Diet and cabinet are far more likely to oversee policy than the 465 elected representatives or 245 councilors (senators). Most legislation comes from the bureaucrats in the cabinet. Without getting into the significant differences in the powers of the Diet versus our Congress, it is necessary to note that bureaucrats have more power in Japan than congressional staff in the US. US congressional staff rotate rapidly—some fear too rapidly to develop expertise. Term limits might increase staff turnover further and reduce Congress's policy knowledge.

> Citizens should ask if the membership changed rapidly, where would the power go?

Another point typically not raised by proponents of term limits is that incumbents unable to seek reelection have little reason to listen to their constituents. For example, following the vote on the impeachment of President Trump, there were efforts to remove House or Senate Members who did not vote the way certain factions preferred. That was especially evident in the Senate, where several senators who'd announced they would not be seeking election in 2022 strayed from what constituents desired.

Why would Members of Congress think about reflecting the will of the folks back home if they were legally prohibited from seeking reelection? Or, if they knew they could not seek reelection, would they concentrate on getting promoted to higher office instead? When students visit the Capitol, they frequently ask about the number of Members in each House. The answer is an old joke: 435 representatives who want to be senators, and one hundred senators who want to be President. Getting reelected or seeking higher office helps keep representatives focused on representing the folks at home.

Here's another of those big problems deserving consideration, debate, and action: campaigns.

FINANCING CAMPAIGNS

Another reform idea that addresses the fundamental structure of our political process and influences the governmental/legislative process is to change the way we finance political campaigns. The campaign financing complaints are many.

- Too much money is spent.
- Too many wealthy outsiders meddle in local campaigns.
- Fundraising is a disadvantage for challengers.

- Too many independently wealthy candidates run.
- There should be public financing to level the playing field.

US House and Senate candidates require tens of millions of dollars to run a competitive race. The typical sources for candidates are:

- Personal wealth, for which there is no spending limit;
- Donations from individuals, which are limited to $3,300 per election for the 2023–2024 election cycle, according to the Federal Election Commission. This amount is far more than the average voter can afford to give, thereby giving more incentive to solicit contributions from wealthier individuals;
- Donations from Political Action Committees (PACs) and Super-PACs, which may or may not even have significant interests in that congressional district or state; and
- Political parties are also subject to higher limits on how much they can contribute.

A quick note on the last two sources: Political parties and PACs raise their funds nationwide from small and big donors. They are more concerned about which party will control Congress or what committees the Member will serve on and how the candidate will vote on issues of interest to them but not necessarily the candidate's home state or district.

Other sources of campaign money are highly questionable to candidates who don't receive the contributions directly. For example, wealthy individuals and organizations spend millions on issue endorsements, issue advocacy, political advertising, and grassroots organizations. They make candidate endorsements, finance advertising, and pay for get-out-the-vote initiatives. This independent spending, in theory not coordinated with a candidate's campaign, exercises sizeable influence, pro or con, over election outcomes. Still, the public cannot see where the funds originated.

Survey research suggests that many Americans believe campaign money has become too influential in politics and government. Of course, some of that perception results from biased media hype. But it is not surprising that campaign fundraising raises questions for voters about how and from whom it is raised and how it is spent.

Although the public is critical of the role of money in campaigns, polls indicate they are just as opposed to public funding of campaigns, an option that has been debated for years but usually gets revisited when finance reform is on the table. When incumbent Members of Congress draft public financing proposals, they always find ways to protect incumbents. Reformers want all candidates to receive the same amount, thus creating 435 real, competitive House races each election. That is unacceptable to the incumbents, who then let the idea die.

WHAT TO DO?

There's a lot wrong with the campaign finance system, including a complete lack of perspective. One solution is often discussed but not liked by the political class. It would probably require a Constitutional amendment. First, it would require that all federal-level donations to candidates must come from individuals capable of voting for them. In other words, everyone of voting age could contribute to presidential campaigns. Everyone living in a state could contribute to candidates running for the US Senate from that state but not from a neighboring state or one on the other end of the country. Lastly, individuals could contribute only to candidates running in their congressional district. Said another way: A voter can contribute only to a contest in which they can vote for or against a candidate.

Such a reform forces candidates to focus on their constituents, not lobbyists, not PAC directors, not fat cats, nor influence peddlers. Why go to Hollywood or Wall Street with cup in hand if you can't accept money from that source? Why spend time romancing the PAC director of a company with no operations in the home district if the PAC can't contribute?

Limiting political contributions to those capable of voting in the election would radically reduce the influence of out-of-state or out-of-district money, put incumbents and challengers on a more even footing, and probably reduce the overall amount of money spent on campaigns. However, that is not the primary objective.

Opponents of this system are numerous. They contend this formula for financing puts wealthy candidates at an even greater advantage over middle-class candidates and gives incumbents a greater advantage because they have the resources of incumbency to promote themselves in the off-year and election year. They also consider the formula impractical for candidates who run in poorer districts where media markets of nearby urban areas put advertising costs out of reach. They suggest that for House races, contributions could be restricted to an entire state rather than the individual district. There are also legal and constitutional issues that could be raised, as mentioned previously.

A related reform idea, again advanced by former Senator Sasse for senators, is to restrict the time they can engage in fundraising activities to only periods in which the Senate is not in session. That could also apply to Members of the House who, like senators, rush back and forth from events or phone-calling sessions to raise money and then rush back to the Floor or committee deliberations to vote on pending legislation without participating in deliberations. But, as one cynic noted, such a change would probably lead to much longer recesses.

ENDING POWER STRUGGLE IN HOUSE LEADERSHIP

Speakers of the House are powerful figures. They are the highest-ranking officer in Congress, second in line to the Presidency after the Vice President, and enjoy almost unlimited access to the media. To a certain extent, strong Speakers could be viewed as essential to an effective body. But, to another, they can be viewed as contrary to the Founders' intent that the House be highly reflective of the populace and that individual Members be assured a voice in the legislative process.

A strong Speaker or a die-hard partisan may not reflect the views of most citizens, and their control of the legislative agenda may thwart what the public would like to see done. All they need to do is to retain the support of their party. Because of the Speaker's ability to influence committee assignments and which legislation gets to the Floor for a vote, it is not hard to retain that support. That leverage is supplemented by the Speaker's ability to raise campaign contributions. In the 2021–2022 cycle, Speaker Pelosi's leadership PAC raised $26 million.

The Speaker's partisanship and abuse of the power of the office have often produced uncivil, sometimes hostile, conditions that lead to gridlock and bitter partisan unrest that spreads among an electorate frustrated that nothing is getting done. It may be time to make a historic change to the system of selecting House Speakers.

Throughout history, the Speaker of the House has been elected by members of the de facto majority. At the outset of each Congress, the minority and majority parties nominate their candidate for the top job, and the majority party's candidate almost always wins the Speaker's chair.

However, what is not well known is that, although not proposed by the Founders, the Speaker of the House may be an individual who is not an elected Member of the House. The Speaker is the only designated constitutional officer of the House, Article I reads: "The House of Representatives shall chuse their Speaker and other Officers; and shall have the sole Power of Impeachment." The Framers intended the Speaker to be of the whole House, not just one partisan faction. Since that is the case, the Speaker could be elected directly by the people, just as the President is. If every voter in every corner of the nation could vote for the Speaker, candidates thought most likely to manage the House fairly and effectively, regardless of party, could be elected Speaker.

Proponents suggest it would help alleviate or subdue the inherent conflicts that make legislating nearly impossible. In the 117th Congress (2021–2022), Democrats outnumbered Republicans by a very narrow majority of eight seats, which fell to seven before the Congress ended. But Democrat

Nancy Pelosi was reelected Speaker, snuffing out much hope of the bipartisan cooperation that is often necessary when margins are that thin. The same numerical situation existed in the 118th Congress (2022–2024) but with Republicans in charge. A Speaker elected nationally may have had the credibility and political capital to level the playing field and create an environment more favorable to bipartisan compromise and governance.

There was a time when straight party-line votes were relatively rare. A level playing field would probably lead to more votes on more amendments by both parties instead of just one politically charged option, with no change for modification that now accompanies most Floor debates and votes. In the past, most bills were subject to voting on numerous amendments; this rarely happens today. It is now an over-simplified, take-or-leave-it approach that makes it hard for most legislation to earn bipartisan support.

This direct-election proposal is a modification of the long-used system for selecting the Speaker of the British Parliament. Their system selects the Speaker from within the House of Commons membership, but the person selected must resign from his or her party and is not allowed to be partisan, even in retirement. Unfortunately, that's not been the history of US Speaker selection.

The states would probably have to propose an amendment to the Constitution to move to the direct election of the Speaker because there is no reason to think either party would willingly reduce their current power within the House. Moreover, although the Constitution gives the House the authority to elect a non-member of the House to the Speakership, there is no motivation to do so, and even if the majority did so, they would probably select a civilian just as partisan as any speaker.

FIXING THE EXECUTIVE-LEGISLATIVE-SUPREME COURT RELATIONSHIP

In the earliest days, Presidents nominated respected lawyers to serve on the Supreme Court, and they were confirmed in very short order. George

Washington nominated James Iredell of Edenton, North Carolina, as an associate justice, and he was confirmed two days later. Recent Presidents have seen their nominations linger for months without a confirmation vote.

Throughout most of our modern history, politics has been part of the process of naming justices. But until recently, legislators resisted putting nominees to a litmus test on how they would vote on issues that might come before the Court. The hypothetical questions implied that a Justice could decide a case without seeing the specifics of the case, something like Members of Congress deciding on a piece of legislation without reading it. It was considered both an insult to the expected objectivity of the nominee and an insult to senators fulfilling their duty to provide "Advice and Consent" to such nominations.

In the beginning, there were six seats on the Court; that number has varied a bit over time, with ten at one point in 1863, then settled at nine around 1868. It is safe to say that every time the number of justices has been changed, it reflected political gamesmanship, attempting to tip the balance of political leanings of the Court.

The year 2021 saw the issue of packing (enlarging the court) publicly discussed once again; there was no effort to disguise the move as anything other than political. A Constitutional amendment would be needed to end the politicization of the Supreme Court and fix the number at nine, the current number, and maybe add an age restriction on service for future nominees.

Because Congress is at or near ideological and partisan parity, such an effort would probably have to start at the state legislative level. If that process is followed, once thirty-four states (two-thirds) adopt an *identical* call for action on this or any other amendments, Congress must call a convention to finalize amendments. However, in 2021, S.J.Res.4, S.J.Res.9, and S.J.Res.11 were introduced in the Senate to set the number of Justices at not more than nine. Whether by Senate or state legislative action, proposed amendments, once ratified by thirty-eight states (three-fourths), would amend the Constitution.

IMPROVING THE CONGRESS FROM THE INSIDE

Aside from the strategic reforms needed to transform Congress into a working legislative and representative body—those we have discussed here are just a few that have been proposed—there are several structural changes that need attention. Many of these were considered by the House Select Committee on the Modernization of Congress, which, regrettably, was discontinued in the 118th Congress. In addition, other changes are more functional and intended to improve how Congress works and alter processes when it doesn't.

Because we touched on a few of them in the past, we include them here in a highly abbreviated form:

1. *Reform the budget process*, which has been a virtual and embarrassing failure for several decades. The process and the politics of budgeting for the national government must change dramatically. A host of reforms have been offered, from changing the fiscal year to calendar, changing the committee's make-up, moving to a two-year budget cycle instead of one, eliminating specific spending categories, focusing on macro-levels of revenue and spending, and many more.

2. *Restore congressional authorizations* of federal programs and require reconsideration of authorizing legislation in committees of jurisdiction.

3. *Re-enforce congressional authority over appropriating funding* for federal programs and agencies so that individual appropriation bills are enacted in each Congress and restrictions are placed on the large and bloated omnibus bills on which Congress now depends and few, if any, Members read.

4. *Streamline committees' jurisdiction* so that too many committees and subcommittees are not addressing the same issues, taking the same time-consuming testimony from the same Executive branch officials. Streamlining would hopefully speed up consideration of

important issues and get legislation to the Floors of both bodies more quickly and effectively.

5. *Open consideration and debate of legislation* on the Floor to more Members with more amendments and extended debates on critical issues. Require legislators to be in attendance when significant issues are debated.

6. *Consider sunsetting more federal programs and agencies,* forcing lawmakers to engage in greater oversight and reconsider the value and cost of government activities.

7. *Initiate a review of the influence and presence of the partisan political parties* in the functions of the House and the Senate and the role they play in the leadership structures, the time and energies of Members and staff, and the evolution of the obliteration of the distinctions between year-around campaigns and governing.

8. *Restructure the congressional calendar* to make Members' time more efficient, enabling them to spend more time in their districts and more concentrated time legislating.

9. *Encourage Members to improve personal relationships* with one another to avoid conflict and uncivil behavior.

10. *Provide greater educational opportunities for Members and staff.* They often begin work in Congress without an adequate grounding in the history of the institution. They are not schooled in the constitutional interactions with the other branches of government. In short, they need to understand the unique culture of the two legislative bodies better and acquire more detailed knowledge of processes and procedures.

Reform #4 is important enough to require further explanation. Streamlining of the committee jurisdictions and membership would represent a significant change in congressional procedures and significantly increase the efficiency of the institution, to say nothing of improving the prospects for bipartisan decision-making and a smoother transition in legislation getting from the committees to the Floors of the House and Senate.

We have discussed in previous chapters what and why Members are appointed to committees and the loosely configured seniority system that plays a key role in those appointments. The current committee system, dating back to 1946, has been subject to shortsighted, piecemeal, and politicized change to the point of organizational exhaustion.

The same holds true for the committee jurisdictions and missions, which have also been bandied back and forth, forward, and backward, and up and down until they have become a discombobulated, confusing, and overlapping hindrance to efficient legislation. Adding to the inherent weaknesses is the inadequate staffing of the committees, not just in terms of their numbers but in their expertise to keep up with rapidly changing technologies, science, public knowledge, and many other professional skill levels. It takes a long time to develop the expertise and experience to meet new challenges. But pay levels for congressional staff that encourage them to seek outside careers and term limits for Members serving as committee chairmen (only in the House and imposed by Republican rules) often handicap both Members and staff.

Another inhibiting factor is the movement of Members from one committee to another. Each committee assignment in the House is for just two years. Many Members move to other committees as they build seniority. Some committees are more important to some Members than others. A Member from a rural agricultural district who farmed before they came to Congress would likely consider the Agriculture Committee more important than other committees, so moving to that committee would make sense strategically and politically. In contrast, for other Members, perhaps most, the assignment would be considered an appointment to Siberia.

Another consideration in reforming the committee system is assessing the number of standing, select, special, and joint committees in both the House and Senate and determining whether they are all needed.

It is also important that Congress establish special procedures and mechanisms necessary to ensure that reforms are considered, shaped into new laws, rules, and procedures, and adopted by both houses of Congress. The former House Select Committee on the Modernization of the Congress engaged in ground-breaking bipartisan reform debates and recommended reforms to the House for enactment. Many of the committee's recommendations were adopted by the House in a rare display of bipartisan cooperation from the inception of the Select Committee to final consideration on the House Floor. While the Senate does not have such a committee, it should. Regrettably, the Select Committee was dissolved by House Republicans at the outset of the 118th Congress, leaving its work to a subcommittee of the House Administration Committee.

The House and the Senate should form a bipartisan joint committee of both houses to consider reforms affecting both houses and look critically at the relationship between the two bodies, which share responsibility for the failure of the budget, appropriations, and authorization processes.

There are dozens of other strategic and tactical reforms that could and should be considered by Congress. It is a huge undertaking. That's because there is a lot wrong with the functions of our governmental institutions and the political system that is supposed to produce individuals capable enough and dedicated enough to fix what's broken. Politicians like to say there are no easy answers, but dumbing those solutions down so they can be squeezed into media soundbites, X (Twitter) posts, campaign slogans, and promises isn't beneficial. You could write a book about the intricacies of each of the solutions we've highlighted here.

Sometimes simplicity makes sense, but this isn't one of those times, so it is incumbent upon an involved citizenry to make sure representatives and senators are committed and able to achieve serious change.

While many of the reforms outlined above would make a significant difference in the operations of the people's branch of government, combining some of them would be even more effective. Some of these efforts need to begin in state legislatures. In the end, citizens must insist that candidates for Congress discuss and then act on internal reforms to earn back their trust and continued support.

Willm Hogarth Inv.^t

Etch'd by J. H. Sherwin.

The Politician.

Etch'd from an Original Sketch of Wm Hogarth's, in the Posession of Mr Forrest: Pub.^d as the Act directs by Jane Hogarth, 1775.
31 October

Effective politicians listen to the views of their constituents.

Chapter 15

Call to Action

I do not say that democracy has been more pernicious on the whole, and in the long run, than monarchy or aristocracy. Democracy has never been and never can be so durable as aristocracy or monarchy; but while it lasts, it is more bloody than either. ... Remember, democracy never lasts long. It soon wastes, exhausts, and murders itself. There never was a democracy yet that did not commit suicide.
—From the Letters of John Adams

Over the past fourteen chapters, we have discussed the basic structure of Congress, the specific roles of Members and their staff, and explored in-depth issues related to campaign finance, congressional district populations, distinctions between the House and the Senate, the exaggerated influence of media, special interest groups, and the resulting inadequacies and failures of the US Congress.

The Founders knew they were creating something different and, hopefully, lasting. They were visionary. No constitutional democratic republic has survived as long as ours. Maybe our longevity is to the credit of Adams and the other Founders who were smart enough not to create a pure democracy or a monarchy, as some preferred, but a democratic republic with three branches of government, each serving as a check and balance of the other.

They built in safeguards against empire builders, oligarchs, and wannabe dictators. They safeguarded our liberties and citizen-government within the framework of national cohesion, shared responsibilities, and the pursuit of common interests.

The Declaration of Independence clearly illustrates this point using three key words: We the People. As discussed previously, numerous mini-revolutionary changes have occurred in the past 250 years. Some unintentionally changed the Founders' intent and, more importantly, the outcome of governance in the United States.

As we discussed, the decision one hundred years ago to freeze the size of the House of Representatives resulted in an enormous reduction in the influence of any one citizen. Many other entities have assumed that influence. They range from special interests and political action committees (PACs) to organized parties, social groups, churches, academics, and most importantly, media.

So now, what do we do about it?

Obviously, the first and easy answer is to vote, of course, but also to make your vote count. And to do that responsibly means educating yourself about issues and candidates. Is simply following your heart sufficient? Is it responsible to just make your voting decisions based on a single issue or the promises of a single candidate? Or to simply follow the leadership of your normal political party affiliation? Or to follow the siren sounds of media that oversimplify and tell you what you want to hear?

The answer is almost always no.

Good decision-making requires more. It has taken much more from the citizenry to get where we are today. Consider that the American people have accomplished that which not even the most visionary imagination could have conceived a century ago, or even fifty years ago. Change has been and continues to occur at the speed of light, but the nation has kept up. The nation has been a world leader. Through it all, the American people have come together many times in the face of the most trying circumstances, and with good leadership, have gone in the right direction and made the right decisions.

It suggests the future of our republic is still in the ascendancy, not in decline.

But is it? Was Adams right in assuming that democratic systems of self-government eventually fall under the weight of human excesses and self-interest? The plague of power, wealth, and fame that always runs through the bloodstream of politics can infect and ultimately destroy any system.

That can be avoided if we inoculate ourselves from it.

The challenges ahead require more public knowledge, more citizen involvement, and more discerning judgment, all in the framework of a civil discourse that enables sound, common sense and reasoned decisions.

Assuming you have found things in this book with which you agree, your challenge is to seek those solutions and find ways to bring them to the attention of your fellow citizens, then collectively bring pressure on the elected who have the power to act. There is strength in numbers and leverage in unity.

By knowing more about how Congress works, citizens can have a hand in making it work better. Citizens can influence the process and have an impact, even if, for example, reforms require a constitutional amendment to change the way campaigns are funded—or change the way senators are elected if that is where people choose to devote their energies.

Education is our shield against tyranny. So, it will require collective pressure to restore civic education in elementary, secondary, and higher education and ensure that civics education does not end with the award of a diploma.

Meeting the challenges we all face will require major changes in the way Congress is organized and fulfills its role and the way members of Congress behave. It will require restoration in the relationship between the Legislative and Executive branches, so they perform their constitutionally prescribed duties.

It will require your Members of Congress to make basic changes in the budget, authorizing and appropriations processes, the procedures for amending legislation, and much more so that your representatives have greater influence in the decision-making.

There are other complex challenges that demand the attention of the citizenry if we are to restore a democratic republican ideal. One is to preserve a national asset, an objective media, an indispensable resource that we noted in previous chapters, is threatened with extinction. The percentage of the population receiving their news from social media and various digital tools continues to grow. Voicing your opinion for objectivity and transparency on those platforms is essential.

Lastly, it is critical that responsible citizens learn about and engage in the evolution of artificial intelligence (AI). This digital phenomenon of unparalleled potential has become both a threat and a powerful ally. Knowing more about it, knowing how to influence it, and knowing how to harness it is exceedingly critical. It is so new and spreading so rapidly that Members of Congress do not have intuitive knowledge of its impact and thus need the informed counsel of their constituents. Realistically, this is one more issue that demonstrates the need to have more members with more than political winner backgrounds.

None of this is going to be easy. The American public has for years been losing faith and trust in the government and those who govern. They have lost faith in once-great public and private institutions that were designed to support them. Most Americans believe the nation is on the wrong track. It could mean further degradation of our democratic republican ideals getting baked into the system.

America today seems chronically divided and its citizens sadly disillusioned, a good many convinced they have been left behind and see little reason to engage. Politics, a once popular and accepted topic at the water cooler and backyard barbeques is now verboten (one reason, of course, is that the water cooler is gone too).

Even if the environment is not exactly conducive to major change, knowing more gives you greater influence, and the bar for getting something accomplished is placed on a lower peg.

We have throughout this book offered suggestions on what citizens can do to have more influence. In speech class, they teach you to tell them what you're going to tell them, tell them, and then tell them what you told them. In this case, key actions—some pretty simple—can bear repeating here:

- Focus on a limited number of reforms you feel strongly about to make your case;
- Learn more about them from politicians, resources, and organizations that have differing views;
- Make your views known;
- Write letters to the editor on one or two key points;
- Communicate with legislative offices and ask for a response;
- Meet with your state or federal legislators and ask them about the issue(s), what they think, and what they can do to bring about change; insist that they follow up with you;
- Motivate social, political, or religious groups to speak up and write letters and speak to representatives and senators;
- Communicate with others in your community who are already engaged in politics in a way that is compatible with what you want to accomplish; and,
- Do not tolerate or engage in communicating in an uncivil, angry, or excessively partisan attitude or behavior.

Because you have read this far, odds are you are interested. You are already engaged intellectually. You will recall that this chapter started with the idea that our ongoing responsibility is to sustain our freedom. Despite the best of our efforts, there is no guarantee we will be successful. Like life, politics is not fair. There is no natural law that says the United States is a permanent fixture in the pantheon of global governments. In fact, history argues the opposite is true.

What will you do to preserve democracy? Start by working to bring us together again.

This is our final chapter, but not yours. Future chapters must be written by you.

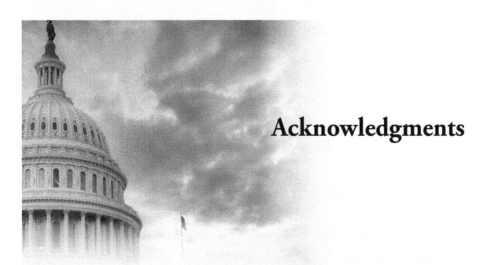

Acknowledgments

This book was conceived years ago and draws on many sources, including the decades of personal experience we gained serving as Congressional staff and in professional capacities in the congressional orbit. We also drew on the expertise of current and former members of Congress and staff and various outside experts from politics, business, survey research, academia, and, most importantly, citizens affected by government action or inaction.

We realized early in the process that writing a book for average citizens would be a challenge, given the challenge of deciphering congressional language and practices and providing insights into how citizens can have a greater influence on the process of self-governance. Some of the ideas and information originated in our work with the Congressional Institute as co-authors of *Surviving Inside Congress, Surviving* was intended as a "handbook" for new Members of Congress and staff. It is now entering its Sixth Edition. We acknowledge the work of Institute staff, particularly then President Mark Strand, in constantly improving *Surviving* and the assistance of the Institute's Timothy Lang. We also congratulate Kelle Strickland, the new President/CEO of the Institute, as she finalizes the 6th edition. However, the Institute is not responsible for the contents of this book.

We also acknowledge the contributions of our families and many friends who offered their guidance on the views of the citizenry and their experiences with the government, the news media, and many more elements of the book, including the professional graphics produced by Mike's daughter Jessica Vergano.

Thanks also to the members of Congress for whom we worked and their professional staff. There were many in the office of the late Republican Leader Bob Michel who were inspirations and whose experience and expertise were invaluable to both of us in researching and drafting this book.

We are also grateful to the professionals at Morgan James Publishing, who guided us through the mysterious publishing maze. We give special thanks to our editor, Cortney Donelson of vocem LLC.

With this effort, we intended to produce a considerably different book that citizens can use to understand better and maybe recapture control over their Congress. Our intent was moved closer to reality by so many individuals and organizations that have championed the causes of civics education, civility in public discourse, consensus policymaking, the restoration of American values, and the broader participation of the citizenry in both politics and public policy. When we began this endeavor, there weren't many in the vanguard among those champions, but today, there are, with more committing themselves every day. We are grateful to them and their work to educate and empower the public. We hope this project will advance those goals.

References and Resources

Here is a list of some of the books we drew on for inspiration or information and some suggested additional reading to enhance your understanding of the history and behaviors of the People's House, your US Congress.

- *All Too Human* by George Stephanopoulos, Little Brown and Company 1999
- *Benjamin Franklin* by Walter Isaacson, Simon and Schuster, 2003
- *Bill of Rights, James Madison's Legacy* by Richard T. Burress, Hoover Institute, 1989
- *The Bully Pulpit* by Doris Kearns Goodwin, Simon & Schuster, 2013
- *Burning Down the House* by Julian E. Zelizer, Penguin Random House, 2020
- *The Centrist Solution* by Joe Lieberman, Diversion Publishing 2021
- *Combat* by Warren Rudman, Random House, 1996
- *Common Sense* by Thomas Paine, Barnes &Noble, 1995
- *Congressional Travels* by Richard F. Fenno Jr., Pearson Longman Education Inc., 2007
- *Debates in the Federal Convention of 1787* by James Madison edited by Gordon Lloyd, Ashbrook Center, Ashland University

- *Destiny and Power* by John Meacham, Random House, 2015
- *The Federalist Papers Made Easier* by Paul A. Skousen, Independently published, 2022
- *The Fourth Turning* by Neil Howe and William Strauss, Crown Publishing, 1997
- *Founding Brothers* by Joseph Ellis, Alfred Knopp, 2001
- *Henry Clay* by David Heidler and Jeannine Heidler, Random House, 2011
- *Herding Cats* by Trent Lott, William Morrow, 2005
- *Hero Tales from American History* by Henry Cabot Lodge and Theodore Roosevelt, Fireworks Press, 1895
- *History of the House of Representatives by the Committee on House Administration*, Government Printing Office, 1965
- *Indelible Ink* by Richard Kluger, W.W. Norton Company, 2016
- *Kings of the Hill* by Lynne Cheney and Richard Cheney, Continuum Publishing, 1983
- *The Man Who Ran Washington* by Peter Baker and Susan Glasser, Double Day, 2020
- *Managing at the Speed of Change* by Daryl Connor, Random House, 2000
- *On the House* by John Boehner, St. Martin's Press, 2021
- *Palace Politics* by Robert Hartmann, McGraw Hill, 1980
- *The Parties Versus the People* by Mickey Edwards, Yale University Press, 2012
- *A Question of Respect* by Ed Goaes and Celinda Lake, Morgan James Publishing, 2022
- *Robert H. Michel* edited by Frank Mackaman and Sean Kelly, University Press of Kansas
- *Seeking Bipartisanship* by Ray LaHood, Cambria Publishing, 2015
- *Speaker* by Dennis Hastert, Regnery Publishing Inc., 2004
- *Speaker Jim Wright* by J Brooks Flippen, University of Texas Press, 2018

- *Street Corner Conservative* by William F. Gavin, Arlington House Publishers, 1975
- *Surviving Inside Congress* by Mark Strand, Mike Johnson and Jerry Climer, Congressional Institute
- *Tip and the Gipper* by Christ Matthews, Simon and Schuster, 2013
- *We the People* by Richard T. Burress, Hoover Institution, 1987
- *The Windmill Chaser* by Bob Livingston, University of Louisiana at Lafayette Press, 2018
- *1776* by David McCullough, Simon & Schuster, 2005

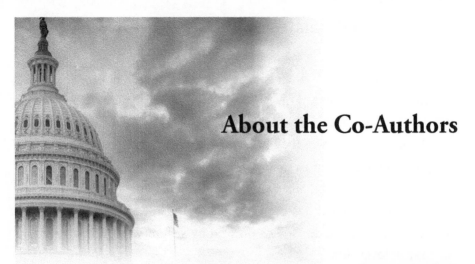

About the Co-Authors

Michael S. Johnson

Mike spent forty-seven years serving in the White House, Congress, private sector media relations and advocacy as well as a number of nonprofit organizations dedicated to improving the work of the Legislative and Executive branches. Prior to that he spent seven years in print journalism. Mike co-authored a book *Surviving Inside Congress*, published by the Congressional Institute, now in its fifth edition. Mike has also written occasional columns for the website NewGOPForum.com, written articles for many publications, appeared on news shows as well as appeared on podcasts for numerous organizations.

Jerome F. Climer

Jerry graduated from the University of Arkansas with a degree in public administration. He interrupted his master's degree work to join the staff of an Arkansas congressman, for what he intended to be a two-year experience. Forty years later he left Capitol Hill having served other Members of Congress, the Secretary of the Department of Agriculture, five years on the House Minority Leadership staff, and twenty as President of the Congressional Institute. This experience enabled him to master the intricacies of the House and Senate and develop perspective about the historic intent for the institution against present day realities. Most of his writing was anonymous, for members of Congress and published as their work, or on behalf of The Congressional Institute. He co-authored *Surviving Inside Congress* of which there are now five editions. The book has been distributed to staff of both parties in the House and the Senate, as well as utilized by several academic institutions for college level study.

Image Credits

Chapter 1, *This is the Team that Will Win Every Time,* Mar. 27, 1898, by Clifford K. Berryman, National Archives Catalog Number: 6010254, Public Domain.

Chapter 2, *Organization and Decision-Making,* 2023 by Jessica Vergano, original art by permission of the artist.

Chapter 3, *The House in Session (According to the Minority Point of View),* Apr. 16, 1908, by Clifford K. Berryman, National Archives Catalog Number: 6010752, Public Domain.

Chapter 4, *Congressional Staff: The Influence of the Unelected,* 2023, by Jessica Vergano, original art by permission of the artist.

Chapter 5, *Anyone Home?* Feb. 24, 1920, by Clifford K. Berryman, National Archives Catalog Number: 6011590, Public Domain.

Chapter 6, *Miss Democracy,* Nov. 7, 1912, by Clifford K. Berryman, National Archives Catalog Number: 306174, Public Domain.

Chapter 7, *Not Yet But Soon,* Aug. 26, 1912, by Clifford K. Berryman - National Archives Catalog Number: 306171, Public Domain.

Chapter 9, *Have you considered that all your fears may be 'media driven'?* CartoonStock, *www.CartoonStock.com.*

Chapter 10, *Puzzle—Find the Committee Chairmen,* Aug. 6, 1909, by Clifford K. Berryman, National Archives Catalog Number: 6010808, Public Domain.

Chapter 11, *That Group of Constituents I'm Meeting . . . is that Feedback or Blowback?* CartoonStock, *www.CartoonStock.com.*

Chapter 13, *Southern Chivalry – Argument versus Clubs,* by J. L. Magee, 1856, Boston Athenaeum, https://bostonathenaeum.org, Public Domain

Chapter 14, *Reforms to Make Congress Work for You,* 2023, by Jessica Vergano, original art by permission of the artist.

Chapter 15, *The Politician,* John Keyse Sherwin,1775, The Met, metmuseum. org 416967, Public Domain.

Endnotes

1   Precedents established in the First Congress by George Galloway/Legislative Reference Service, Library of Congress (George B. Galloway/ The Western Political Quarterly Vol. 11, No. 3 (Sept. 1958), pp. 454–468, https://www.jstor.org/stable/444560, (JSTOR is "Journal Storage," a digital library founded in 1994)

2   United States Senate. https://www.senate.gov/about/origins-foundations. htm. Also: "The requisites ... residents among them," from Democracy and the Federal Constitution: Notes from the Constitutional Convention, May-Sept. 1787, https://userpages.umbc.edu/~bouton/History101/ ConstitutionalConvention.htm.

3   Zemler, Ph.D., Jeffrey A. "James Madison." Washington Library, https:// www.mountvernon.org/library/digitalhistory/digital-encyclopedia/article/ james-madison/.

4   "Address of the President to Congress, [30 April] 1789," Founders Online, National Archives, https://founders.archives.gov/documents/Madison/01-12-02-0078. [Original source: The Papers of James Madison, vol. 12, 2 March 1789–20 January 1790 and supplement 24 October 1775–24 January 1789, ed. Charles F. Hobson and Robert A. Rutland. Charlottesville: University Press of Virginia, 1979, pp. 120–124.]

5   "Amendments to the Constitution, [15 August] 1789," *Founders Online,* National Archives, https://founders.archives.gov/documents/Madison/

01-12-02-0224. [Original source: *The Papers of James Madison*, vol. 12, *2 March 1789–20 January 1790 and supplement 24 October 1775–24 January 1789*, ed. Charles F. Hobson and Robert A. Rutland. Charlottesville: University Press of Virginia, 1979, pp. 339–342.]

6 Azerrad, Ph.D., David. "How James Madison Saved the Constitution This Month by Writing the Bill Of Rights." The Heritage Foundation, Dec 28, 2016, https://www.heritage.org/the-constitution/commentary/how-james-madison-saved-the-constitution-month-writing-the-bill-rights.

7 Malsberger, John W. "The Political Thought of Fisher Ames." *Journal of the Early Republic* 2, no. 1 (1982): 1–20. https://doi.org/10.2307/3122532.

8 Remini, Robert V. 2006, *The House: The History of the House of Representatives,* New York: Smithsonian Books in association with HarperCollins, accessed from https://archive.org/details/househistoryo00remi.

9 Heidler, David W. and Jeanne T. Hediler. 2010. *Henry Clay*. New York: Random House, p 148.

10 Cheney, Richard B. and Lynne V. Cheney. 1983. *Kings of the Hill: Power and Personality in the House of Representatives.* New York: Continuum Intl Pub Group.

11 Simkin, John. "Arthur Vandenberg." Spartacus Educational, March 2022 (update), https://spartacus-educational.com/USAvandenbergA.htm.

12 Taft, Robert A. and Senate Leaders, "More than 'Mr. Republican'." United States Senate, accessed Sept 8, 2023, https://www.senate.gov/about/origins-foundations/parties-leadership/taft-a-robert.htm.

13 "Arthur Vandenberg." Wikipedia, https://en.wikipedia.org/wiki/Arthur_Vandenberg.

14 Bible Portal (no date). Quote by Edmund Burke, accessed Sept 8, 2023, https://bibleportal.com/bible-quote/to-make-a-government-requires-no-great-prudence-settle-the-seat-of-power-teach-obedience-and-the-work-is-done.

15 Thomas, George. "Madison and the Perils of Populism," (quoting from Reflections on the Revolution in France by Edmund Burke), reposted from Fall 2016, National Affairs No. 56, Summer 2023, https://national

affairs.com/publications/detail/madison-and-the-perils-of-populism.

16 Goeas, Ed and Celinda Lake. 2022. *A Question of Respect: Bringing Us Together in a Deeply Divided Nation*, New York: Morgan James Publishing, Foreword.

17 Patterson, Thomas E. "Pre-Primary News Coverage of the 2016 Presidential Race: Trump's Rise, Sanders' Emergence, Clinton's Struggle." Harvard Kennedy School's Shorenstein Center on Media, Politics and Public Policy, June 13, 2016, https://shorensteincenter.org/pre-primary-news-coverage-2016-trump-clinton-sanders/.

18 Carney, Jordain. "Legislation slows to crawl in divided Washington." The Hill. April 07, 2019, https://thehill.com/homenews/senate/437657-legislation-slows-to-crawl-in-divided-washington/.

19 Ibid.

20 Sultan, Niv M. "Election 2016: Trump's free media helped keep cost down, but fewer donors provided more of the cash." Open Secrets, April 13, 2017, https://www.opensecrets.org/news/2017/04/election-2016-trump-fewer-donors-provided-more-of-the-cash/.

21 OpenSecrets.org. "Most expensive midterm ever: Cost of 2018 election surpasses $5.7 billion." Open Secrets, Feb. 6, 2019, https://www.opensecrets.org/news/2019/02/cost-of-2018-election-5pnt7bil/.

22 Navarro, J. G. "Advertising revenue in the U.S. 2014–2027." April 28, 2023. Statista, https://www.statista.com/statistics/236958/advertising-spending-in-the-us/.

23 Sherlock, James C. "Out-of-State Money Floods to Incumbent Democrats in Virginia's Competitive Congressional Races." Bacon's Rebellion Blog, 10/26/2022, https://www.baconsrebellion.com/wp/out-of-state-money-floods-to-incumbent-democrats-in-virginias-competitive-congressional-races/.

24 Vogel, Kenneth and Shane Goldmacher. "Democrats Decried Dark Money. Then They Won With It in 2020." *New York Times,* January 29, 2022, https://www.nytimes.com/2022/01/29/us/politics/democrats-dark-money-donors.html.

25 Warren, Michael. "Major outside spending boosts Trump-backed Budd in North Carolina Senate primary." CNN, May 16, 2022, https://www.cnn.com/2022/05/16/politics/nc-republican-senate-primary-election/index.html.

26 Ruane, Kate and Sonia Gill. "Congress, Let's Fix the Problems in H.R. 1 So We Can Enact the Bill's Much-Needed Reforms." ACLU, March 5, 2019, https://www.aclu.org/news/free-speech/congress-lets-fix-problems-hr-1-so-we-can-enact-bills-much.

27 Hoppe, David. "The Filibuster Made the Civil Rights Act Possible." *Wall Street Journal,* April 11, 2021, https://www.wsj.com/articles/the-filibuster-made-the-civil-rights-act-possible-11618174288.

28 Ibid.

29 Ibid.

30 Desjardins, Lisa. "What every Senate Democrat has said about filibuster reform." PBS | Politics, June 23, 2021, https://www.pbs.org/newshour/politics/what-every-senate-democrat-has-said-about-filibuster-reform.

31 Words from Senator Mitch McConnell. "Democrats Hypocritically Killing the Filibuster Would Break the Senate." March 16, 2021, https://www.republicanleader.senate.gov/newsroom/remarks/democrats-hypocritically-killing-the-filibuster-would-break-the-senate#:~:-text="Quote%3A%20%27The%20legislative%20filibuster,of%20short%2Dterm%20electoral%20change.

32 Ibid.

33 Peter Carlson. "A Short History of the Filibuster." Peter Carlson - Accessed 9/8/2023, https://www.historynet.com/a-short-history-of-the-filibuster/.

34 Ibid.

35 Kluger, Richard. 2016. *Indelible Ink: The Trials of John Peter Zenger and the Birth of the Free Press.* New York: W. W. Norton & Company, p 267–268.

36 Goodwin, Doris Kearns. 2014. The Bully Pulpit: Theodore Roosevelt, William Howard Taft, and the Golden Age of Journalism. New York: Simon and Schuster, p 324.

37 Ibid. p 326.

38 Goodwin, Kearns Doris. The Bully Pulpit: Theodore Roosevelt, William Howard Taft, and the Golden Age of Journalism. New York: Simon and Schuster. 2014, p 324.

39 Statista. "Number of Daily Newspapers in the United States from 1975–2018 – Accessed Sept. 8, 2023, https://www.statista.com/statistics/183408/number-of-us-daily-newspapers-since-1975/.

40 Bauder, David. "US Newspapers Continuing to Die at a Rate of 2 Each Week." Associated Press, June 30, 2022, https://apnews.com/article/journalism-united-states-39ef84c1131267233768bbb4dcaa181b.

41 Ibid.

42 PEW Research Center. "State of the News Media 2016 Fact Sheet," June 15, 2016 - Assessed Sept. 8, 2023, https://www.pewresearch.org/journalism/2016/06/15/NEWSPAPERS-FACT-SHEET/.

43 Bauder, David. "US Newspapers Continuing to Die at a Rate of 2 Each Week." Associated Press, June 30, 2022, https://apnews.com/article/journalism-united-states-39ef84c1131267233768bbb4dcaa181b.

44 Pengue, Maria." 21 Extraordinary Newspaper Statistics You Should Know about in 2023." (Quoting Pew Research Center) Feb. 23, 2021, https://letter.ly/newspaper-statistics/.

45 PEW Research Center. Newspapers Fact Sheet, June 29, 2021, https://www.pewresearch.org/journalism/fact-sheet/newspapers/.

46 "Barack Obama and the Freedom to Write." PEN America | YouTube. December 10, 2020. Video, 35:14:00, https://www.youtube.com/watch?v=YOQVvikud0Q.

47 Farris, Scott. "Opinion: The Most Important Losers in American Politics." Washington Post. Dec. 30, 2011, https://www.washingtonpost.com/opinions/the-most-important-losers-in-american-politics/2011/12/15/gIQAQLeiQP_story.html.

48 Shedden, David. "Early TV Anchors," Poynter Institute Archive, April 4, 2006, https://www.poynter.org/archive/2006/early-tv-anchors/.

49 Nielsen. "Nielsen Estimates 119.9 Million TV Homes in the U.S. for the 2018–2019 TV Season," September 2018, https://www.nielsen.com/

insights/2018/nielsen-estimates-119-9-million-tv-homes-in-the-us-for-the-2018-19-season/.

50 Nielsen. "Nielsen Estimates 121 Million TV Homes in the U.S. for the 2020-2021 Season," August 2020, https://www.nielsen.com/insights/2020/nielsen-estimates-121-million-tv-homes-in-the-u-s-for-the-2020-2021-tv-season/.

51 "Walter Cronkite Editorial on Tet and Vietnam." Alpha History, Feb. 28, 1968, https://alphahistory.com/vietnamwar/walter-cronkite-editorial-1968/.

52 Burman, Marc. "Celebrating 20 Years: 'Face The Nation' Moderator Margaret Brennan Reflects On Two Decades In The Changing News Landscape." Forbes, Jan. 18, 2022, https://www.forbes.com/sites/marc-berman1/2022/01/18/celebrating-20-years-face-the-nation-moderator-margaret-brennan-reflects-on-two-decades-in-the-changing-news-land-scape/?sh=372d7b3e7efe.

53 Bach, Natasha. "Social Media is the go-to resource for Millennials and Gen-Z, but that doesn't mean they trust it." PRWeek. 01/11/2022, https://www.prweek.com/article/1737192/social-media-go-to-news-source-mil-lennials-gen-z-doesnt-mean-trust.

54 Shearer, Elisha. "More than eight-in-ten Americans get news from digital devices." PEW Research Center, 1/12/2021, https://www.pewresearch.org/short-reads/2021/01/12/more-than-eight-in-ten-americans-get-news-from-digital-devices/.

55 Goeas, Ed and Celinda Lake. 2022. A Question of Respect: Bringing Us Together in a Deeply Divided Nation, New York: Morgan James Publishing, p 97.

56 "Hannah-Jones: All Journalism Is Activism." Jonathan Turley. July 20, 2021, https://jonathanturley.org/2021/07/20/hannah-jones-all-journalism-is-activism/.

57 "Your Unethical Nature" Northwestern Journalism Professor Trashes Columnist for Waiting for the Facts on Police Shooting." Jonathan Turley. June 21, 2021, https://jonathanturley.org/2021/06/21/murder-he-wrote-northwestern-journalism-professor-trashes-columnist-for-waiting-

for-the-facts-on-police-shooting/.

58 "Lifetime Achievement Awards Ceremony with Lester Holt." Murrow College | YouTube. March 30, 2021. Video, 44:16, https://www.youtube.com/watch?v=AWIbAKI9PSA.

59 Sullivan, Maragaret. What's a journalist supposed to be now—an activist? A stenographer? You're asking the wrong question." *Washington Post,* June 7, 2020, https://www.washingtonpost.com/lifestyle/media/whats-a-journalist-supposed-to-be-now--an-activist-a-stenographer-youre-asking-the-wrong-question/2020/06/06/60fdfb86-a73b-11ea-b619-3f9133bbb482_story.html.

60 Gessen, Masha. Why are Some Journalists Afraid of "Moral Clarity" The New Yorker, June 24, 2020, https://www.newyorker.com/news/our-columnists/why-are-some-journalists-afraid-of-moral-clarity.

61 McBride, Kelly. "New NPR Ethics Policy: It's OK For Journalists To Demonstrate (Sometimes)." NPR, June 29, 2021, https://www.npr.org/sections/publiceditor/2021/07/29/1021802098/new-npr-ethics-policy-its-ok-for-journalists-to-demonstrate-sometimes. Note: (The new NPR policy reads, "NPR editorial staff may express support for democratic, civic values that are core to NPR's work, such as, but not limited to the freedom and dignity of human beings, the rights of a free and independent press, the right to thrive in society without facing discrimination on the basis of race, ethnicity, gender, sexual identity, disability, or religion." Link to NPR Ethics website for actual document: https://www.npr.org/ethics).

62 Blatchford, Taylor. "Student Journalists Ask: Is Objectivity Becoming Obsolete?" Poynter.org, Nov. 10, 2021, https://www.poynter.org/educators-students/2021/student-journalists-ask-is-objectivity-becoming-obsolete/.

63 Ray, Justin. "New York Times Reporters Frustrated Over Outside Work Policies." Business Insider, March 7, 2022, https://www.businessinsider.com/new-york-times-reporters-frustrated-over-outside-work-policies-2022-3.

64 Willnat, Lars, Weaver, David H. & Cleve Wilhoit. "Survey of journalists, conducted by researchers at the Newhouse School, provides insights into the state of journalism today." S.I. Newhouse School of Communications

at Syracuse University, May 5, 2022, https://newhouse.syracuse.edu/news/survey-of-journalists-provides-insights-into-the-state-of-journalism-today/.

65 Willnat, Lars, Weaver, David H. & Cleve Wilhoit The American Journalist Under Attack, Media, Trust and Democracy: Key Findings 2022," S.I. Newhouse School of Public Communications at Syracuse University, 2002, https://www.theamericanjournalist.org/post/american-journalist-findings.

66 Baron, Martin. We want objective judges and doctors. Why not journalists too? (Opinion)" Washington Post, March 24, 2023, https://www.washingtonpost.com/opinions/2023/03/24/journalism-objectivity-trump-misinformation-marty-baron/.

67 Hussman, Walter. "Bring Back Objective Journalism." Wall Street Journal, Feb. 15, 2023, https://www.wsj.com/articles/bring-back-objective-journalism-news-reporting-objectivity-public-opinion-trust-fourth-estate-reporters-media-newspaper-8a2c6ba.

68 Grabowski, Mark . "Objectivity didn't fail journalism. Journalists failed it." Washington Examiner, June 17, 2020, https://www.washingtonexaminer.com/opinion/objectivity-didnt-fail-journalism-journalists-failed-it.

69 2021 Edelman Trust Barometer. Edelman.com. March 16, 2021, https://www.edelman.com/trust/2021-trust-barometer.

70 Edelman, Richard. "Declaring Information Bankruptcy." Edelman.com. Jan. 12, 2021, https://www.edelman.com/trust/2021-trust-barometer/insights/declaring-information-bankruptcy.

71 Turley, Jonathan. "Only 21 Percent of Americans Trust Newspapers." JonathanTurley.org. July 15, 2021, https://jonathanturley.org/2021/07/15/gallup-poll-only-21-percent-of-americans-trust-newspapers/.

72 Ibid.

73 Ibid.

74 "A new understanding: What makes people trust and rely on news." America Press Institute. April 17, 2016, https://www.americanpress institute.org/publications/reports/survey-research/trust-news/.

75 Knight Foundation. "Indicators of News Media Trust: Survey." Sept. 11, 2018, https://knightfoundation.org/reports/indicators-of-news-media-trust.

76 "The Mueller Conclusions." The Editorial Board *Wall Street Journal.* March 24, 2019, https://www.wsj.com/articles/the-mueller-conclusions-11553468979.

77 Koppel/Kalb interview; Carnegie Endowment for International Peace. March 7, 2019, https://carnegieendowment.org/2019/03/07/war-on-press-event-7061.

78 Thiessen, Mark. "The Trump-Russia collusion hall of shame." Washington Post. March 28, 2019, http://www.washingtonpost.com/opinions/the-trump-russia-collusion-hall-of-shame/2019/03/28/306b5168-5173-11e9-a3f7-78b7525a8d5f_story.html.

79 "Report on Matters Related to Intelligence Activities and Investigations Arising Out of the 2016 Presidential Campaigns." Justice.gov. May 12, 2023, https://www.justice.gov/storage/durhamreport.pdf.

80 Mikkelson, David. "We have a Bad News Problem, Not a Fake News Problem," Snopes.com: Nov. 17, 2016, https://www.snopes.com/news/2016/11/17/we-have-a-bad-news-problem-not-a-fake-news-problem/.

81 Harper, Jennifer. "Inside the Beltway: Fake news now a worldwide concern." Washington Times. June 27, 2019, https://www.washingtontimes.com/news/2019/jun/27/inside-the-beltway-fake-news-now-a-worldwide-issue/.

82 Farhi, Paul. "Sarah Sanders promotes an altered video of CNN reporter, sparking allegations of visual propaganda." Washington Post. Nov. 8, 2018, https://www.washingtonpost.com/lifestyle/style/sarah-sanders-promotes-an-altered-video-of-cnn-reporter-sparking-allegations-of-visual-propaganda/2018/11/08/33210126-e375-11e8-b759-3d88a5ce9e19_story.html.

83 Perticone, Joe. "The 20 lobbying groups that spent the most money to get their voice heard in Washington last year." *Business Insider* (India). March 8, 2019, https://www.businessinsider.in/the-20-lobbying-groups-that-spent-the-most-money-to-get-their-voice-heard-in-washington-last-year/articleshow/68323849.cms.

84 Dilorenzo, Thomas. "The Truth About the 'Robber Barons'." Ludwig von Mises Institute.

85 Statista. "Leading lobbying industries in the United States in 2022, by total lobbying spending." April 5, 2023, https://www.statista.com/statistics/257364/top-lobbying-industries-in-the-us/.

86 Leonhardt, David. "'A Black Eye': Why Political Polling Missed the Mark. Again." NY Times, Nov. 12, 2020, https://www.nytimes.com/2020/11/12/us/politics/election-polls-trump-biden.html.

87 Keeter, Scott; Kennedy, Courtney & Claudia Deane. "Understanding how 2020 election polls performed and what it might mean for other kinds of survey work." PEW Research Center: Nov. 13, 2020, https://www.pewresearch.org/short-reads/2020/11/13/understanding-how-2020s-election-polls-performed-and-what-it-might-mean-for-other-kinds-of-survey-work/.

88 "Legendary Campaign: Pepper vs. Smathers in '50 By Howell Raines, Special To the New York Times," *New York Times*, Feb. 24, 1983, https://www.nytimes.com/1983/02/24/us/legendary-campaign-pepper-vs-smathers-in-50.html.

89 Barrett, Devlin. "Ex-congressman from Abscam scandal faces new vote-buying charges." Washington Post. July 23, 2020, https://www.washingtonpost.com/national-security/ex-congressman-from-abscam-scandal-faces-new-vote-buying-charges/2020/07/23/f59bbc4a-ccf4-11ea-91f1-28aca4d833a0_story.html.

90 govtrack.us, accessed Sept. 11, 2023, https://www.govtrack.us/misconduct.

91 Terris, Ben. "He's got a 'Downton Abbey'-inspired office, but Rep. Aaron Schock won't talk about it." *Washington Post.* Feb. 2, 2015, https://www.washingtonpost.com/lifestyle/style/hes-got-a-downton-abbey-inspired-office-but-rep-aaron-schock-wont-talk-about-it/2015/02/02/1d3f1466-ab1f-11e4-abe8-e1ef60ca26de_story.html.

92 Mullins, Brody; McGinty, Tom & Jason Zweig. "Congressional Staffers Gain From Trading in Stocks" *Wall Street Journal.* Oct. 11, 2010, https://www.wsj.com/articles/SB10001424052748703431604575522434188603198.

93 CBS *60 Minutes*, Insiders. "The road to the STOCK Act." Steve Kroft, correspondent; Ira Rosen and Gabrielle Schonder, producers. June 17, 2012 (originally aired on Nov. 13, 2011), https://www.cbsnews.com/

news/insiders-the-road-to-the-stock-act/.

94 *Tillison, Tom.* "Rep. Alan Grayson slams Paul Ryan, Saying He Wants Americans to Work Until They Die.*" Business and Politics. March 13,* 2013, https://www.bizpacreview.com/2013/03/13/alan-grayson-paul-ryan-wants-poor-people-to-die-55418/.

95 Rogers, Alex. Harry Reid: No Regrets Over False Romney Charges." *Time Magazine.* March 31, 2015, https://time.com/3765158/harry-reid-mitt-romney-no-taxes/#.

96 Baker, *Peter.* "Trump Says Tillerson Is 'Dumb as a Rock' After Former Secretary of State Criticizes Him." Dec. 7, 2018, New York Times,https://www.nytimes.com/2018/12/07/us/politics/trump-tillerson.html#:~:text="Mike%20Pompeo%20is%20doing%20a,rid%20of%20him%20fast%20enough.

97 Smock, Ray. Incivility and Dysfunction in Congress is a National Crisis by Ray Smock for History News Network." Columbian College of Arts & Sciences, George Washington University. Nd, https://historynews network.org/article/142484.

98 Ibid.

99 Jenkins, Pam. "Politics Is Driving Incivility in America, According to New National Poll." WeberShandwick/Powell Tate with KRC Research. June 13, 2012, https://webershandwick.com/news/politics-is-driving-incivility-in-america-according-to-new-national-poll.

100 Civility in America 2019: Solutions for Tomorrow." Weber Shandwick/Powell Tate with KRC Research. June 26, 2019, https://webershandwick.com/news/civility-in-america-2019-solutions-for-tomorrow.

101 Statista. "U.S. Congress public approval rating 2021–2023." August 17, 2023, https://www.statista.com/statistics/207579/public-approval-rating-of-the-us-congress/.

102 Ibid.

103 Bond, Paul. "Leslie Moonves on Donald Trump: 'It May Not Be Good for America, but It's Damn Good for CBS.'" Hollywood Reporter. Feb.

29, 2016, https://www.hollywoodreporter.com/news/general-news/leslie-moonves-donald-trump-may-871464/#!.

104 Ignatius, David. "America seems to be on a death trip. We can't fix it by demonizing one another." *Washington Post.* June 25, 2019, https://www.washingtonpost.com/opinions/america-seems-to-be-on-a-death-trip-we-cant-fix-it-by-demonizing-one-another/2019/06/25/db955036-9785-11e9-830a-21b9b36b64ad_story.html.

105 Milbank, Dana. No wonder Jonathan Turley's dog is mad." *Washington Post.* June 4, 2019, https://www.washingtonpost.com/opinions/2019/12/04/no-wonder-jonathan-turleys-dog-is-mad/.

106 Turley, Jonathan. "The Impeachment Inquiry Into President Donald J. Trump: The Constitutional Basis For Presidential Impeachment." Written Statement, US House of Representatives/Committee on the Judiciary. The George Washington University Law School Dec. 4, 2019, https://int.nyt.com/data/documenthelper/6547-jonathan-turley-s-opening-stat/739d-3374f20a9ed69157/optimized/full.pdf.

107 Laloggia, John. "Republicans and Democrats agree: They can't agree on basic facts." PEW Research Center. August 23, 2018, https://www.pewresearch.org/short-reads/2018/08/23/republicans-and-democrats-agree-they-cant-agree-on-basic-facts/.

108 Fingerhut, Hannah. "In 'political correctness' debate, most Americans think too many people are easily offended." PEW Research Center. 07/16/2016, https://www.pewresearch.org/short-reads/2016/07/20/in-political-correctness-debate-most-americans-think-too-many-people-are-easily-offended/.

109 Oliphant, J Baster. "For many Americans, views of offensive speech aren't necessarily clear-cut." PEW Research Center. Dec. 14, 2021, https://www.pewresearch.org/short-reads/2021/12/14/for-many-americans-views-of-offensive-speech-arent-necessarily-clear-cut/.

110 Gecewicz, Claire. "Few Americans say their house of worship is open, but a quarter say their faith has grown amid pandemic" PEW Research Center. Apr. 30, 2020, https://www.pewresearch.org/short-

reads/2020/04/30/few-americans-say-their-house-of-worship-is-open-but-a-quarter-say-their-religious-faith-has-grown-amid-pandemic/.

111 Williams, Walter. "Is racism responsible for today's Black problems?" Special to The Daily Home/St. Clair Star. July 30, 2020, https://www.annistonstar.com/the_daily_home/free/walter-williams-is-racism-responsible-for-todays-black-problems-column/article_64fdcc2c-d2e0-11ea-808e-ffc470a4fe36.html.

112 Cillizza, Chris. "Nancy Pelosi turns 75 today. She's still the most effective leader in Congress." *Washington Post.* March 26, 2015, https://www.washingtonpost.com/news/the-fix/wp/2015/03/26/nancy-pelosi-turns-75-today-shes-still-the-most-effective-leader-in-congress/.

113 Tumulty, Karen. "How Nancy Pelosi's unlikely rise turned her into the most powerful woman in U.S. history." *Washington Post.* March 25, 2020, https://www.washingtonpost.com/opinions/2020/03/25/how-nancy-pelosis-unlikely-rise-turned-her-into-most-powerful-woman-us-history/.

114 "Why did the United States begin directly electing Senators in 1913." DailyHistory.org, nd, https://dailyhistory.org/Why_did_the_United_States_begin_directly_electing_Senators_in_1913.

115 Ibid.

116 Skelley, Geoffrey. How The House Got Stuck At 435 Seats. After 110 years, a look at the benefits—and drawbacks—to expanding the chamber." FiveThirtyEight. August 12, 2021, https://fivethirtyeight.com/features/how-the-house-got-stuck-at-435-seats/.

117 Brian Frederick. *Congressional Representation & Constituents: The Case for Increasing the U.S. House of Representatives.* Oxford, England: Routledge Publishing. 2010, p 243–245.

A free ebook edition
is available with the
purchase of this book.

To claim your free ebook edition:

1. Visit MorganJamesBOGO.com
2. Sign your name CLEARLY in the space
3. Complete the form and submit a photo of the entire copyright page
4. You or your friend can download the ebook to your preferred device

Print & Digital Together Forever.

Snap a photo   Free ebook   Read anywhere